WANT TO BE A SCREENWRITER?
THEN ASK YOURSELF:

- What is the key ingredient of any good film script?
- What did Aristotle know about powerful storytelling that I'd better find out?
- Which pays better and offers better opportunities: writing for film or for TV?
- What is a guaranteed method for reaching an agent?
- Where are the best places in a screenplay to make dramatic enhancements and revisions?
- Why do scenes in restaurants, cars, and bars make a screenplay dull?
- How do you make it through the lean times and squeeze the most out of the good times?

The answers to these and all your other questions are part of

THE WHOLE PICTURE

D0951062

Richard Walter is the Chairman of the UCLA Film and Television writing program. He is a screenwriter, a novelist, and the author of *Screenwriting: The Art, Craft and Business of Film and Television Writing* (Plume). He lives in Los Angeles.

THE WHOLE PICTURE

STRATEGIES FOR SCREENWRITING SUCCESS IN THE NEW HOLLYWOOD

RICHARD WALTER

A PLUME BOOK

PLUME
Published by the Penguin Group
Penguin Books USA Inc., 375 Hudson Street,
New York, New York 10014, U.S.A.
Penguin Books Ltd, 27 Wrights Lane, London W8 5TZ, England
Penguin Books Australia Ltd, Ringwood, Victoria, Australia
Penguin Books Canada Ltd, 10 Alcorn Avenue,
Toronto, Ontario, Canada M4V 3B2
Penguin Books (N.Z.) Ltd, 182–190 Wairau Road,
Auckland 10, New Zealand

Penguin Books Ltd, Registered Offices:
Harmondsworth, Middlesex, England

First published by Plume, an imprint of Dutton Signet,
a division of Penguin Books USA Inc.
Excerpt from *The River*, pages 180–83, screenplay by Neal Jimenez.

First Printing, August, 1997
10   9   8   7   6

Library of Congress Cataloging-in-Publication Data is available.
ISBN: 0-452-27179-7

Printed in the United States of America
Set in Times Roman

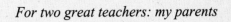

For two great teachers: my parents

ACKNOWLEDGMENTS

■ ■

From my curious and commodious perch in Westwood I serve up copious commentary to legions of writers. This much is certain: advice is easier to dish out than to take.

So I praise God in heaven—to say nothing of publisher Arnold Dolin—for sending me Peter K. Borland, senior editor, without whose affectionate, affirmative guidance this book would represent but a catalogue of Richie's Greatest Hits. Thanks for all of that, Peter, and also for your infinite patience and understanding. And thanks to editor Julia Serebrinsky, pinch hitter/utility infielder, for her generous and capable support when and where it counts the most: in the end.

I'm grateful also to Henry Dunow, my faithful representative at Harold Ober Associates, who is more available and supportive than any neurotic writer has any right to expect of any self-respecting agent.

I am blessed also at UCLA's film school with the world's best students and colleagues.

Of the former there are far too many to mention, but I salute each and every one of them for kicking my butt, for brightening my days, and for challenging me hourly to avoid the ruts and traps working-stiff writers inevitably confront not only in Hollywood but everywhere across the landscape of creative expression.

Among the latter I am especially grateful to Professors Lew Hunter, Hal Ackerman, Dee Caruso, Velina Houston, Nancy Sackett, Cynthia Whitcomb, Dan Pyne and so many others for their boundless faith and for their perpetual expansion of my horizons.

Thanks also to research associates over many academic seasons who generously and cheerfully lent time and energy to this volume: Michael Stinson, Lara Runnels, Vesta Winston, Dawn Fratini, Kathy Anne Stumpe, Scott Sublett and others. They're not only wonderful supporters but also splendid writers, each and every one of them.

I would have been lost without my resourceful transcriber and spelling/punctuation/grammar maven Allan Hollingsworth, an authentic soul of light.

Thanks to Dr. Rod Gorney for his encouragement over many years and especially for teaching me—and the world—about the end of scarcity and the privilege and burden of choices.

Thanks to Steven Bach, USC film school crony, studio chief, author, for so many things but especially for explaining to readers and movie audiences and myself the yin and yang of commerce and art.

Thanks to Professor Janet Neipris of New York University for helping forge the UCLA-NYU screenwriting axis and for informing and affirming my life and for being so loving a friend. Likewise, Donald Wille. Knowing you guys truly enriches my days.

Thanks to Chairman Robert Rosen and Dean Gil Cates, uniquely intelligent fellows whose devotion to teaching and learning is invaluable not only for students but for professors as well.

And extra special appreciation to Leslie B. Kallen of Leslie Kallen Seminars for providing endless time and patience and toleration—and infinite toil—and for helping to communicate worthy screenwriting principles far beyond Westwood's walls.

And finally, again and always, with love for Pat, Susanna and Danny, who provide more fun and greater inspiration than any mere movie, and who remind me when I come home each night just who it is I really am and what it is that truly matters.

CONTENTS

■ ■ ■ ■ ■ ■ ■ ■ ■ ■ ■ ■ ■ ■ ■ ■ ■ ■ ■ ■

THE WHOLE PICTURE

Is there anyone who's not writing a screenplay?

Settling into the taxi at the airport on my return from a screen-writing seminar back east, in as casual a tone as I could muster I asked the driver, "So how's the script coming along?"

He turned and looked me full in the face, his eyes as wide as basketballs. He gasped, "How did you know?"

Not only screenplays but screenwriting books, journals, newsletters, courses, conferences, colloquia, seminars, software, workshops, programs and panels continue to proliferate. One could easily get the impression there are not a half-dozen souls in the entire nation who do not have at least a work in progress.

And many of these writers appear to have one other thing in common: my address.

I am an easy target. Screenplays mailed to me eventually wend their way through the seemingly impenetrable bureau-cracy of a vast university, arriving without fanfare at my humble scholar's warren in the sweet backwater of our arts campus. Frankly, such attention represents for me the most splendid sort of privilege. But occasionally, it's just a bit of a burden.

In my experience, most of these over-the-transom drafts are

not yet ready for referral to the professional community. But here and there is one that is worthy. And when a script is of such quality as to merit recommendation to an agent or producer, I am always happy to oblige.

Every day I receive calls from such souls seeking new talent.

It surprises many writers to know that the agents and producers who call generally implore, "Send me writers who have no credits."

As I argue in my previous book on screenwriting, having no credits is often a writer's best credit. A writer without credits has not seen thousands or even millions of dollars squandered in so-called "development deals" that never developed—that is to say, that never became movies. A writer without credits does not have to live down an earlier effort that eventually, somewhere along the road to exhibition, was badly botched.

One thing is certain about even the most successful screenwriters: every single one of them—without even a wisp of an exception—was once wholly unknown. Each among them was once as obscure, as remote, as anonymous, as unlikely ever to succeed as today's humblest novice.

Success in screenwriting is elusive, I assure you. Certainly the form represents a uniquely daunting challenge. For one thing, movies constitute a most curious admixture of the practical and the impractical. This book's central struggle is to integrate such seemingly irreconcilable aspects of an otherwise impossible enterprise.

That's why I call it *The Whole Picture*.

We examine the screenplay first from afar, as if viewed from across a lake, seeking its overall shape, gauging its major dimensions, gleaning the outline of its broadest configuration. Just like viewing a painting in a gallery, we approach it gradually until we arrive scant inches before the canvas, inspecting the individual brush strokes, the otherwise disconnected whirls and whorls and eddies, the scribbles and scratches that collectively constitute the whole picture.

Part 1, "Show," may seem on the surface to be very much at

odds with Part 2, "Business." For perhaps the greatest hoax perpetrated upon screenwriters is the notion that they must choose between two wholly different directions. They can write a film that is meaningful and personal, providing profound, provocative insights into the human condition. Or they can toss off a down-and-dirty ditty dedicated exclusively to chasing dollars. That is to say, they can write scripts that are either artistic or commercial.

But Part 3, "The End of Adversity," demonstrates that screenwriting is not about opposition but collaboration. As one former studio chief writes, the conflict between art and commerce is in fact ". . . a false dichotomy, less 'either/or' than 'both/and.' "

Indeed, history confirms that since the invention of dramatic expression in Greece, some hundreds of years before the birth of Christ, works now regarded as classics were not discovered after their time but during the lives of their creators. They are marked not only by artistic merit but also by substantial commercial success. And they have been celebrated through the centuries and into the modern epoch.

Thanks in part to the plethora of new books and seminars on screenwriting, a new phenomenon is taking over Hollywood: major scripts are skillfully, seductively shaped, yet they are soulless. They tend to be shiny but superficial. They proffer pat prescriptions for chrome-plated stories, with all the right parts in all the right places, but in the end they have no heft.

Call them movies-lite.

They provide the sense of structure but none of the substance of sincerely compelling dramatic expression. I would personally prefer to read a misshapen, all-over-the-place screenplay that violates all of the rules but nevertheless moves me, provokes and even disturbs me, than one which presents a generally pleasing prospect without providing an occasion to laugh, cry, cringe, gasp, groan, recoil or a combination thereof.

The first chapter, "The Personal Screenplay," argues that all screenplays ultimately deal with a single subject: the writer himself. A writer intent on creating and selling a worthy script needs to look not outward to whatever it is that Hollywood appears to be buying this particular week, but inward, deep into his own heart, his own treasure chest of triumph and torment. Professional page-formatting techniques, the sharpest tips on show business etiquette and marketing ploys, the most highly sophisticated analysis of puported movie trends are all useless if the product to be marketed—the screenplay—is at its core as heartless and hollow as the Tin Man.

The second chapter, "Creative Choices," confronts the decision-making nature of artistic expression in general, and articulates the kinds of choices facing screenwriters, in particular with respect to three essential components: idea, story and theme.

Chapter 3, "Identity," argues that all choices lead to the same destination: the unique personality that is the writer's alone. This is achieved not intellectually through a recitation of procedures but through an exploration of the way working writers work.

This chapter poses a story craft challenge encouraging writers to achieve a smart and solid narrative sensibility. We demonstrate through concrete tale construction the Swiss-watch relationship of each component to the other. I will outline the precise principles and methodologies enabling writers to recognize more effectively—if also more painfully—what it is within themselves that translates to the screen and, every bit as important, what does not.

The fourth chapter, "Challenges in Story Craft," presents an array of examples that put into use principles articulated in the previous chapters. Here is a purposeful examination of methods by which the screenwriter can achieve what he needs to achieve: the marriage of illusion and reality. You will have the opportunity to complete partly realized plots with an eye toward enhancing your tale-assembly skills and attain a richer understanding of the choice-making nature of creative expression.

The chapter "Rewriting" presents a catalogue of Notes on Notes, an inventory and translation of the handwritten commentary I inscribe in the margins of scripts I analyze in advanced graduate classes at UCLA and throughout the motion picture industry. This is offered in the interest of facilitating the forever-perplexing—and always necessary—revision process. The commentary derives from consultations with actual writers of actual scripts.

I'll include useful rewrite principles pertaining not exclusively to a particular screenplay analyzed but to all screenplays. The diverse challenges confronting various scribes are more similar than at first apparent. By focusing upon one here and another there, we shed light on all.

From there we move into Part 2, which elucidates considerations more directly related to the business of professional screenwriting.

Chapter 6, "Gratitude Versus Attitude," addresses a writer's need affirmatively—instead of destructively and self-defeatingly—to apply his rage to the page, to exploit his emotions in a way that offers rewards both to the writer and the audience.

Chapter 7, "Agents," contains hitherto-unrevealed methods that virtually guarantee consideration of material—feature-length film scripts as well as television fare—by legitimate, licensed, franchised artists' representatives who are signatory to the appropriate Hollywood talent guild contracts.

Then, in Part 3, we will explore The End of Adversity, ways in which borders blend and metaphors merge between the reel and the real world. This chapter confronts the manner in which—through collective creativity—film has come to represent the highest form of human cooperation and collaboration.

By the book's conclusion, writers—new and experienced—ought to have developed fresh strategies for success, both creatively and professionally. They ought to own not just the skills to structure a solid story but also a sense of the magic and the awe that is such an integral component in the screenwriting equation.

In the end, writers will see that there are different paths to success and, amazingly, that there is no way in which a wholly enlightened, expanded, informed writer can fail. For at the bottom and the top of it, among the vast family of artists and craftspeople who contribute to the making of a film, it is the screenwriter alone whose name means nothing.

All that matters is the script.

PART ONE

SHOW

CHAPTER I

The Personal Screenplay: Integration and Gender

Recently I was packing for a trip to Las Vegas, neither to gamble nor gambol but to offer a screenwriting seminar at the University of Nevada. The phone rang with a call from a campus administrator instructing me to bring my passport.

"Passport?" I asked. Spoofing the bandit's timeless dialogue from *Treasure of the Sierra Madre*, I quipped, "I don't need no steeenking passport."

"Not to enter Nevada," my caller patiently affirmed. "But you do need a passport to teach on this campus." Stringent new immigration legislation, she explained, compels employers to verify each worker's status. Accordingly, university policy now requires legal-resident aliens to provide their work permits—the fabled green card—and United States citizens to present their passports.

There are many immigrants from Mexico and Central America throughout the Southwest, and not all are documented. Many of them are economically disadvantaged, and the jobs they seek tend to be semiskilled. On a college campus, such work exists primarily among the facilities and maintenance crews.

I was told that while it seemed unnecessary for visiting faculty to document their citizenship, the university couldn't exactly require verification solely from women and men who "appear" Latino. That would be blatantly racist. So the university created a solution typical of progressive academic institutions: it refused to discriminate against any particular group, and decided instead to mistreat *all* groups.

Thus, the requirement to provide the passport.

As it happens, I easily lose things—keys, documents, my train of thought—and because I was reluctant to risk misplacing an item as critical as my current passport, I suggested that I bring instead a recently expired one.

"That won't do," the administrator told me.

"Why not? I couldn't have been issued the now-expired passport if I had not been a citizen in the first place."

"That's true," the voice on the phone conceded. And then, with dreadful reluctance, it continued, "But how does the University of Nevada know that subsequent to the passport's expiration you have not renounced your citizenship?"

For a second, I was completely speechless.

"If you think that's crazy," the voice rasped wearily, "I quite agree. But I'm powerless to waive the rule. I have to advise you that if you do not bring your passport the seminar will be canceled."

So I brought my passport.

Recounting such circumstances and scanning the ads and articles in newspapers, magazines and movie trade journals, one could easily get the impression that there is a serious problem in our nation: huddled, teeming masses of foreigners, yearning to breathe free, storming the borders in what can only be a desperate attempt to teach screenwriting.

For screenwriting education in recent years has not merely burgeoned but exploded. And this phenomenon is by no means limited to accredited film schools. An itinerant army of self-appointed instructors treks back and forth across the nation and the globe. Indeed, so many amateurs now dabble in the discipline that screenwriting might well be considered today's macramé.

Certainly there are differences among various teachers' approaches. One lecturer preaches that the properly constructed screenplay contains five stations on the story continuum. Another refers to these as "plot points" and "turning points" (I've never quite figured out the distinction) and asserts that there are not five but nine—or was it eleven?—of them, more or less. Still another pundit identifies no fewer than two dozen "building blocks" at the core of story structure.

But these differences all pale beside commonly agreed upon principles. For example, virtually all the popular screenwriting teachers concur that among the myriad screen elements—character, dialogue, setting and more—story is preeminent. And all of us agree that underlying every story is something called "structure."

From my own point of view, these other worthy teachers provide merely their own particular spin on Aristotle's timeless work, *The Poetics*, which argues that story structure is divided not into five or nine or two dozen but only three essential parts. This is often wrongly referred to as the three-act paradigm (this season's hot word), but keep in mind that Aristotle never mentions the word "acts."

Aristotelian Story Structure

Aristotle writes instead of beginnings, middles and ends. Perhaps, with the new millennium hard upon us, the time has come finally to deconstruct all that canonical Greek dogma, but personally, if I have to choose among an array of approaches, I'm going with Aristotle.

I predict the old fellow will last.

Aristotle's so-called theory regarding story structure is no theory at all. It merely represents his observations of specific traits shared by the classical plays performed during his lifetime but written centuries earlier. His *Poetics* simply catalogues the characteristics he believed account for the works' longevity. He hoped to enable writers of any era to identify the fundamental techniques that drive dramatic narrative, much like the tales from ancient Greece which have held audiences' attention millennia after their creation.

My UCLA film faculty sidekick, Professor Lew Hunter, points out that many among our extracurricular screenwriting cohorts and colleagues have a vested interest in mystifying this creature called "story structure." If they can convince writers that they alone hold the recipe for some magic formula, they can sell more tickets to their seminars. Lew and I, on the other hand, desire instead to demystify the process.

And there's nothing even a bit mysterious about Aristotle's view. He asserts that each story has a beginning, a middle and an end. In the well-turned tale the beginning is the part before which there is nothing. The middle, however, is preceded by the beginning and followed by the end. The end is that part after which there is nothing.

This may seem so brazenly obvious as to appear valueless, but, in fact, among the most common mistakes in the thousands of screenplays I have seen over the decades is that they start not at but before the beginning.

And they end not at but after the end.

Spike Lee is an example of an adept screenwriter who simply cannot end at the end. In the otherwise splendid *Do the Right Thing*, for instance, the action culminates in the burning and looting of the neighborhood. What is "the right thing" for protagonist Mookie under such circumstances? Should he protect his employer's pizza shop from destruction by the mob? Or should he join his brothers in trashing the joint?

Mookie contemplates his dilemma, then hurls a trash can through the plateglass window, clearly affirming the righteousness of violence, at least in this particular character's view and in this particular instance. This action, Lee seems to say, is the right thing for Mookie to do.

Or perhaps he means to assert that it is the wrong thing.

In postrelease interviews Lee argues he is intentionally ambiguous here. He does not believe the artist's role is to dispense neat, pat, clean, approved, authorized, sanitized solutions to society's most excruciating and complex challenges. He demands instead that each member of the audience decide the issue for himself.

Some viewers will endorse Mookie's action; others will protest it. But surely all can welcome the invitation the film provides for further debate, as public airing of difficult issues inevitably sheds light upon the human condition.

Moral ambiguity aside, however, all can agree on at least this much: when Mookie trashes the pizza palace the movie is truly complete. This moment clearly constitutes the authentic Aristotelian end of the film, the point after which there is nothing left to say.

And indeed, at precisely this point the screen fades to black. There is every expectation that we are about to witness the tail credits scroll across the screen.

Instead, the image fades in once again and we are treated to a vision of actor Danny Aiello, who portrays the pizza store owner, and Spike as Mookie, discussing the various issues. It seems possible Ted Koppel will, at any moment, drop in from the sky to moderate the exchange. The debate drags on and on with no other effect than to sap, squander and debilitate the power of this otherwise uniquely potent American film.

What does it add to the picture besides time? Is the tale advanced in any identifiable way? Is the audience's appreciation of the characters expanded?

Not a bit.

The artist tells us only what he has already told us.

He acts too much like the little kid at a family party whose parents importune him to play the violin for the gathered relatives. The child balks and protests and resists but finally, reluctantly, consents.

And after mauling, say, the Dvořák *Humoresque*, it's time to assemble around the dinner table to chow down, but by this time the kid is fully into his fiddle-scraping and will not quit.

Too many films suffer due to too many writers' inability to know when to quit, to locate the Aristotelian ending and to conclude at that point where nothing more is needed.

Moreover, this beginning/middle/end construct applies not just to the whole picture but also to its particular parts. Each and every individual scene within a movie has its own beginning, middle and end.

As does, for that matter, each and every line of dialogue.

Educators differ on how this structure can be attained and perfected. But they all agree that whichever approach is taken, the primary focus should be the story.

There is more to screenwriting than that alone, but first of all there is that. And all by itself that ought to be enough to encourage us to stifle petty disagreements arising from time to time among the extended family of screenwriting theoreticians.

Nevertheless, one popular entrepreneurial instructor suggests a couple of linked notions that are sufficiently different from my own as to warrant consideration here. My purpose is not to engage in any pedagogical turf war but to demonstrate two essential principles at the center of screenwriting specifically and creative expression in general.

The Personal Screenplay

This colleague insists that whatever else writers may write, what they must not write is their own personal story. Nobody cares a whit, he cautions, about a particular writer's private, personal plight—except, of course, the writer himself.

Moreover, this esteemed compatriot asserts that the purported error of writing the personal screenplay is committed primarily by writers who happen to be women. Now, if writing the personal screenplay is a mistake, and if that mistake is usually committed by women, it follows logically that one who embraces such principles believes also that, compared with men, women are inferior writers.

Here, then, is the first corner of our disagreement. More than a quarter century of professional writing and decades spent teaching writing have convinced me that writers' own personal stories are all they should write.

Please note that I do not suggest writers may write their own personal story if they feel the desire or compulsion to do so. I assert instead something far more strident than that.

Principle 1: Whenever writers sit down before blank paper or glowing green (or amber) phosphor, their personal story is all they *can* write.

Even if a writer attempts vigorously to do something else, even if he works on an assignment writing a script for hire based on someone else's idea that is totally alien to his own experience, he will nonetheless end up telling nothing other than his own personal tale. For whatever the original concept, however specific, however narrow, it will in all instances be filtered through the peculiar sensibilities of the specific writer. In the end, despite himself, the writer will create a tale that is personal.

Why fight it?

My advice: surrender.

It is one battle in which defeat actually amounts to victory.

Women, Men and Screenwriting

My own view, which runs quite contrary to that of our colleague, is that women, not men, are the stronger writers. Indeed, compared with men, women are not only better writers, they are better people.

Is this statement not sexist?

Of course it is. I offer it not as a boast but a confession. Intellectually, I understand that it represents bias incarnate. It is always a mistake to generalize. Generalizing does not merely lead to prejudice; it is prejudice itself.

Yet here I generalize most shamelessly. For we must face the fact that it is impossible to grow up in a culture without carrying some of the ideological and intellectual baggage that it hands you. Western (and not only Western) industrial (and not only industrial) culture permits—even encourages—women to be self-revealing, to show and to express their emotions. Conversely, men are trained to be quite the opposite: untouchable, unreachable, invulnerable, inscrutable, closemouthed, close-to-the-chest, poker-faced, cagey, closeted, secretive.

The Georgetown University linguistics professor Deborah Tannen—among other experts—observes that women engage in conversation primarily to share cares and concerns and to offer one another mutual support. Men, on the other hand, confront conversation as competition, a chance to gain and hold ground, an opportunity for entrenchment of posture and position.

I do not doubt, for example, that my wife and her female pals know far more about each other's private, personal, intimate lives than I know about those of my male cronies.

I struggle to live otherwise, but a culture's burden is what it is.

In the early days of the feminist movement—the middle and late sixties—my bride and I and other recently married couples met regularly for dinner parties. After the meal was concluded, the fellows went off to the living room to sip brandy and smoke cigars—although perhaps in that era it was not precisely cigars that we smoked—and the women took to the kitchen to wash the dishes.

To me, conversation among men seemed predictable and tedious in the extreme. There were two safe, approved subjects:

cars and sports. But as far as I am concerned, an automobile is transportation. And—dare I admit it?—athletic competition bores me to tears.

Increasingly, I found myself joining the women in the kitchen, assisting in the cleanup. This was for purely selfish reasons. Simply stated, I prefer conversations among women. They seem to deal not with inconsequential matters but with risky subjects actually worth considering: relationships, heartache, hope, fear—all the glorious and dreadful paraphernalia that renders life interesting.

Ignorance of sports, of course, can prove quite a handicap for a professional male writer. Many show business meetings start with small talk. All too often the subject is sports. But the subtext—the true substance of these conversations—has nothing whatever to do with football or basketball. It is instead the primitive, ceremonial reassurance that we men do not intend to disembowel one another. It is the same reason, anthropologists say, that upon meeting, men shake hands: the gesture's purpose is to demonstrate that we wield no weapons.

What counts in men's conversations, therefore, is not the topic but the rhythm, the cadence, the rising and falling inflection, the strutting and posturing, the bobbing and weaving, the pecking and chirping. In short, it is ritual. Luckily for me, I was able to discover early enough that one needs to know nothing about sports to sound informed.

When I meet with men to conduct business I commonly open with the mindless, breathy, generic gambit: "How about that game!"

My male counterpart—agent, producer, executive—never challenges me. He never inquires as to precisely what game I am referring. He never even asks me to identify the particular sport. To do so would be to reveal his ignorance. Not knowing whether I speak of hockey, basketball, Ping-Pong or rugby, he invariably responds in guttural, phlegm-rattling, vigorous agreement: "Yeah, man. That was *something*!"

One can usually drop the pretense then and there and get on to the true purpose of the meeting, whatever it might happen to be. But after years of mumbling this mantra I admit I've grown cocky and I'm not likely to let go so easily. Instead of getting down to business, I'll volunteer something on the order of: "Do you *believe* that guy?"

Instead of asking "Believe *what* about *which* guy?" my male associate will shake his head mock-knowingly and say something like: "How does he get away with it?"

Such are the grunting, groaning, feinting exchanges, the surrogates for conversation that pass for interaction among men.

Amusing as this lack of sincerity may seem, it represents a dreadful deficit for male writers. Self-revelation is, after all, at the center not of screenwriting alone but all creative expression. Is not self-protection likely to suppress, to stifle, to strangle, to suffocate the genuine emotion that ought to lie at all art's heart?

This is why I preach that with regard to worthy creative expression, it is not men but women who possess the distinct advantage. Advantage aside, however, it is also now widely recognized that within every man and woman there are both masculine and feminine traits. And from this we can now derive an additional fundamental consideration screenwriters are well advised to contemplate.

Principle 2: Screenwriters must embrace authentic self-disclosure, no matter how painful, as nothing less than the organizing principle of their creative lives.

Writing that is guarded, devoid of emotion, evenhanded, objective and dispassionate might be thoroughly proper in a corporate prospectus or annual earnings report to shareholders, and might also serve adequately for instructions regarding the assembly of a backyard barbecue grill.

With regard to screenwriting, however, such expression violates the most fundamental artistic principle of all: it's boring.

The Integrated Screenplay

Integration is an essential, elusive quality informing all creative expression. Integration transcends mere parts—tale, character, dialogue and the rest—and instead embraces the whole picture.

And what precisely is integration?

Integration is every bit as easy to understand as it is difficult to achieve. The integrated screenplay is one whose every aspect—each bit of action, every line of dialogue—accomplishes simultaneously the twin tasks of 1) advancing plot and 2) expanding character. Perhaps this is just another way of saying that each piece of information needs to tell the audience something new.

Call integration screenwriting's great equalizer. If in a palpable, measurable, identifiable way the material simultaneously advances story and character, all rules are off, all prohibitions are rendered null and void. Integrate your whole picture and you can write anything at all.

Indeed, if from beginning to end a screenplay is genuinely integrated, the writer can successfully do even *nothing at all*. If that sounds crazy, remember that crazy is precisely what worthy art is.

Let us demonstrate.

My earlier book on screenwriting preaches that scenes in restaurants, as an example, are to be avoided. Turn on the TV right now, or slap a recent—or not-so-recent—cassette in the VCR and you're likely to encounter actors sitting around tables in restaurants, not acting out the tale but narrating it as they engage in action that is no action at all: sawing away at their meal with silverware.

It is no more than a wretched excuse for lazy writers to have actors recite a tale while engaging in bogus "action": wielding knives and forks, sipping water and wine, blotting lips with napkins, sprinkling pepper and salt and, of course, flapping their jaws.

Still worse, such scenes inevitably begin too early, long before the true Aristotelian beginning, the point before which nothing is needed. In the rare instance where a writer absolutely must place a scene in a restaurant, he certainly does not need to start with the characters entering the establishment, then being greeted by the greeter, seated by the seater, and introduced to the busboy and kitchen staff. One certainly need not have the waiter describe today's specials; indeed, there's no need whatever to have the folks order their food. A writer can and should cut directly to the meat of the scene.

And a writer's best bet, again, is to avoid scenes in restaurants altogether.

Unless they're integrated.

In John Patrick Shanley's *Moonstruck*, the character portrayed by Cher is seated with a man at a table in a restaurant. The waiter arrives to take their order. Cher's companion wants fish. Paraphrasing, Cher says, "Fish? You're eating fish?"

"Why not fish?"

"Because you're going to be fourteen hours on a plane to Sicily. That fish will sit in your stomach and rot. You'll turn green."

"I don't want fish?"

"No."

"So what do I want?"

Cher prescribes precisely what he should eat. "You want a light angel-hair pasta primavera." Her dining partner nods to the waiter, agreeing that this is his order. Now he turns to Cher. "You really know how to take care of a man," he tells her. "You're exactly the kind of woman I need. Marry me."

"You call that a proposal?" she protests. "On your knees!"

He shrugs, rises from his chair, drops to his knees, proposes marriage.

She accepts.

Note first that even though the setting is a restaurant, the characters are not exclusively eating and talking. Right there, smack in the middle of the restaurant—amidst the astonished diners— the suitor gets down on his knees to propose marriage.

This is no car chase. This is no saloon brawl.

Nevertheless, it is exciting dramatic action.

Indeed, it is a whole lot fresher and more exciting than yet another car chase, or another too-familiar movie fight in a movie bar.

It is something that is happening, something that is visual; it is not merely a discussion among actors. It is a scene to be seen, not one merely to be heard. It represents activity instead of stasis. In many ways, because it is subtle, because it is something small—ordering dinner—that sheds light on something big—the protagonist's character—it represents the most exquisite sort of movie action.

How do we know it is integrated?

Because in a clear way, first of all, it advances the story. *Moonstruck* is at its heart the tale of a woman who falls in love with her fiancé's brother. In order to have a fiancé she must become engaged. If there is no fiancé, there is no fiancé's brother. If there is no fiancé's brother, there is no story. If there is no story, there is no movie.

Beyond the scene's lame venue—the restaurant—there is also the forbidden ordering of food. Does the discussion regarding entrees constitute dialogue that is genuinely integrated? Yes, because it expands our appreciation of Cher's character. At this early juncture in the picture she is something of an Earth Mother, a woman who knows how to nourish a man in the most traditional, maternal way.

The dialogue surrounding the food establishes this nurturing aspect of her character. Indeed, she is a woman who holds erotic love in contempt. The example of her parents' wretched marriage is more than sufficient to have taught her this sorry lesson.

Eventually, of course, she will become quite another kind of woman. She will realize that a woman is entitled also to passion, to steamy, seamy, searing, soaring romance. She'll discover that love is not a hoax, a trick, a trap, a burden. Love, Cher will eventually determine, is the only reason we are here. Better to burn in hell for eternity than to endure a loveless, sterile life on earth.

In this fashion the characters are rendered fleshy and real; in this fashion they develop and grow instead of remaining static. And in this fashion, also, the tale moves forward.

What is usually prohibited is perfectly legitimate here because it is integrated; it provides story and character information previously not known to the reader of the script and the audience in the theater. A film scene that is not repetitive but that instead offers new information draws the audience closer to the screen, very much in the manner of a primitive shaman drawing his tribal brothers and sisters more closely around the fire to better absorb his tale.

As I mentioned earlier, integration is such a powerful aspect of the cleverly crafted script that, in the truly integrated movie, it is possible to do absolutely nothing at all and still advance the tale and expand character.

In the made-for-television movie *Golda*, for example, Ingrid Bergman (in the final performance of her career) portrays the late Prime Minister of Israel. In one scene the chairman of the United States Senate's Armed Services Committee meets with her. He intends to inform her that he can sell only military weaponry that does not quite meet Israeli security requirements.

The senator arrives at the modest official residence in Jerusalem to find himself completely alone with the prime minister—no aides or assistants or secretaries. And her very first act—on its face nothing more than a quick, chitchatty line of dialogue, the sort of courtesy and politeness movies need generally to avoid—seemingly violates one of our most stringent screenwriting prohibitions: she offers him a cup of coffee.

Collectively, in terms of person-hours, I do not doubt that fourteen trillion aeons have been consumed by audiences across the globe watching actors in films and on television talk about, pour and drink oceans of coffee. And acres of rain forest have fallen to provide paper upon which inept screenwriters can inscribe time-squandering, wheel-spinning dialogue surrounding the beverage.

Decaf or regular? Cream and/or sugar? Dairy substitute and/or artificial sweetener? If the latter, NutraSweet, saccharine, Sweet'n Low, Sugar Twin? Half-and-half instead of cream? Milk instead of half-and-half? If milk, whole? Extrarich? Low-fat? Extralight? Skimmed? Condensed? Powdered? Boxed? Canned?

Pasteurized or certified raw?

Homogenized?

Cow? Goat? Camel? Buffalo? Yak?

Inevitably it's an unsubtle attempt by a movie writer to stall, to stretch, to fill, to pad, to bloat with air. Or it's an act of desperation by an out-of-ideas television writer hoping to kill time until the next commercial.

But it is in life that we kill time; in movies time kills us.

Nevertheless, integration in the writing of *Golda* justifies even the coffee.

When the senator accepts the prime minister's offer of coffee, she goes to fetch it, leaving him all alone in the diminutive apartment's cramped living room. He sits on the couch and waits. And he sits. And he waits. And he sits. And he waits. Perhaps twenty seconds elapse—an eternity on film—in which absolutely nothing happens.

From the audience's perspective those twenty seconds feel like three whole days.

This nothingness soon becomes wondrously disquieting for both audience and character. At long last the senator rises and searches the apartment for the prime minister. He discovers her in the kitchen. She is just now setting his coffee on the table, along with a piece of pastry. She pulls out a chair, beckoning him to sit.

Even before a line is spoken we are provided a bounty of information. Subtextually we see that Israel, for all its strategic importance, is but a speck of a nation, a land so modest, so humble that its prime minister all by herself prepares coffee for high-level official visitors in her downscale one-bedroom official digs.

If that were the end of it, the business would be justified because it is integrated—character and story alike are moved some measurable distance. But it is not the end; it is merely the beginning.

The senator settles in at the kitchen table and begins to consume both the coffee and some of the prime minister's home-baked strudel. He mentions the inferior military equipment his government is willing to sell. Golda expresses her dismay. Out of the unlikely mouth of a little old Jewish mother, a former Milwaukee schoolteacher, there now spills the most informed military jargon anybody ever heard. She comments on retro-fitting bomb racks with titanium struts, speaks of explosive tonnage, cites statistics relating to radar range and weapons and ordnance and kill ratios and a host of pertinent high-tech considerations.

The senator is awestruck by this expertise from such an unlikely source; quickly he is converted to her cause. And why not? Madam Prime Minister is, after all, a mother. Perhaps still more to the point, she is a Jewish mother. And she's got her prey exactly where she wants him: at her kitchen table.

He hasn't a chance!

Thanks therefore to integration—plot expansion combined with character enhancement—nothing is turned into something. A character sits on a couch in a living room engaged in absolutely no activity beyond breathing. Yet the writer wields this apparent inaction so splendidly that the story is moved forward, with substantial dramatic impact. And in the next moment, the otherwise mundane offer of a cup of coffee does not stifle the tale but instead richly intensifies it.

Notwithstanding my earlier caution to avoid generalizing, it is now possible to offer a broad, sweeping generalization that is nonetheless true for screenwriting in all cases, without exception:

Principle 3: **If a screenplay is truly personal and genuinely integrated, it does not matter what the script is about.**

Movies contain, after all is said and done, only two kinds of information: sight and sound. If every single sight and each and every sound genuinely advances the story and enhances the audience's appreciation of the characters, and if the tale represents the intimate, personal experience and sensibilities of the writer, audiences will be enthralled by it, regardless of its subject or setting.

Example #1: A Jail Tale

Not many years ago I received a letter from a prisoner in a California penal institution. He had heard me discuss screenwriting on a San Francisco radio talk show.

"During the past few years," he wrote, "I have devoted a great deal of energy to learning the craft of screenwriting, and I have completed four scripts."

Of course, this impressed me most favorably. Writers have to write a bundle of scripts just in order to become familiar with the form and with the fiercely formidable challenge of the craft, and to find their own voice. That this writer had four scripts under his belt seemed to bode well for him.

His next sentence struck me as still more encouraging. "I write very much from my life's experiences," the letter continued, "based upon my rather intimate knowledge of cops and cons and the things men do in the dark."

Cops and cons and the things men do in the dark.

It's not quite poetry from Shakespeare, but it is nevertheless nifty, dazzling, sexy, sparkling stuff. It's punchy and to-the-point; it represents language that is original. More important, with a minimum of words it communicates a great deal. And it testifies to, among other things, the personal nature of the writer's efforts.

My correspondent went on to explain that he would have loved to attend the screenwriting seminar I was offering in the Bay Area just a few days hence. But, he told me, upon checking his calendar he'd discovered that on that particular weekend he would once again be a guest of the state at the same luxury facility, exactly as he had been for scores of previous weekends and, indeed, as he would be for weeks and months and years to come.

The fact that he was humorously self-deprecating about his sorry situation impressed me even further; writers who take themselves too seriously are the most difficult among a group of naturally difficult creatures.

He asked for permission to send me one of his scripts.

That he did not simply enclose the script but sought my permission to do so demonstrated to me that here was a writer who understood the etiquette regarding screenplay submissions. A smart query letter will win the approval of any agent, any producer, any screenwriting professor. The smartly shaped query is the way a sharp writer turns an unsolicited script into one that is solicited.

Of course, I granted him permission to mail me the script.

It arrived, accompanied by a brief cover letter. The letter thanked me for my consideration and went on to express in a number of gorgeously rendered sentences some of the most poetic contemplations I have ever read treating the subject of writing.

He wrote:

> This work gives me a new life, or a new sense of life
> in a way that has been, for me, most remarkable.
>
> I have come to believe that any person of talent, any
> person involved in the great task of bringing that talent
> to form and life in any worthy piece of work, brings at
> the same time life and form to his own soul.

An authentic chill took possession of me. The stunning simplicity of his language, its deceptively easy skill, caused me to think, perhaps a bit ruefully: Next to this guy I'm just a typist.

His letter continued:

> When I write I stand with my future behind me
> and my past stretches out before me as far as my
> mind can see.

I could not even figure out precisely what he meant by that, but nonetheless it struck me as so magnificent that I seriously considered hanging up my word processor.

What followed, however, was most amazing of all.

> And all the characters I have known, all the lovers
> and warriors and barkers and painters and scene-shifters
> and criminals come round. And as I look back, I am
> coming to the conclusion that the rather bitter dispute
> I've had with the world was never more than a simple
> lovers' quarrel.

Cannot anyone understand why I excitedly awaited receipt of this screenplay? When it arrived at my office, however, my eager expectation turned quickly to dismay.

The script's length alone—174 pages—offered ample evidence of what could only be its amateurish nature. Sight unseen, I already knew the writer needed to lose sixty pages or more.

Even worse, a mere scanning of the screenplay revealed that it was a violent prison tale involving gangs and drugs and riots and rapes. While I assert that strong conflict is essential to every corner of every worthy screenplay, the last thing in the world I wanted to read was a macho-men-with-hair-on-their-chests jail tale with hordes of hard-boiled cons strutting and posturing, plotting and suffering, banging their spoons Jimmy Cagney style on the mess hall's steel tables, plotting their escapes, calculating their revenge upon The System.

Certainly I was under no obligation to read this convicted

felon's work. Nevertheless, to ignore this hapless soul seemed more loathsome than to offer at least some token response.

I sat down one night just before bedtime, anticipating that one minute was perhaps thirty seconds more than I would spend with the script. I told myself I would glance at the first few pages, jump to the middle, scan the conclusion.

Then I would dictate a quick letter saluting the writer's talent and discipline. I would refer specifically to one or two points in the script so that he'd get the impression I had read it somewhat more carefully—in fact, *lots* more carefully—than I actually had. I would advise him that before showing it to potential representatives or purchasers he would need to trim it—as my three-year-old son could have told him. And finally, I would wish him every success in the world.

Surely, I mused, God in heaven would credit my Good Works merit badge account.

Instead I was up half the night, biting my nails in terror, brimming with compassion for the characters and their astonishing horror, glory, desperation, courage, greed, generosity, rage and love.

What appeared at first to be a loss-of-innocence story turned out instead to be a tale of innocence regained.

In the opening, Nasty, a veteran con in his forties, receives a new cell mate, a youngster of nineteen, Richie. Nasty takes a liking to the youth and hopes to educate him in prison etiquette, expecting to spare him at least some of the darkness that can cost a prisoner not only his soul but his very life.

All the same, Richie succumbs to dope and prison gangs. Nasty, however, in his futile struggle to save Richie, learns important life lessons himself.

At one critical point, for example, Nasty receives a letter from his sister notifying him that six months earlier their mother died. Nasty grieves, of course, to learn of his mother's passing, and all the more so when he contemplates that he has fallen to such a low station that he did not even learn this fundamental information until half a year after the fact.

Worse than that, however, is his sister's assertion that it is he who killed their mother, as surely as if he had personally plunged a knife into her heart. "It was your disgrace, your humiliation," the sister writes, "that destroyed her. Your outlaw legacy shamed her and brought misery and ruination upon her days."

Nasty goes crazy with sorrow and rage, torching his cell and earning himself a long stint in solitary confinement. In the hole his only warm-blooded companion is a rat, with whom he shares his bread-and-water ration.

At long last a confederate working the food detail asks Nasty through the grate if he would like some drugs. "I would die for a taste of some decent dope," Nasty responds. He is advised that prison policy routinely grants requests, even from prisoners in solitary confinement, to attend chapel on Sunday. If he will sit in the chapel's back row, Nasty is instructed, someone will pass him a package.

Nasty goes to chapel, but before anybody has a chance to slip him any contraband he becomes mesmerized by the sermon delivered by an evangelical Christian preacher, a visiting pastor from the local community. She is the victim of a rape that occurred some ten years earlier, and has never recovered from the degradation and despair that quickly and wholly enveloped her existence. In an attempt to move on with her life, she sought refuge in Christ. And to this end she now ministers to the self-same sorts of souls who victimized her. Perhaps if she can teach a bunch of violent male criminals to pursue peace and find forgiveness she, too, can at long last achieve some manner of tranquillity.

Her straightforward, simple eloquence—the poetic lilt of her testimony—rattles Nasty to his core. The young woman's sermon rocks his tormented soul. Right then and there, in response to her glorious witness, he forever renounces drugs and all manner of evil. He pleads with God for forgiveness.

He is, in short, converted to the faith.

I admit that at this point I found occasion for misgiving and even suspicion. Savvy felons appreciate that religious conversions play well with parole boards. I wondered if our writer was falsely posturing in a sophisticated attempt to win early release, and if I was myself being exploited, utilized in a nefarious probation scam. Certainly it could not harm a prisoner's cause to have in his corner a university professor, available perhaps to write a letter on his behalf or even to testify in person in support of clemency and early release.

Moreover, I was also fearful that the script would become from this point on no more than a religious tract that, even if wholly sincere, would be marked only by narrowness of purpose. I worried that instead of the expanded vision that is the essence of all creative expression, the screenplay would descend into limitation and stultification.

But our writer at this point instead moves quickly from Christian faith to Islam. This skillful transition occurs through the good offices of another character—a convicted serial murderer—who has found serenity and liberation through his devotion to Allah. And in this manner, by moving from one faith to another, the tale transcends any particular creed and becomes instead a story of faith itself.

Eventually the prison is torn by rioting in which our evangelist is taken hostage, only to be rescued by a reborn Nasty, who has discarded his prison name and reclaimed his Christian one: Peter.

Even this name-change testifies to integration's importance. Normally it is foolhardy for a screenwriter to change a character's name in the middle of a script. What possible excuse is there for such a conceit? What can the writer expect to achieve besides creating an unnecessary confusion among his readers?

Yet here the name change expands the character and the story. It is, after all, thoroughly appropriate that Nasty discard his prison name, exactly as he abandons all other trappings of his prison mentality. It is proper that he embrace his Christian name at one and the same time as he commits himself to his Christian faith.

Eventually, over a period involving no small labor of revision, the writer was able to trim the draft to presentable size and to win an agent. At this time, now out of stir, he enjoys a screen-writing career of substantial promise.

His story, one that seemed on the surface so unappealing, turns out in fact to be riveting and heartbreaking. Perhaps best of all, even in its darkest shadows it offers vast cause to rejoice, to celebrate the human heart, to salute the soul and the spirit of woman and man.

Make no mistake about it—all of this derives primarily from only two items: 1) the tale's deeply personal nature and 2) its author's ability to write dialogue and action that is perpetually integrated, consistently advancing story and character.

Example #2: AIDS—A Laff Riot

Permit me another example of a script that at first appeared extremely unlikely to be worthy. This one, however, was written not in prison but in another well-regulated institution: the graduate screenwriting program at UCLA.

Our advanced screenplay workshops are the meat and pota-toes of our Master of Fine Arts in Screenwriting program. Each convenes once a week for three hours and enrolls only eight writers. There are no assigned readings, no exams. There is but a single assignment: write a professional-quality feature-length screenplay.

At the first session of each semester, typically, far too many writers attempt to enroll. In order to choose the participants, I hear each applicant's story proposal. Based partly upon my affection for the projected tale, I decide whom to admit.

I recall one such class in particular. As usual, we went around the table from student to student, listening to the writers pitch their notions. In due course we came to a writer we'll call Carl Farrow. Carl appeared grim. He had hobbled into the classroom with the aid of a cane; his skin looked pasty and pale, and on his face were telltale splotches, the discolorations typical of Kaposi's sarcoma, a form of skin cancer common among victims of AIDS.

The story he proposed in the class that particular Monday night told of a man who, upon hearing his HIV-positive diagnosis, decides at long last openly to confront his sexuality, to emerge from the closet.

"Sounds good," I said, awkwardly stroking my scratchy professorial beard, nodding sagely before moving on to the next student.

But I lied.

In every pore I dreaded yet another such tale depicting gay coming-out, all the more so when combined with AIDS. By no means do I doubt that there resides exquisite human drama in such an arena. It is only that in the past couple of decades we have witnessed so many such stories, some of them splendid, some of them not. And here was yet another of them. I viewed this latest effort as by definition redundant, repetitive, superfluous. It struck me as a woefully misguided outlet for Carl's precious time and talent.

I thought to myself: Is this what the world really needs? Do we require yet another AIDS/gay-coming-out tale? Had not the subject been wrung dry years ago?

Nevertheless, I suppressed an urge to discourage the writer. As if I were standing outside of myself, as if I were watching myself and listening to myself from afar, I stumbled through the motions of approval and affirmation. Given Carl's medical state, I simply did not have the heart to tell him the truth regarding my own dim view of his project's prospects.

Nor could I exclude him from the class. Even though I regarded his proposal as one of the least promising in the group, there was simply no way in the world I could tell someone in such condition that he was not welcome in my course.

Reluctantly, I enrolled him.

When the script was handed to me at the end of the semester I put off reading it until I'd evaluated all the others. Finally, at long, long last, and with abundant trepidation, I opened the screenplay.

I was astounded by what I read.

First of all, the tragic story was told with great humor; in fact, the script was a straight-ahead, breakneck comedy that was nothing short of hilarious. I roared aloud as I read through it, no small tribute.

Comedy is, after all, not a lower but a higher form. It is not the least but the most demanding genre. Compared with action/adventure or melodrama, for example, it is simply intolerant of any wobbling. Comedy is either funny or it is not. The people laugh or they do not.

And I laughed a lot reading Carl's story.

The script tells of a narcissistic, primping gay man who logs a lot of time peering at himself in any and all available mirrors. In his thirties, he already worries about encroaching wrinkles.

Upon his HIV diagnosis, however, he comes to worry not about getting wrinkles but about not getting wrinkles. His concern is, of course, that he will not live long enough to suffer the burdens of aging.

The script was splendid in virtually every way.

About the only problem in the screenplay's execution was the unsympathetic treatment of the protagonist's brother. He was portrayed as a Christian fundamentalist zealot who believed that AIDS was merely Satan's handiwork. In the brother's view, if the protagonist would only deliver himself over to the Lord and beg forgiveness, his AIDS would vanish, would blow away like so much dandruff. Carl felt, understandably, that this attitude trivialized the problem and, still more grievously, discounted his nature and denied his identity.

Since the beginning of my experience as a writer and as a writing educator, however, I have argued that *all* characters in a screenplay—including even the most villainous—should be rendered sympathetic. Unreconstructed monsters from Jupiter are a lot less dramatic than flesh-and-blood human beings right here on earth who remind us not of aliens but of ourselves.

I implored Carl to soften the brother's attitude.

"But that's based upon my own real brother and that's the way he really is," the writer insisted.

"I don't care how your brother really is," I said. "I care only about what is most dramatic. You fault your brother for his failure to understand and to forgive, but can you find it in your own heart to forgive him? You want him to appreciate your point of view but you are unwilling—even for a moment—to appreciate his perspective. Can you not imagine his pain in contemplating your situation? He did not spring whole in a religious vision from the head of Zeus. Like the rest of us," I told Carl, "your brother carries the emotional and psychological luggage that was handed to him. How does he explain your situation to others, or to himself? How does he deal with the fact that his baby brother suffers from a fatal disease? Can you not sense his shame and rage, his frustration and grief?"

Perhaps reluctantly, Carl rewrote the brother's role, producing a far more sympathetic portrait, a more fully realized character who was palpably human and humane instead of stereotypical, predictable, flat.

The revised version won not only an A from this instructor, it also won first prize in a prestigious screenwriting competition. And it won Carl representation at a reputable literary agency. It launched for the writer something very much resembling a career.

Alas, Carl was so inconsiderate as suddenly to die and make liars of all of us who knew for a fact that he would, like ourselves, live forever.

At the Quaker funeral service, I was deeply touched to see so many of our UCLA screenwriting students, Carl's classmates, in attendance. Many offered eloquent testimonials to his memory.

And I witnessed also a man whom I had never met, a member of Carl's family, arise to offer compelling, respectful, grieving, loving testimony to this newly departed writer whose life and gift was cut too, too short by the ravages of this era's peculiar blight. I realized, plain as day, that this could only be the brother

I had read about in the screenplay. Clearly, in Carl's elegant, poetic tale, some substantial healing had been provided for the spirits of both brothers.

Thus it was demonstrated to me yet again that the personal, integrated tale merits attention and consideration regardless of readers' expectations, of audiences' predispositions, of subject matter, of time, of place, of setting.

From this notion a new screenwriting principle emerges:

> **Principle 4:** Even if you do not know that you are writing your own personal story, that is what you are writing. Your own heart and your own hand make every script you write only that: your own.

A script may be an assignment from a studio based upon somebody else's idea. It may be the commissioned adaptation of a novel that the writer only pretends to appreciate. In any and all cases, if the writer is capable, the script will be personal and integrated, and worthy of audiences' time and attention, to say nothing of the money required to purchase a ticket.

I had occasion to witness the truth of this proposition a few years ago while lecturing and consulting on screenwriting in the Middle East. I met with a group of writers in, among other places, Tel Aviv. One of the best of their stories was called *The New Room*.

Example #3: Middle Eastern Adultery

A woman in a suburb of Haifa bids good-bye to her husband as he departs their home for an extended business trip. "When you return one month from now," she tells him, "there will be a surprise for you—a new room."

"You studied construction at the University Extension and now you believe you can build an addition to the house?" he asks. "Such projects require substantial labor. And here that kind of labor is typically performed by Arabs. You are a woman, an Israeli, a Jew. Arab laborers will not work for you."

"I will engage an Arab contractor who has been recommended to me. He will hire and supervise the workers."

The husband cannot persuade his wife to give up her foolish scheme. "Whatever you do," he cautions, "don't let them in the house. The work can be done from the outside. If they need to use the bathroom, they can go to the pub down the street."

At this moment the couple's young child toddles up to his father, who lifts him high off the ground for a farewell embrace. But before he can quite hug the kid, he is repelled by the stench of a diaper in desperate need of changing. He wrinkles his nose and thrusts his son abruptly at the mother.

Father leaves. A bearded, disheveled, scruffy but affable, capable Arab contractor is engaged. He hires laborers and work commences on the new room. It proceeds apace. Midway through the job, however, at the conclusion of one particular day's sweaty, gritty toil, the contractor knocks on the door seeking permission to use the bathroom. Face-to-face with her reliable, responsible employee, the wife cannot find it in her heart to refuse him and, reluctantly, she grants his request.

He enters the bathroom. A minute goes by. Two. Ten. Twenty. There are the sounds of a phenomenal amount of activity within, and it is perhaps a half hour before our contractor emerges.

He is unrecognizable.

Clean-shaven, combed and scrubbed, dressed now in a suit and tie, he is handsome beyond description; Omar Sharif is Danny DeVito next to this dude. "Forgive me," he apologizes to his employer, who stands there gaping at him, dumbstruck. "I have abused your generous offer to utilize the bath. My cousin, you see, is being married in the village a mile from here and I needed to wash up and change my clothes for the ceremony."

The woman stands there, drinking in the vision of the man, as if meeting him for the first time. At this moment the child toddles up to him, latches onto his trouser leg. The Arab moves to hoist the boy into the air for a cuddle.

"No!" cautions the mother. "His diaper is soiled. I was just about to change it. He reeks!"

She reaches to reclaim the child, but the contractor hangs on tight. "Please, madam," he protests, deeply inhaling the dreadful fumes. "This smell I love like life itself! And why not? Life itself is exactly what is, no?" He waxes enthusiastic on the subject of children, procreation and plain old love. Our housewife is enormously taken with this attractive, alluring, affirmative soul who presents so stark a contrast to her clinical, sanitized, saran-wrapped husband.

Soon enough a sensual love story emerges.

The script is truly a feast of human action and interaction of the most fundamental nature. When I met with the writer in order to discuss it, I started off with casual chitchat. Did she live here in Tel Aviv? No, in fact she lived in Haifa, she informed me.

"Central Haifa?"

"Actually, a suburb."

"In an apartment?"

"No."

"Your home is a detached structure, a house?"

"Yes," she told me. She seemed increasingly uncomfortable with my questions. Everything she told me of her life was, of course, fully in keeping with the script's details.

"Has a new room been added to the house since you moved in?"

"What's the difference?" she asked me with thinly veiled annoyance. "In fact, yes. A new room has been added to the house since we moved in. So what?"

I simply could not resist asking: "Did you design the room yourself and hire a contractor?"

"Enough questions!" she snapped. "I refuse to be interrogated! Can we not talk about the script?"

The script, of course, was precisely what we were talking

about. It was, indeed, no mere movie script but—like every solid screenplay—a depiction of the writer's own life, in more ways than the writer herself had even realized.

The heartbreaking scandal that not long ago enveloped Woody Allen's personal life springs to mind. Among its many wild aspects, what amazes me most is the artist's refusal to acknowledge that his films—"fictions" though he may properly call them—are in so many ways reflections and replications of his soul, his psyche and the actual experience of his own, true life.

Similarly, I do not doubt for a moment that our Middle Eastern writer truly believed she wrote fiction, and to some extent she was quite correct; surely she took liberties with the facts, with the data, reorganizing them into a better-fitting order, eliminating some real-life situations altogether while inventing others that never actually occurred.

Most likely there were just enough changes from reality that she was able to write her own personal integrated tale without quite realizing that she was doing it. And such is the nature of all worthy creative narrative expression. One hugely gifted writer from America's midsection states it this way: "We write our own lives; and then we write our own obituaries."

For if a writer struggles to write something other than her personal story, if she does not personalize it, if she fails to make it her own unique tale, regardless of how well turned it may be it will nonetheless also be flat, hollow, heatless, heartless, pale, frail, laminated, not wholly human.

For each and every movie explores only one and the same theme. Whatever else writers may think they're writing about, in fact we all treat but a single subject: ourselves. And that is why it does not matter what particular configuration of incidents and anecdotes convect a screenplay's vapors as long as the picture is whole and as long as it is informed by a vision and a voice every bit as singular as the author who creates it.

But do not particular kinds of people favor particular kinds of films?

Frankly, no. Often they think they do, but experience demonstrates otherwise.

In academic circles, where careers often appear to rise and fall upon a scholar's ability to utilize three syllables where two would suffice, "story" is often referred to as "narrative." But whatever it is called, story's power resides in its ability to replicate the shape of life itself. Beginnings, middles and ends do just that; they model nothing less than the human agenda. The healthy, integrated screenplay, like the healthy, integrated life, contains a beginning (childhood) that is relatively short and a middle (adulthood) that generally occupies the vast majority of an individual's days. And who among us seeks a long, slow, painfully drawn-out end with intravenous tubes and huffing, wheezing resuscitators jammed down our throats? In good lives and good movies alike, ends come quickly; they're short, abrupt and to the point.

To be sure, there is something sweetly narcissistic in the experience. I used to think of the movie screen as a window through which we spy on the lives of others. But lately, I've come to realize that it is actually a mirror, in which we view reflections not of others but of ourselves.

This is why integrated tale craft—the wholly shaped story—transcends mere genre. If its story is integrated, we appreciate a film even when we'd expected to dislike it. The shapely tale, through its structure, presents us with a reflection of nothing other than the idealized, romanticized human life. And in doing so it provides us with the curious reassurance we demand of all creative expression.

For example, I have always had something resembling an anti-science fiction bias. Space travel and alien creatures often bore me to tears. It all strikes me as the stuff of daytime talk show/tabloid wackos. Glistening titanium-and-vinyl alternative futures? A wearying, all-too-familiar film-student conceit. Is there not enough drama to be found right here on earth?

Nevertheless, when such films are genuinely integrated—when they are personal and perpetually advance story and character—I treasure them. *E.T.*, *2001* and *Robocop* are but three examples of pictures I expected to find unappealing yet wound up adoring.

They're at once fast and funny and scary and silly and profound. They are, in short, everything one wants a picture to be. And most important, for all their gadgetry, for all their tricks and gimmicks and quirks and eccentricities, they're splendidly human. Each moves tale and character continuously and therefore attracts vast audiences.

In a discussion sometime ago, a group of writers considered the concepts discussed in this chapter. One participant challenged the notion that all good films are personal. Did I mean to argue that *Star Wars*, for example, is something more than a skillful Saturday morning sci-fi serial adventure? Could I claim that *Star Wars* represents George Lucas's own personal identity tale?

The short answer: Yes.

Note first of all—to begin with the most superficial level—that the protagonist in *Star Wars* is a fellow named Luke. Can anyone doubt that George Lucas—who calls his company Lucasfilm and locates its headquarters on Lucas Valley Road—chose the name "Luke" for the central role other than purposefully and deliberately?

Similarly, can anyone imagine that the *Star Wars* trilogy is not representative of George Lucas's particular and wondrously curious worldview, most especially his innocent, affectionately loopy notions regarding good and evil, love and hate?

Note that the antagonist, Darth Vader, is a man whose last name sounds awfully like "father." In fact "vater" in German actually means "father."

And who is Darth Vader revealed to be at the end of the film?

Why, nobody but Luke's father.

And is not one's father at least to some extent a reflection also of oneself?

Those who are close with George Lucas allow that his relationship with his late father was perhaps more than just a little strained. Clearly, there is much in *Star Wars*, perhaps even more than its own creator realizes, that is deeply, profoundly personal.

Go ahead, then, and write a science fiction picture if it suits you. Or write a goofy screwball comedy. Write a soap opera. Write a machismo, hair-on-your-chest, blood-and-guts action/adventure prison tale. Write a gay coming-of-age story or a tale about a woman who builds an addition to her house. No matter what is written, no matter who writes it, if it is integrated and personal, it treats one and the same subject.

Weave a crafty tale that is thoroughly integrated and personal; you'll win audiences regardless of your subject. And you'll succeed, too, in saying to audiences something that is worth hearing.

CHAPTER 2

■ ■ ■ ■ ■ ■ ■ ■ ■ ■ ■ ■ ■ ■ ■ ■ ■

Creative Choices: Idea, Story, Theme

Art is choice.

A painter may work in oil or tempera, watercolor or acrylic. He may choose a single hue or many thousands. He may apply the pigment to canvas or cardboard, to leather, plywood or glass. He may smear it on thick or thin, with brushes that are fat or frail, with a pallet knife, a toothpick, a pipe cleaner, a finger or directly from the tube.

The completed painting may be square, round, a cameo, a mural, a panel, a triptych. It could be abstract, surreal or representational; a portrait, a landscape, a still life.

But however it turns out in the end, all paintings represent one and the same thing: the record of choices made by the artist.

The same applies to music.

A composer may score for solo violin, clarinet, flügelhorn, kettledrum, voice. He may write a duet or a trio, a sonata, an entire symphony. His composition may be loud, soft, fast, slow, legato, staccato or all of the above. Whatever else it may be, however, one note follows a second and a third and so on throughout the course of the piece until it is finished.

And in the end it is nothing other than these combined choices that collectively constitute the entire composition.

If choice-making lies at the heart of all creative expression, it is especially true for film. For it is film's creators who confront by far the greatest number of artistic choices. This is because movies by their very nature integrate both light and language, information that is not only visual but also aural. In addition, a movie is presented not in a single flash but over an extended period of time. And all the images and all the sounds mean nothing unless they are deployed inside the interlocking matrices of choices that come finally to constitute context and narrative.

Therefore, the screenwriter's choices are clearly limitless. From the writer's standpoint, decision-making is involved continually and at every imaginable level. What happens in the next scene? What is its setting? What is the next bit of action? What is the next line of dialogue? What is the next sentence? What is the next word?

Ironically, making these choices does not reduce the universe of possibilities but actually expands it. This is because new choices, rather than removing themselves from the overall body of available alternatives, create still newer configurations for further choice-making. The writer's universe, very much like the cosmos in which we live, continues over time not to diminish but to expand.

Movies, more than any other form of artistic expression, derive from a veritable blizzard of sources: infinite ideas, scattered snatches of dialogue, combined characters and stories and props and wardrobe and music and hairstyles and more.

But there is only one theme.

Principle 5: **All movies—no matter how diverse their subjects—treat but one and the same theme: identity.**

Grasping this principle completely requires us to embrace "theme" as working writers do, not with our intellect but with our hands and hearts. This is because film, as I argue repeatedly, is not so much about understanding as it is about feeling.

Therefore, in order to exploit thematic considerations in a screenplay most effectively, writers need not merely know their theme, they must own it. And to accomplish this, they need to grasp theme's relation to idea and story, for it is from idea and story that theme is ultimately derived and articulated.

A Case Study

To explore theme, then, in an encapsulated way, let us walk through a humble episode of a half-hour television situation comedy scripted by a writer who happened at the time to be a UCLA screenwriting student. Then, we'll look at the beginning of a longer tale of my own invention—call it a romantic comedy/thriller—involving adultery and murder in and around the New York publishing scene. We will recount the story up to the end of the beginning, the point at which it is necessary to make a critical choice. And in doing so we'll demonstrate the ways in which choice drives story.

We'll also pose a particular story craft challenge in order to confront screenwriters with not only the burden but also the beauty of choice-making.

In addition, we'll survey various solutions to the challenge as offered by writers I've met across the country and around the globe over the past decade.

And finally, I'll provide my own particular resolution to the story craft challenge.

We'll prove the proposition that even as writers are writing about every imaginable subject under the sun, in fact all treat but a single theme: identity. We'll show that whatever else writers write about, each work is merely another articulation of that singular theme, the writer's own identity, the one theme that has arrested the attention of every writer and every viewer since the invention of written narrative nearly three thousand years ago.

First, let's review briefly how the writer of the sitcom episode won the assignment in the first place. It provides an enlightening example of a fairly typical way in which TV writing careers are launched.

The writer had originally written a spec episode of *Cheers*. "Spec" is short for "speculate." When writers speculate—and it may well be the main thing writers do—they write without any guarantee of compensation in the hope that eventually whatever it is they create will sell. And even if it does not sell, its merit ought serve as a sample of the writer's craft, a showcase demonstrating in cold, black ink upon bright, white paper that she or he can truly write. It could be a "calling card" for future, paid assignments.

Speculating is the activity that occupies television writers as they struggle to break into episodic series TV. Even for writers of theatrical feature films, and for others who are well established, speculating is the predominant activity throughout the length and breadth of their careers.

It so happened that *Cheers* was, at that time, sold out for the season; no further assignments were available. Nevertheless, the writer was able to find an agent willing to read the spec episode. This agent considered the script to be worthy and submitted it instead to *Who's the Boss?* as a sample of the writer's work.

This is standard practice in TV. Write a spec episode in a particular genre—in this instance the thirty-minute, "three-camera/taped-before-a-live-audience" situation comedy—and it may serve in the search for assignments on other shows within that same genre.

The *Who's the Boss?* staff agreed that the script was skillful, even if it treated a subject they had already covered. They invited the writer to meet with them to "pitch" proposals for their show—that is, orally to propose outlines for future episodes. At the meeting, the staff listened to all the proposals and purchased none.

Devastated, the writer prepared to leave, but surprisingly was instructed to remain. As is routine in episodic TV, the staff of *Who's the Boss?* had compiled a comprehensive list of their own ideas which freelancers would be hired to bring to fruition. They felt that one particular idea would be suitable for this writer.

For those who may not be familiar with the format of *Who's the Boss?*, it was a sitcom based on the following setup: the protagonist, Tony, is a man in his mid-thirties who, in exchange for room and board for himself and his early-adolescent daughter, keeps house for an attractive and prospering businesswoman.

American television seems to love last year's—or last decade's—controversy. Even with the modern women's movement long under way, television found it provocative, even downright hilarious, to present a situation in which a woman was boss over a man rather than the other way around, particularly where the man's chores were domestic: laundering, vacuuming, ironing, cooking. Can't you see the network meeting at which the proposal was originally pitched? "Tony vacuuming! Imagine! *Vacuuming!* I'm gonna have a heart attack! *Tony!* Vacuuming!"

In any case, the episode our writer ended up scripting was based on the idea that Tony has a friend who's a priest. It opens with Tony's young daughter angrily returning toys to her pal, the girl next door. They've suffered a spat and vowed to return each other's dollies and dishes, borrowed over the years; never again will they have anything to do with one another.

"That's a mistake," Tony advises his daughter. Friendship, he explains, is all that really counts in life. It is true that from time to time friends argue, Tony explains, but they also make peace. Forgiveness is the name of the game. He pleads with the girl to reconcile with her friend.

"Never!" the daughter responds.

Tony pleads with her to reconsider. He recalls a disagreement of his own with a pal from his old neighborhood. The two were fast friends until one day they argued over something—he doesn't even remember what—and went their separate ways, never again to have any contact whatever. "It is already ten years since that happened," Tony laments, "and not one day has passed, not an hour, that I have not felt impoverished by my ruptured relationship with this former friend."

Tony asserts that his daughter will be committing a profound error if she fails to heal the rift with the neighbor.

But if friendship is so important, the daughter challenges her father, why doesn't Tony make peace with *his* pal?

Because, Tony explains, it's been so long since they've had anything to do with each other that he wouldn't even know how to find the guy.

Nonsense, the daughter protests; two or three phone calls will easily track down his lost friend. If Tony's not just blowing air, she goes on, if he truly means what he says, if he's not merely handing down the standard parental hypocrisy, he ought to reconcile with his old buddy. If Tony will set that example, the daughter promises, she will make peace with her own friend next door.

In this way, Tony's daughter shames him into seeking out his long-lost pal. The mechanics of his tracking down the friend are not presented in the show. All that matters is that a reunion is arranged. (A lesser writer would have squandered a substantial amount of time and language cataloguing Tony's activities in locating his former friend.)

When the friend actually appears on-screen for the first time, it is a wonderful surprise to see that he wears the collar of a Roman Catholic priest.

Note the writer's skill here. Even within the limited context of television's small screen, there is nevertheless a great deal that a writer can graphically communicate. The episode at hand offers commendable examples. Here, for example, upon first sight of the old pal we are exposed in a flash to the fact of his stature: the former street tough is now a holy presence, a man of the cloth. His priest's collar is all we need see to learn this. It is a splendid bit of action that is visual instead of talky.

Another trap this writer avoided was tipping her hand.

A less skillful writer would have had some character say, "I hear that Callahan became a priest." But where's the purpose in prematurely exposing such information except to blunt the thrust—to debauch the dramatic impact—of seeing the friend in his religious collar the first time we meet him?

Aristotle in his *Poetics* urges the poet—surely he meant the screenwriter—to find the true beginning not only in a play but even in a part of a play. Not only whole plays but even mere parts of plays have their own beginnings, middles and ends. And the beginning, he tells us, is the part before which we need nothing.

And we need nothing in this scene before the two now-reunited pals, already reconciled, quaff coffee in the kitchen, exchange old neighborhood lore, and in doing so revitalize their previously dormant relationship. A less adept writer would have wasted a good deal of time and language detailing the early moments of the reconciliation. Our writer, however, places the characters smack-dab in the middle of their rapprochement.

And that "middle" is the authentic Aristotelian "beginning" of the scene; it is, again, the part before which nothing is needed. Tony and Father Callahan, at the kitchen table, swap fond memories—pranks played on one another and on mutual pals—laughing and scratching and enjoying each other's company as if nothing had ever separated them, as if over all these years there has been lost not even a moment.

Now, however, Tony recalls a particularly nefarious prank perpetrated decades earlier at the young Callahan's expense. And upon hearing the ancient prank recounted, the priest's demeanor transforms most abruptly.

"You're the guy who did that?" the priest asks Tony, incredulous, still clearly hurt by the prank even after all the ensuing years. "That was you?"

"Of course it was me," Tony boasts. "You didn't know that?"

Callahan reports that indeed he did not know. The priest again asks Tony, "You did that? You? That really hurt me a lot. It was really you?"

Tony smiles broadly and nods proudly, a broad Cheshire-cat grin smeared across his smug, self-satisfied face.

Callahan, reexperiencing his ancient pain, loses control. To his surprise—and that of everyone else—he cold-cocks Tony, delivering a roundhouse punch to the jaw that sends him sprawling.

No one is more horrified than Callahan himself. He apologizes profusely, asserting that he now realizes he's never lost his street-tough soul, that he has no business posing and posturing and strutting as any kind of priest, as a devoted servant of Christ. He'd thought that when God called him to His service he had surrendered that gritty, ugly, let's-fight aspect of himself. Now he sees that it was all a wretched, sorry joke.

Not to worry, Tony reassures him, rubbing his jaw, picking himself up off the floor. "I really had it coming."

"It's not your fault," Callahan protests. "You didn't punch anybody in the face." The priest tears off his clerical collar. "I am leaving the Church," he announces. "I have no right to represent myself as a man of God."

"Nonsense," Tony argues. All men and women—even priests—are sinners in the eyes of the Lord, he insists. To be saved, a man needs only to ask forgiveness.

But Callahan will have none of this. He storms out of the house, his collar abandoned on the floor beside the table, his life as a priest now ended.

Tony is mortified. He feels responsible for the turmoil he has caused. For one thing, Callahan was supposed to serve a spaghetti dinner at the local senior citizens' center, as he does every Thursday night. Now no one will be there to support the old folks. The least Tony can do is to go to the seniors' center and provide the dinner.

Tony and his family show up at the center, spaghetti dinner at the ready. "Where's Callahan?" the elderly folks want to know. Tony creates lame excuses.

Now, suddenly, Callahan appears.

The collar is gone; he wears civilian clothes. He announces

that he is leaving the priesthood, and that he feels obligated to explain personally to the seniors that he will no longer be providing Thursday-night spaghetti dinners.

Everyone pleads with him to reconsider, but he resists. "If God wants me to return to His service, let Him show me a sign."

Promptly, there is a sharp knock at the door. A man enters carrying a huge sign that a local sign-painting company is just now delivering. It reads: BINGO WEDNESDAY NIGHTS—SENIOR CITIZENS CENTER—50 CENTS.

"There!" everyone joyfully observes. "A sign!"

"That's not what I meant," Callahan protests.

"You said 'a sign.' "

There is quite a lot of fun in the dialogue here revolving around the word "sign."

"I didn't mean a 'sign' sign. I meant a *sign*."

"A sign is a sign."

"I meant a biblical sign," Callahan pleads. "The Red Sea parting. An earthquake. At the very least thunder and lightning."

"You asked God for a sign and he gives you a sign and you're still not satisfied?" Tony asks. "You think God has no sense of humor?"

And at last Callahan is persuaded to resume his priestly role and return to the Church.

The last thing that happens in the episode, of course, is that Tony's daughter reconciles with the girl next door.

And right there, in a humble TV episode, is a perfect example, among other things, of Aristotelian story structure: beginning, middle, end. The end of the beginning is the point at which Tony is shamed into seeking reunion with the priest. The middle ends with the appearance of the sign. The end, of course, is all that follows.

The episode also offers a perfect example of a fundamental screenwriting trinity: idea, story, theme.

Again, the idea: Tony has a friend who's a priest.

What value in that? Precious little. Indeed, all by itself it is virtually worthless. This fact allows us to underscore a most fundamental screenwriting principle.

Principle 6: **The least important, most overappreciated element in screenwriting is the idea.**

What truly counts is not the idea for the story but the story itself, the sustained, integrated enterprise that combines character and tale and dialogue and all of the other elements that collectively constitute the whole picture.

It is, however, neither idea nor story but theme upon which we wish to focus here. What is the theme that underlies this tale? What is its overarching principle?

Simply this: faith exists solely to be challenged. Faith untested is no faith at all. A challenge to one's faith offers the opportunity to revitalize and renew that faith.

Moreover, the greater the challenge to a faith, the greater the potential for expansion. Exactly as a weight lifter pressing only a pound or two will not derive much benefit, so also will a weak-kneed challenge to faith fail to strengthen that faith. To build muscles one needs to press a hundred pounds; the greater the struggle, the greater the growth.

If the truth be told, critics, pundits and educators do not have high expectations regarding sitcom episodes offered up on mainstream, commercial television. Nevertheless, the night this particular *Who's the Boss?* episode aired, some forty million people were exposed to a wondrous lesson in human faith and healing.

It was not intellectual or conscious, but it was there, as clear as light. Millions of everyday folks learned that if they someday experience a crisis of faith—and what life is without such crises?—instead of succumbing to dread and fear, they might actually rejoice in the opportunity provided to forge what could prove to be a still greater faith.

All of this in an ordinary episode of a wearisomely familiar TV series episode, with prearranged characters in preordained situations. Here is testimony aplenty to the power of narrative expression and to the preeminence of story among all the elements that constitute a screenplay.

Principle 7: It is in the story, not in the mere idea, that the theme is ultimately articulated.

In sum, a lame television show with a facile, shallow idea, put into the hands of a talented, disciplined writer, wields power that is infinite. A vast, common audience is confronted with profound questions about the nature of life itself. And that same audience is provided with insights into religion, theology, God, clergy, family, friendship and more.

Note, finally, that the theme was no doubt a complete surprise even to the writer. The writer probably did not consciously acknowledge that the tale revealed her own particular view of faith, or the role faith plays in defining identity.

The producers certainly did not ask for a story commenting upon the nature of human faith. If that's where the tale eventually ended up, it was as much a surprise to them as to the writer. Indeed, theme is in its nature a surprise to all parties. Remember, all that the producers sought was a story in which "Tony has a friend who's a priest."

The lesson? It is possible to start with a narrow, slight, pale idea and end up with a theme that is hefty, substantial and profound. Start with a profound theme, however, and what is guaranteed is this: a tale that is self-conscious, self-important, heavy-handed and unworthy of the time, attention and consideration of any audience.

Having examined a completed TV episode and achieved a hands-on deconstruction of theme's special nature, let us confront a story craft challenge—wherein the reader is invited actively to participate in the construction of a movie tale and to explore theme's singularity from within.

Story Craft Challenge: What's in the Bags?

Let me detail the beginning of a tale of my own invention. We'll call it *Creature Comforts*. Before getting into concrete details of the story, let me briefly review the manner in which the original idea occurred to me, as it demonstrates the principle that ideas are virtually worthless unless and until they are worked out into stories.

Years ago I was in Manhattan on business. My first book, a novel, was about to be published. As I made my way toward Rockefeller Center for a meeting with my editor, I passed the entrance to the modest Piccadilly Hotel on West 48th Street. As I strode past the front doors—twin glass panels—I glanced inside and briefly witnessed a man and a woman leaning wearily against the front desk.

I saw no luggage, although it is quite possible that there was luggage aplenty just beyond my view.

No big deal.

My observation of this scene could not possibly have taken longer than two seconds. Nevertheless, for a year, I continually thought about it: Who are these people? Where is their luggage? What is the nature of their relationship?

I am not saying this is the only thing I did all year. Of course, I continued to live my life—to write, to teach, to breathe, to eat, to take out the garbage, and even to brush my teeth occasionally. But I also thought perpetually of that splendidly boring, monumentally inconsequential moment that had caught my eye on an ordinary summer day.

Eventually, it led to the following collection of incidents and anecdotes that we can label a story.

In the early-morning light a taxi pulls up to the entrance of the Jacob K. Javits Convention Center, the vast facility on Manhattan's West Side. The entrance is festooned with banners on which is emblazoned the legend: WELCOME, BOOKSELLERS!!! Clearly, the American Booksellers Association's annual trade show is opening.

Out of the taxi steps our protagonist, wimpy, nerdy, geeky, fortyish Herb Castle. Herb is every bit as creased and crumpled as his olive-drab corduroy suit. One look at his glazed, bleary expression easily gives any viewer the impression that Herb has just arrived via the so-called red-eye, the low-budget all-night flight from the West Coast.

As he steps from the cab, the catch on his abused salesman's sample case snaps open; its contents spill to the gutter. Even a cursory glance reveals them to be books: obscure technical and scientific texts. Clearly, Herb is a regional sales representative for a publisher of such volumes.

As he scrambles awkwardly to gather the books, the impatient taxi driver complains, "That's thirty-two forty on the meter, pal."

Herb pulls his wallet from his pocket. He rifles through his cash with dismay. He has nothing but a hundred-dollar bill. Sheepishly he proffers it to the driver, saying, "I hope a hundred's not a problem."

"Not for me it ain't," the cabby responds cavalierly in a thick Noo Yawk drawl, pocketing the bill, gunning the engine and sprinting away onto the avenue.

"Officer!" Herb yells to a policeman directing traffic nearby. "That cabby just split with my change!"

The policeman, however, does not exactly spring to action. "The white zone is for the loading and unloading of passengers only," he recites in numb, flat, bureaucratic cop-babble. "Please do not obstruct ingress to and egress from the facility." The sleek crime-fighting machine that is the New York City Police Department is not about to unleash its legions to seek justice in the case of yet another cabby absconding with too generous a tip.

Let us pause for just a moment in order to record some observations.

Certainly I make no claim that this is a passage of poetic genius to rival Shakespeare. Nevertheless, in its workmanlike way it establishes important information regarding our protagonist. And, notably, it accomplishes this for the most part not through dialogue but through action that is aural rather than visual.

The medium is, after all, not radio but moving pictures.

We quickly establish that Herb is a man who is often abused, cheated and just generally exploited. We know already—in substantially less than a minute—quite a lot about his profession and his purpose. And even if the telling is not exactly a laff riot, we can concede at the very least that there's a ghost of a giggle somewhere in here.

At least a modest little chuckle.

And in the movie business you don't cut funny.

In precious little time, then, without squandering a lot of language, without spectacular fireworks, with neither a car chase nor a chain saw massacre, we deliver substantial story and character freight.

Normally I urge screenwriters to avoid designating credit sequences; let the director and editor and other collaborators decide precisely where it is most appropriate to roll the main title and opening credits. Having just said that, allow me to suggest that the next sequence is ideal for rolling the main title and opening credits.

We travel through the convention facility's vast central chamber—a squadron of 747s could fly loop-the-loop stunts in this space—where the mainstream, upscale publishers have their plush, upholstered, laminated, carpeted booths featuring lavish displays replete with every kind of giveaway: book bags and trinkets and trophies and posters and even books. The floor swarms with buyers, sellers, agents, editors and authors.

We linger momentarily over a particular publisher's unique feature: a boxed set, the body of reissued works by a reclusive best-selling author who writes under the nom de plume Page Turner. Through posters displayed around the booth it is apparent that over a decade "Turner" has written a dozen hot thrillers, all of which have made the *New York Times* best-seller list. Half have been hit movies; several have become popular television series. Furthermore, it is apparent that after all these years in anonymity, the author is planning to go public and to participate in the promotion of his collected works.

At long last, as the final opening credit crawls across the screen, we find ourselves off the main chamber, in a modest backwater, clearly the convention center's low-rent district, where the handful of scientific and technical textbook publishers have their downscale booths.

Herb's booth is hardly a booth at all. It's more like a point along the corridor, a spot against the wall, consisting entirely of a bridge table and a hard metal folding chair upon which Herb uneasily dozes, dead to the world, his chin on his chest.

And why not? The corridor is virtually deserted.

On the table before him, arrayed standing on their spines, are his publisher's handful of current offerings. A crude homemade easel—felt-tipped marker on folded shirt cardboard—lists the company's leading titles.

Now, suddenly, a startlingly beautiful young woman enters the frame. She is smartly, stunningly dressed. She moves right up to Herb's station, regarding his sleeping form wryly, shaking her head slowly from side to side. A big, broad, ear-to-ear smile brightens her face and the whole long, otherwise dim corridor.

As if her presence alone—the glowing, pulsing aura created by her sheer beauty—is sufficient to wake him, Herb returns to consciousness, opening his eyes, clumsily stifling a yawn.

As always, he hits the ground apologizing. "Sorry. Must've dozed off there for a minute. Thanks so much for stopping by. We've just reissued Olivewood and Crawford's *Curvilinear Dysfunction in Crystalline Entropy Mechanisms*—it's part of our *Rotational Divergent Immunoglobulin* series. There's also an updated edition of *Nonperiodicity in Central Euclidean Tessellations* and. . . ."

Herb runs out of steam, grinding mid-sentence to a breathy halt. All the while the young woman simply smiles at him with an expression that communicates both affection and toleration.

She says nothing.

"Laura," the startled Herb finally says. "I hardly recognize you."

"Want to see some ID? Driver's license? Bloomie's charge plate?"

"You look beautiful. Radiant. Like a whole new person."

"A whole new person is precisely what I am, living a whole new life. For one thing, Carl and I are through. The marriage is over. Finito. I've moved out of the house in Brooklyn Heights."

"I'm so sorry."

"Don't be. My life hasn't ended; it's just begun. Take me to lunch and I'll tell you all the bloody details, all the gory gossip."

"I'd love to," Herb responds. "But I can't. I've got to hold down the fort here."

Together they scan the empty aisle. Clearly, there isn't much of a fort to hold down.

Screenwriting problems do not arise in neatly ordered, conveniently configured, prepackaged bundles. They leap out at writers in clusters. It is appropriate for us, therefore, to pause here for a few observations regarding craft.

First, this little bit of dialogue has provided readers of the script and viewers of the film with substantial information regarding the characters and their situation. Without spoon-feeding, without spelling it all out in too-on-the-nose chatter, we already appreciate, for example, that Herb and Laura go back a long way in their lives, and that they haven't seen each other in quite some while.

We also learn from the dialogue that Laura has just now ended an unhappy marriage to some guy named Carl.

We've moved the dialogue along with rising and falling inflections, interrogatories and responses, stress and resolution that mark and replicate the rhythms characterizing authentic speech. It is not, of course, real speech but reel speech. It may have the sense, the feel of true-to-life dialogue, but it also simultaneously advances character and plot. In real life, people stumble and stammer and beat around the bush before coming to the point.

But this is not real life; this is a movie.

And if we are to succeed, we need to write dialogue that is integrated. The dialogue must expand the audience's appreciation of the characters and at the same time move the story forward.

The lines of dialogue here are short and purposeful, not blocky, not speechy. We do not hear the characters lecturing one another. Instead they swap snappy, quick lines, creating a Ping-Pong match, the rocking up-and-back sounds that seem to color genuine dialogue.

Since I am the writer of this screenplay, let me cheat just a little and tell you something that I would not tell the reader of the screenplay: I need, for the purposes of the story, to get Herb and Laura out of here, away from the convention.

One way I can attempt to do this is by struggling to craft dialogue for Laura that will finally persuade Herb to run off with her to the next scene. But I do not need to waste even a minute. In a movie it is possible to have a character absolutely refuse to do something, yet promptly in the next scene have him do whatever it was he said he absolutely could not under any circumstances do.

We can, therefore, have Herb point-blank refuse to agree to take Laura to lunch. And in the very next scene they are having lunch together at an East Side cafe.

But in concurrence with Aristotelian precepts, we start the scene not *before* the beginning but *at* the beginning.

And the true beginning of this scene—the part before which nothing is needed—is not at the beginning but at the end of their meal.

We find them, in fact, having finished lunch, lingering at the table as Laura orders yet another bottle of wine, perhaps their third. The two are warmly aglow—even a bit woozy—under the influence of the grape.

Laura finishes the description of her marriage's crash landing: "... And so I said to myself, 'That's the final straw,' picked up my hat and coat and walked out the door of our house in Brooklyn Heights."

"You and Carl are taking time off, then, to allow each other a bit of place and space, as intelligent, advantaged, enlightened, aware couples do from time to time these days?" Herb inquires.

"Spare me that mellow feel-good California new-age drivel," Laura responds. "Carl and I hate each other."

"I see," Herb remarks, ruefully. He tries to reassure her. "Oh, it may be a little hairy at first, a little lonely," he says. "There may be moments you get to feeling more than a trifle shaky, even panicky. From time to time you may feel a certain despair, a dark and dingy doom, a gloomy sense of hopelessness—"

"Herb," Laura interrupts, pouring him more wine, "shut up a minute, will you? I feel great."

"I feel sloshed."

"We're both a little blotto," Laura says, "and it's a good thing, too, because there's something I've always wanted to tell you, and I think I'm just sloppy enough to say it straight out. I love you. I've always loved you."

"I'm fond of you too, Laura."

"I'm not talking 'fond,' " Laura says. "I'm talking love."

"I understand completely," Herb insists, nodding sagely, not understanding at all.

"Do you?" Laura asks him. "Then let's get out of here. Let's go somewhere—some cool, secure place. I know a hotel nearby—let's have sex. Do you understand? Do you? I'm saying let's go somewhere right now, get naked and ball till we're black and blue and blind."

Herb promptly knocks over the wine bottle. He quickly rights it, pours himself another glass. "You're merely reacting to the trauma of the separation," he says. "Overreacting. It's perfectly natural."

"Translation," Laura says. "You're turning me down."

"Of course I'm turning you down. This is all too fast for me."

"Fast? I've obsessed about you for decades. There hasn't been a day, not an hour, that I haven't thought of you."

"Ridiculous," Herb insists. "I'm the selfsame nerd you knew in the neighborhood."

Laura leans forward and gazes into his eyes. "It took tremendous courage for me to seek you out. You're in town for the day. We have a chance for a sweet, crazy moment together. Something special just for us. When it's over, it's over—you go back to Santa Monica; I stay here in New York. We never see each other again. But when we're old and feeble with Alzheimer's, after everything else has faded, this crazy afternoon in Manhattan is all we'll remember."

"I hadn't a clue you felt this way," Herb confesses.

"I don't blame you for hesitating," Laura says. "It won't even be any good. First times tend to be a little clumsy, a little awkward. Still, the issue looms between us like a wall. We can address it or ignore it but it is nonetheless there, unfinished business, an ancient account that's got to be settled."

"I don't mind telling you I'm flattered," Herb says after a hefty pause. "And tempted. But, frankly, what with your recent separation, I doubt you could handle such an event emotionally just now."

"Speak for yourself."

"You're absolutely right," Herb realizes. "I'm the one who couldn't handle it. It's not my style. I'm a middle-class kid. A married guy. You asked me a direct question and you're entitled to a direct answer. No. Impossible. Absolutely not. Forget it. It's out of the question."

While Herb and Laura argue about whether or not they should cheat, let me also cheat a little and offer what would be totally unacceptable in the script itself: a revelation of my design.

Just as I earlier needed to get Herb and Laura away from the book fair, for the purposes of the story I need now to get them into bed. If you recall, I waived much potential dialogue at the convention center pertaining to Laura's effort to persuade Herb to join her for lunch. Here, too, I've chosen not to create a lot of dialogue for her to persuade Herb to cooperate with the new scheme.

We can do precisely what we did in the earlier instance: Herb flat-out refuses to join her at a hotel.

At which point, of course, we cut directly to the exterior of the Gramercy Hotel, a charming, romantic hideaway in the East Twenties. Over this we hear the voice of the desk clerk saying, "And precisely how long will you require the room, Mr. Murphy?"

And now we're inside the lobby of the hotel, with Herb and Laura arrayed awkwardly against the front desk and the clerk peering at the registration card which Herb has just now fraudulently filled out.

At this juncture, let's pause briefly for a couple of observations.

First, right here is the point at which we catch up with the limp, lame idea that launched this whole convoluted plot: my vision years earlier of the two apparently lost souls leaning against the desk of the Piccadilly Hotel in Manhattan's West Forties. A moment's glance at a couple of strangers triggered everything. This goes some distance toward underscoring the proposition that an idea all by itself—as compared with a story that will sustain a whole screenplay—is, at best, of trivial value.

Second, let us argue a bit about the placement of the just-concluded scene in a cafe. Am I not one to caution writers against playing out scenes in restaurants? Are not eateries places where characters typically engage in action that is not truly action—wielding knives, forks, spoons—and recite the tale through dialogue instead of acting it out? After all, the word "drama" derives from the Greek word meaning "to do." It does not mean "to talk."

On the other hand, all rules are null and void in the face of integration. You can do anything, even nothing at all, if somehow or other character and story are palpably, measurably, identifiably advanced.

And this is the case with the East Side cafe, in a number of ways. For one thing, it is in perfect keeping with motivation soon to be revealed: Laura's need to get Herb rip-roaring drunk in order to win his cooperation in a scheme that has yet to be exposed. Certainly a cafe is a reasonable location for one character to ply another with booze.

Herb and Laura stand now before the desk clerk as he inquires of Herb—falsely registering as "Murphy"—precisely how long he'll need the room.

"Depends," Herb stutters, fidgeting, looking to Laura for help. But she has no help to offer. "That depends on a number of factors," Herb continues, turning back to the clerk. "It's entirely possible," he finally babbles, "that we'll require the room only tonight."

"That's fine," the clerk reassures him. "Where are your bags?"

Herb panics; his mind races with a trillion questions. Bags? Don't you need bags to check into a hotel? Maybe you can check into a motel with no bags, but in a hotel, where you have to enter and exit in plain sight of the front desk, are guests not required to possess luggage? Is it not suspicious to check in without bags? Does it not provide the unmistakable appearance of an afternoon's adulterous sprawl in the straw? If there are no bags to schlepp past the desk on the way out, is it not too easy to skip the joint without settling one's account?

All of the above queries, of course, are appropriate to spell out in, say, a novel. But they have no place in any screenplay. Screenplays consist entirely of information that is visual and aural—what is seen and what is heard. Screenwriters attempt through sight and sound to replicate for the reader of the pages the experience of the viewer in the theater. Internal, interior, mental calisthenics can be made manifest to the audience viewing the film only through facial contortions, physical gestures and clues provided through agitated, awkward dialogue.

This is why I argue that novels are actually easier to write than screenplays. Even if many regard the novel—literature—as a higher form, especially when compared with something so down-and-dirty, so lowest-common-denominator as movies, it is the novel that is in fact less challenging to write. Authors of novels can assert what a character thinks, recalls, realizes. They can explore and examine any and all mental processes. They can describe not only what happens but also what has happened and what will happen.

But screenwriters are stuck with sight and sound alone. Moreover, we are stranded forever in the numbing, demanding, relentless present tense. Even that over-exploited conceit—the flashback—must be expressed in the present tense.

All the *Creature Comforts* film audience knows of Herb's misgivings about checking into a hotel without luggage—and I expect it is enough—is provided when he unexpectedly blurts out, "American."

What can this possibly mean? It seems to be something of a non sequitur and therefore creates a bit of confusion. Such confusion sets up a sort of welcome gentle stress and tension that involves audiences, keeping them curious and awake.

Not only the audience, but even the characters in the movie appear to be confused by Herb's response. And in that response is an example of a screenwriting precept that derives from a law—the Prudent Person Principle—which we'll examine more extensively later. For now, let us merely note that the principle requires, first of all, that characters within movies respond to a film's circumstances in more or less the same manner as the audience members themselves would likely respond under similar circumstances.

In keeping with this principle, then, both Laura and the desk clerk regard Herb curiously. In unison they ask the very same question the audience would likely ask: "American?"

"Airlines," Herb responds. "American Airlines. They misrouted or rerouted or something. The bags. Sent them to Cleveland or Buffalo or some such godforsaken place." He turns to Laura and says, "I suppose we'll have to purchase complete new wardrobes here in town, darling."

"Just the excuse I've longed for my whole life," she says.

The two are playing little private games, both right in front of the clerk's face and at the same time, metaphorically, behind his back. Here are two about-to-be-first-time-lovers who are understandably anxious. The opportunity for some private banter helps relax them just a bit, brings them closer together in a way they alone can appreciate.

The clerk, however, reassures them. "Don't worry about your bags, please, Mr. and Mrs. Murphy. Airlines lose bags all the time, but they also find them." He reaches for the phone and prepares to dial. "I'll call American Airlines and have them deliver the luggage right here to the hotel as soon as it reaches Kennedy. What flight did you come in on?"

Herb is paralyzed.

Naturally, he has no desire for the clerk to phone any airline in search of phantom bags on a phantom flight. None of this, however, can be reported expressly to the reader of the script. Instead, all the reader is offered is Herb rallying, inventing. "Actually," Herb tells the clerk, "I have to call the airline myself to rearrange our return flight. While I'm at it, I'll tell them we're registered here."

"That's fine," the clerk says, satisfied, hanging up the phone.

But as soon as Herb figures he's outfoxed the guy, the clerk seizes a pad and pencil. "Describe the bags for me. You folks have been inconvenienced enough. I want to make sure the bell captain sends your luggage directly to your room the minute it arrives."

Herb can't shake this dude!

"Describe the bags?" Herb asks. "Sure. Why not?" He exchanges a private glance with Laura, then takes a deep breath. "Let's see. There's an off-white vinyl Samsonite piece, somewhat beat-up, and also a plaid fabric fold-over with a hard black double handle." The clerk scribbles furiously as Herb, with burgeoning enthusiasm, creates his fantasy luggage. "Oh, and also a little carry-on flight bag. With a Braniff logo. Not American." He's about to go on but Laura furtively kicks him beneath the counter, beyond the clerk's view.

"That's all of it," Herb says.

"Front!" the clerk sings out, hitting the bell. A bellhop approaches.

We cut now to a comfy, cozy New York hotel room with one vast, yawning bed. The door opens and Herb and Laura enter. They lock the dead bolt and hook up the restraining chain.

They face each other. "The time has come, I suppose," Herb says, "to be a little clumsy, a little awkward."

This, of course, echoes of the line Laura used in her seduction of Herb at the cafe during lunch. And to that extent, it links the earlier scene with this one and represents another facet of integration: stitching together the separate strands of the tale. Furthermore, the connection is not to something immediately previous but to something still earlier in the narrative. This lends the script a desirable roundness; it makes it appear less straight-line.

After a shy, embarrassed pause, the two slam together in an embrace.

Creative expression in any and all formats is at its core a choice-making enterprise. At the very beginning of this chapter I asserted that every work of art—a painting, a work of sculpture, a musical composition—is a record of the choices made by the artist. I do not believe artists sit alert at their stations consciously contemplating choices, but when the work is complete there can be no denying that a pattern of choices has been created; moreover, it is that pattern which constitutes the work itself.

And we face various choices here in *Creature Comforts*.

We could, at this point, create a big lovemaking scene, a sweetly vulgar hump-romp with Herb and Laura stripping off each other's clothes, tumbling together naked to the bed, nibbling, licking, grabbing, groping, bumping, grinding, stroking, combining. Or they could fall instead to the floor and couple with one another on the scratchy carpet.

Or they could retreat to the closet and in its dim light endlessly commit unnatural acts upon one another, perhaps while one or the other hangs upside down from the clothing rod. Or they could copulate while wriggling all around on the hard, cold, tingling mosaic tile in the bathroom, or while standing together in the shower, or while wrapped around each other in the tub.

Another possible choice is a straight-out, full-tilt, hard-core pornographic sexfest resplendent with penetration involving any permutation of objects and orifices.

Sound good?

To me, frankly, such scenes tend promptly to become boring. Sensuality that is implied—left to the imagination—is far more seductive, more erotic than sexuality that is expressed. Instead of playing out on screen, it plays where all art plays best: in the mind of the viewer or reader.

In *Creature Comforts* we can accomplish this by having the camera tilt up to the ceiling upon the lovers' first embrace. We hold there for a dreadful, heavy beat, and before our eyes the light dissolves from mid-afternoon to dusk. And in this manner we know that several hours have passed.

When we tilt back down to the bed, the lovers are bound together in each other's arms, nude, dead to the world in the afterglow of lovers' slumber. What's more, they lie on the raw mattress; the sheets and blankets and pillows are scattered throughout the chamber, offering ample testimony to the raucous, raunchy, randy, robust romp that has clearly transpired.

Indeed, the lovers' peaceful posture offers a marked contrast to the wrecked and ruined room. There is a deep serenity that is presented against a backdrop of sharply underscored erotic passion. Each enhances the other. Contrast is a useful weapon in all artists' arsenals. A photographer shooting a fur coat, for example, might in the same manner position his subject against a craggy granite rock face so as to bring into palpable relief the fur's rich, plush tactility.

There comes a sharp rapping, a noise very much resembling a knock at the door. Laura remains blissfully asleep but Herb awakens, opening a single curious eye. He wonders: Was it a noise from upstairs, or below, or in the room next door, or across the hall? Was it someone walking in the corridor past the door?

In a movie, of course, we cannot assert what it is any character "wonders," since we are prisoners of sound and light alone. We are prohibited from discussing thought processes. We can present only that which one can see or hear.

And all we see is Herb waiting patiently. At last, after some silence, he once again closes his eye.

At which point the knock sounds again.

This time both of Herb's eyes pop open. Concern clouds his countenance. Cautiously he swings his feet to the side of the bed. Pulling a sheet from the floor and drawing it around his waist like a makeshift toga, he goes to the door. There he cocks his head, almost touching the door with his ear.

At which point there is a clear and unmistakable knock.

Herb is so startled that he is virtually knocked to the ground.

"Who is it?" he calls out in raspy dread.

"Bellhop!" a voice rings out most merrily. "Good news, Mr. Murphy! Your bags have arrived!"

It cannot be said often enough: writing—like all of creative expression—is choice. Script by script, scene by scene, line by line screenwriters have nothing to do but select among an endless array of alternatives. One possible choice here is for Herb to blurt out: "Bags? What bags? I have no bags! I made the whole thing up! I'm a liar and a cheat! My companion and myself are actually engaging in adultery! This is an illicit liaison! I'm betraying my marriage vows in here!"

That might be dramatic in a way; and under certain circumstances it might even be funny.

The problem here, however, is that we are eight or ten minutes into our movie, and if we make this choice now, the movie is over. End the film here and the audience will rise and march en masse to the booth in search of the projectionist's head. They did not drive their cars and poke around for a parking place, stand on line in inclement weather, then fork over seven to ten dollars per ticket for a movie that lasts scant minutes. They've bargained for something that is more on the order of a couple of hours.

And they're entitled to expect the film artists—screenwriters first and foremost—to hold up our end of the bargain.

A better choice would be to have Herb unlock the dead bolt and open the door just the several inches that the restraining chain allows. Through the narrow wedge of doorway he peers out into the hall and sees, indeed, the bellhop and his luggage cart stacked high with bags: an off-white vinyl Samsonite piece, somewhat beat-up, a plaid fabric fold-over with a hard black double handle, a flight bag.

Braniff.

Not American.

And right here is the appropriate moment to pause in order to consider the rule referred to earlier: the Prudent Person Principle.

Principle 8: Audiences will tolerate characters on screen in situations they themselves would never be in, as long as the characters in the movie act the way the audience members themselves would act under those same circumstances.

Precisely what impact can this have upon the potential choices for our narrative in *Creature Comforts*?

Simply this: Herb has to take the bags into the room.

They're the bags, after all, that he described in precisely the same detail to the clerk. Even from his vantage through the partially open door, he can see that they sport identification tags marked "Murphy," and that the tags also bear the phony address Herb invented at the front desk but a handful of hours earlier.

How can Herb deny that these are his bags?

According to the Prudent Person Principle, Herb has to accept the bags.

And so he does, releasing the chain, opening the door wider, allowing the bellhop to place the luggage inside the door. Herb once again locks the dead bolt and reattaches the restraining chain.

"What's all that?" Laura inquires groggily, nodding toward the luggage as she slowly wakens.

According to the Prudent Person Principle, not to mention every other screenwriting rule ever imagined, Herb and Laura must open the bags.

Creating the bags' contents represents for the screenwriter the most critical kind of choice-making, because the bags' contents drive the whole picture.

In my travels around the world addressing screenwriting groups, I often tell just this much of the story. And at this juncture in the narrative I invite writers to imagine that Herb indeed opens the bags.

And I ask them: What's in the bags?

Below are some of the answers I have received over several years. After listing and analyzing them briefly for potential strengths and weaknesses, we'll move on to my own version of the answer, and in doing so we'll try to articulate an extremely important principle regarding the special nature of theme in screenplays.

What's in the Bags: Various Choices

Plane Tickets and Passports

Placing plane (or bus or train or steamship) tickets and passports in the luggage is smart story craft. The tale kicks forward instantaneously. If there are tickets to Paris (or anywhere else), rest assured one or the other or both members of the couple will eventually travel there. And audiences can expect that in the new location adventures will be encountered.

As with tickets, passports also provide screen stories with forward motion. The names on the documents can be "Murphy" or they can be those of Herb and Laura. The documents' photos

can be of Herb and Laura at an earlier age, perhaps in their college years, perhaps as preadolescents.

And such paraphernalia might well herald a journey through
their earlier lives.

Key(s)

The bags could contain among other things a key that fits,
say, a locker at Grand Central Station. Or it could fit the door
and ignition of a car parked across the street from the hotel. Or
the key's mate could surface much later in the film.

In any case, keys suggest motion. Some lock that the key
opens will be found and it will provide another tale thrust.

The introduction of the key at this point in the story offers testimony to the writer's skill, and it reveals an appreciation for the
art of integration. A writer's embrace of the interlocking enterprise represents plot craft itself.

A Body or Body Parts

Judging by the number of occasions in which mild-mannered
writers come up with dead bodies or parts of dead bodies, one
might well get the impression that the screenwriting landscape is
awash in sadists and perverts!

This is not necessarily true, but I have to admit that dead
bodies can be clever components to pack into the bags. They
imply violence, of course. And, like it or not, violence, which
signals emotional conflict, lies at the heart of drama from the
days of the ancient Greeks.

Not only does a body or a body part add stress and tension
and conflict to the tale, desirable commodities in dramatic expression, but all vastly turn the tale on its head, and they do so
quickly. What was up until now something of a mildly comedic
romantic romp instantaneously becomes a tale of terror and
intrigue.

Photos or a Videocassette

We've already touched upon the subject of photos. The pictures of the passport holders can be those of our Herb and Laura. The photos can be contemporaneous or from another time in their lives.

But they can also be pictures of completely different people. If the writer has a good grip on story craft, whoever is portrayed in those passport photos ought to appear in the flesh later.

If instead of—or in addition to—photos there is a videocassette, eventually it will become necessary to pop that tape into a player and view whatever it is that unfolds. It could be images of a crime committed by other characters who would eventually surface in the script.

Or it could be scenes from Herb's and Laura's earlier lives.

Or it could be surreptitiously recorded images of Herb and Laura at the convention, at lunch, entering the hotel, and/or perhaps even images of their lovemaking.

Or it could be scenes from portions of their lives that they have not yet lived and eventually we see them live out these scenes in "real" life! Fascinating thematic issues such as illusion and reality can be explored.

Archaeological Artifacts

Perhaps there are small statues or pottery from some ancient archaeological dig. Perhaps there are merely shards of such items. Eventually the couple travels to the site of the dig. Maybe it's in the midwestern United States. Maybe it's in Iraq. Wherever it is, they piece together certain items that are key to the solution of a current or historical tale of murder and betrayal.

Or it could all be part of an unlawful scheme to import artifacts from a foreign country.

Rhino Horns and/or Tigers' Penises

Similarly, there could be contraband relating to endangered species. Herb and Laura could have stumbled into a convoluted scheme to loot such treasures from some remote corner of the world. Or they could themselves be victims of the perpetrators of such a plot who hope to exploit them in the illegal import of goods presumed to possess curative qualities.

Wardrobe

There could be any and every kind of costume inside the bags.

Let us say, for example, that there are a bridal gown and a groom's tuxedo. Perhaps later in the tale Herb and Laura appear at a wedding as bride and groom.

Perhaps it is not just any wedding gown, but Laura's garment from her own wedding years ago. If this is the choice, there is the added responsibility of explaining it to the audience. It's easy enough to tell the reader of the script that the garment was worn by the character at her wedding, but how will this information be made available to viewers of the film in a theater?

This can be accomplished in any number of ways, such as through scattered bits and pieces of dialogue. Laura could say, "Wow! It's my wedding dress, and there's Carl's tux."

This is, of course, more than a little heavy-handed. I hold in low regard screenwriting where characters brazenly narrate information to the audience. A common example occurs when a character "thinks out loud," speaking lines as he contemplates them. Such self-consciousness simply reminds the audience of what they are entitled to forget: they're at the movies.

A more appropriate way to reveal such information is to delay that revelation and then let it unfold visually. For example, Herb and Laura could eventually come upon a photo album and from the photos inside it could become apparent that the clothes are one and the same.

If the clothes do not include a tuxedo and a wedding gown,

how about throwing in underwater diving outfits that the characters could eventually wear in a perilous dive into a flooded quarry where clues to an earlier mystery are found? Clearly, thinking aloud or other sorts of explanations are not required here.

Furthermore, instead of diving gear the bags could include mountain-climbing equipment: nylon cord, clamps, pitons, spelunking picks and mallets, and the like. This, of course, will take them not to the bottom of a sea but to the top of a mountain—or a sleek, high-rise urban tower. The venues for action and adventure, plot twists and turns, are limitless.

Microfilm

Certainly there could be microfilm.

The frames of the film could represent the results of an international spy operation and we might be launched into a tale of intelligence and counterintelligence.

There's not a thing wrong with any of these tales. Haven't there been scores and even hundreds of them?

But therein, of course, lies the problem. Spy stories are too, too familiar. I do not assert that it is impossible to construct a spy tale that is fresh and new and startling in every way; rather, I argue that it is most difficult to do, given the slew of movies of this type which have appeared over so many decades.

If a writer wants to place microfilm in Herb's and Laura's bags in order to advance a tale of spying, let that spying be industrial instead of international. Covering new territory provides a possibility for freshness.

Let me give you an example. In my experience of writing professionally over many years, I have scripted numerous works in the industrial, corporate, commercial, instructional, educational, and informational film arena. One client was a major toy company. My assignment was to smear wall-to-wall narration over the corporation's annual sales film, a project that more closely resembled an upscale slide show than any movie.

What I remember most about the experience is the staggering

security measures employed by the company to protect its most highly cherished trade secrets—for example, if its equivalent of the Barbie doll would be "anatomically correct" that year. That is to say, would it have breasts? And would the company's Ken knockoff have testicles?

Never in my life—not at any bank, not at any airport—have I ever encountered such massive and comprehensive security precautions as those taken by this manufacturer of toys, tokens, trifles and trinkets. Substantial fun might be derived, it seems to me, by wrapping a nail-biting tale of industrial espionage and intrigue around the details of a particular child's toy.

Or perhaps the tale could involve military secrets that have been betrayed in the manufacture of a particular item in, let's say, the G.I. Joe line. A rifle, or an aircraft, or a submarine is too perfectly detailed for the government's own comfort. Attempts are made to suppress the toy. And how was the information for its manufacture obtained in the first place?

This is not too different from international intrigue, but it is fresher—we don't see this type of thing nearly so frequently on the screen. It also integrates a weighty milieu—that of government security—with the lightweight paraphernalia of the world of children's toys. This provides potentially splendid contrast. And contrast underscores conflict.

In Colin Higgins's *Foul Play*, Chevy Chase and Goldie Hawn portray lovers who possess a piece of microfilm that is sought by international terrorists. While it's a pretty good movie, it's somewhat blunted by the hoary, weary microfilm/international spy conceit.

Wouldn't the story be more interesting if the couple's pursuers instead sought a vial of frozen bull semen, an item that seems at once thoroughly off-putting and enormously valuable? The semen could represent the results of centuries of hybridization, all of it now in jeopardy, all of it now depending upon Chevy and Goldie's ability to protect it. This could create extra tension and add something that we have not seen ten thousand times already.

Nonsense Stuff: Ping-Pong Balls, Condoms, Toenail Clippings

The bags can contain items that make no sense at all.

Ultimately, if it suits the tale, the writer can strive indeed to make some sense of the items. Ping-Pong balls, for example, might represent some metaphorical reference to the diplomatic process that decades ago brought together the Chinese and American governments after our table tennis teams toured and competed in each other's country. (At that time it became difficult to determine whether or not what one watched on television was the news or a lost clip from a newly discovered Marx Brothers movie.)

Condoms, of course, relate readily to the scourge of AIDS, to any and all matters involving human sexuality, and to a substantial number of other naturally dramatic, controversial subjects.

Toenail clippings could eventually be subjected to scientific DNA analysis, revealing that they once belonged to, say, Albert Einstein or Adolf Hitler or John Kennedy or Sonny Bono or Tommy Lasorda or Rin Tin Tin or Screaming Jay Hawkins or anybody else.

Drugs

The suitcases could be stuffed with illicit drugs.

These could be out in the open—plain as day—in plastic bags, clearly visible upon one's lifting the suitcase's lid. Or there could be built into the luggage a hidden compartment, for example a false bottom, in which the contraband is cleverly, elaborately concealed. But luggage with false bottoms and hidden compartments, I must confess, strikes me as tedious and overly familiar.

Instead of drugs, the bags could contain certain other objects—perhaps the archaeological artifacts mentioned earlier—that are themselves eventually discovered to conceal cocaine, heroine or whatever other style of pharmaceutical contraband the screenwriter chooses. Investigators might at first suspect that the artifacts themselves are contraband, then discover that it is what's inside them that is illicit.

But if luggage with false bottoms strikes me as tedious, what can I say regarding the whole notion of illegal drugs? Surely the subject's been done to death. Want to guarantee that I won't attend a movie? Run its trailer with a voice-of-doom narrator talking about cops going undercover in order to bust some dope ring. I hope never again to subject myself to any such movie!

Take, for example, Eddie Murphy's sparkling performance and the various other dazzling aspects of the fish-out-of-water movie *Beverly Hills Cop*. It's great until the plot stumbles into cocaine smuggling, and then the movie becomes merely a third-rate episode of some marginal TV police/action/melodrama.

Steer clear, therefore, of the shoals of familiarity. My advice to screenwriters: avoid at all costs the subject of drug smuggling. It violates screenwriting's lone unbreakable rule: it's boring.

Nothing

When I ask writers to contemplate what is in the bags, it thrills me when one or another of them seizes the true power that resides in writing's choice-making nature and decides that the bags contain nothing whatsoever; they are totally empty. Perhaps the bags themselves are the subject of whatever scheme constitutes the story's substance.

Has not everyone heard the story of the fellow who marches daily through a well-fortified border checkpoint pushing a wheelbarrow loaded with dirt? Each day the guards sift through the dirt, trying to figure out whatever it is that the guy is smuggling, but they continually come up empty. What it turns out that he is actually smuggling, of course, is wheelbarrows.

Perhaps the bags—much less their contents—are of no consequence at all. It is merely the fact that they arrived, and what the arrival says about Herb's mental calisthenics at the front desk when he first "created" the bags, that matters.

The Bags Cannot Be Opened

Another possibility is that Herb and Laura struggle to open the bags but the lids will not budge. The bags could remain sealed throughout the picture, representing some metaphorical aspect of the tale and its theme. Or they could be opened later, perhaps by some other individual encountered along the tale's road who, for some reason, happens to possess the key.

The Twilight Zone Approach

Perhaps the bags' contents change each time they're opened.

One writer suggested, for example, that when Herb opens the bags he finds whatever he finds; perhaps he finds nothing at all, i.e., the bags are empty—an alternative suggested a couple of choices ago. He closes the bags, he closes his eyes, he thinks carefully for a heavy moment and he reopens the bags.

Inside one of the formerly empty suitcases there is now a dia-mond-and-ruby brooch.

He closes the bag again, thinks, then opens it again to find a cup of hot coffee, a steaming plate of scrambled eggs and bacon, home-fried potatoes and whole wheat toast. Each time he closes and opens the bag it is found to contain whatever it is he has just made up in his mind, exactly as he "created" the bags in his mind in the first place during his exchange with the clerk at the front desk.

In this same writer's version the film cuts suddenly to Santa Monica, where Herb is at home, in his study, wearing his bathrobe, seated at his desk before his word processor, thinking and writing, writing and thinking. And each time he writes anew, we return briefly to the hotel room, where the contents change precisely as Herb revises his pages back in Santa Monica.

Herb is revealed to be a writer constructing a tale—*this* tale—and creating the bags' contents exactly as real writers create whatever they wish to create within the universes of their various stories.

A particularly appealing aspect of this treatment is that it integrates the field of writing itself. Herb is presented at the tale's outset, after all, as a member of the book community—a publisher's regional sales representative—on his way to attend an event that centers entirely on the world of books. Why not create him as a writer of books who is writing *this* very "book"—or movie—as he goes along?

I characterize approaches along these lines as *Twilight Zone* methods. They transcend the more familiar reality-based story notions and bleed over into the world of fantasy, magic, illusion and imagination.

This does not mean, however, that under such circumstances the regular rules for story craft are suspended. Not at all. Indeed, this approach places an even greater burden on screenwriters. For they must struggle to find within the inexplicable the same inner logic, the same sense of traditional balance, that any story must possess.

Writers of these fantastic tales cannot decide that, since fantasy and imagination have been invoked, there is no longer any obligation to weave the various story strands into the whole, complete fabric. To fail to confront this challenge is the equivalent of resolving impossible circumstances by having a character wake up at the end of the movie to discover it has all been merely a dream.

What's the problem with that?

It's too easy!

When audiences fork over time and attention and consideration—to say nothing of the fistful of dollars required for a movie ticket—they seek evidence that the film artists have worked hard. And the work of reconciling various story lines in the context of fantasy and imagination is all the more weighty because writers do not have the usual array of potential solutions available to them.

In short, there is no end to the choices writers have at their disposal. The more choices a writer makes, the more still other choices become apparent. The universe of choices does not contract but expands, fully in keeping with the nature of choice itself.

In the next chapter we will move on to my own solution to the What's in the Bags story craft challenge, and the positing of a fundamental screenwriting principle regarding the nature of theme. But first let us present a portion of the tale just now described—the first several pages—as it would appear in proper, professional screenplay format. This allows us the opportunity to appreciate not so much what information ought to be included in a screenplay but, still more important, what needs to be left out.

CREATURE COMFORTS

FADE IN:

EXT   JAVITS CONVENTION CENTER—NEW YORK
MORNING

Banners festooning the entrance read: "Welcome, Booksellers!!!"

A TAXI pulls up.

Harried, harassed, hassled HERB CASTLE, forty, stumbles from the cab lugging an unwieldy SALESMAN'S SAMPLE CASE.

Herb is as creased and crumpled as his drab cord suit; he looks like a man who has just gotten off the all-night, supercheap, red-eye flight from the Coast.

The Sample Case promptly breaks open, spilling TECHNICAL and SCIENTIFIC TEXTBOOKS into the gutter.

The CABDRIVER calls to him, pointing to the meter.

                    CABDRIVER
            That's thirty-two forty, pal.

Ankle-deep in books, Herb struggles to extract his wallet
from his pocket. He removes his one-and-only bill, a crisp,
new HUNDRED, and hands it sheepishly to the Driver.

                      HERB
            Is a hundred a problem?

                    CABDRIVER
            Not for me it ain't.

The Taxi speeds away.

Herb turns to a nearby COP directing traffic.

                      HERB
            Quick! That cabby just split with my change!

                       COP
            You are obstructing ingress to and egress
            from the facility. The white zone is for the
            immediate loading and unloading of
            passengers only.

INT   MAIN EXHIBITION HALL

There are acres of display booths aswarm with BUYERS and
SELLERS.

Publishers hawk books on health and fitness, addiction and
recovery, how to live, how to die, how to diet, how to prosper
in the coming depression and laugh in your friends' faces
while their children starve.

There is even a smattering of fiction.

Prominent in this latter group is the booth representing
PENTANGLE PRESS.

The company's entire display—as its posters attest—is
devoted to the upcoming release of a boxed set of the

collected works of best-selling reclusive author Page
Turner.

CORRIDOR—TEXTRON'S BOOTH

In a hallway off the main floor, clearly the convention's low-
rent district, Herb dozes fitfully at his company's "booth":
a card table and folding chair.

A stunning beauty, LAURA MAYER, late thirties,
approaches the booth. Her mere presence startles Herb into
wakefulness.

> HERB
> We've just reissued Olivewood and
> Crawford's <u>Curvilinear Dysfunction in
> Crystalline Entropy Mechanisms</u>—it's part
> of our <u>Rotational Divergent Immunoglobulin</u>
> series and . . .

He runs out of steam.

> HERB
> (continuing)
> . . . I hardly recognize you.

> LAURA
> Want to see some ID? Driver's license?
> Bloomie's charge plate?

> HERB
> You're beautiful. Radiant. A whole new
> woman.

> LAURA
> A whole new woman living a whole new
> life. For one thing, Carl and I are through.
> Finito. We've separated. I've moved out of
> the house in Brooklyn Heights.

> HERB
> I'm so sorry.

LAURA

Don't be. My life hasn't ended; it's just
begun. Take me to lunch and I'll give you all
the gory gossip.

HERB

I'd love to, but I've got to hold down the fort
here.

Together they scan the empty corridor.

■ ■ ■ ■ ■ ■ ■ ■ ■ ■ ■ ■ ■ ■ ■ ■ ■ ■ ■ ■

CHAPTER 3

Identity:
The Only Choice

Movies, like all other forms of creative expression, in the end represent only different configurations of choice: what you put in and what you leave out.

The specific patterns of decisions constitute the particular stories and characters. But no matter how widely the tales may vary, no matter how diverse the roles, all screenplays inevitably assume a final, common vector.

Just like the snowmelt that gradually carves out a canyon, the route of the tale seems to meander arbitrarily. Yet the underlying principle charting the melt's course is the same for all courses, and it is gravity. The ultimate path may twist this way and that, widen here, narrow there, but its overall track is predetermined—and most precisely so—by nature herself.

As surely as gravity steers the water, so does identity invisibly steer the tale that knits together any screenplay.

And where does it steer it?

Right back to the writer who created it.

To comprehend this in a way that is meaningful not only for critics and theoreticians but also for practitioners—i.e., writers—let us explore story's special nature again in a concrete, practical manner. We will not intellectualize or philosophize here. Let us make this discovery the way it exists in the real world of screen-writers, not as calculated abstracts and mental constructs but within the context of actual choices-in-the-making. Let us pick up where we left off with our story craft challenge in the previous chapter.

Our Own Solution to What's in the Bags

Herb opens the bags to discover, among the various items, all sorts of upscale duds: high-fashion three-piece suits, silk shirts, ties, slacks, fancy-label socks and underwear. He pulls out a cashmere sport coat and slips it on.

It's a perfect fit.

He looks at himself in the oval mirror inside the armoire door. Naked now except for the jacket, for the briefest moment he poses, perhaps even primps and preens. The coat appears custom-tailored to Herb's measurements.

He rifles through the rest of the bags' contents. He withdraws an audiocassette recorder and an army .45 automatic pistol. He finds also fresh, neatly bound and bundled currency—a cool million dollars in lush, green cash.

He reaches deeper and extracts a legal-sized manila envelope and dumps its contents—clipped and stapled documents—onto the bed. One set of papers swarms with microprint legalese; it appears to represent some kind of contract. Another sheaf is a list, an itinerary of dates, times, locations, appointments: a signing at a bookstore, a TV interview, an appearance at a literary society at an upstate college.

Let's pause here for a moment to consider the special problems that arise in the attempt to show printed matter on the screen. It's all so easy in literature—for example in a novel—simply to blurt it all out. The author can state that these papers are an author's contract and a listing of the events that an author on a book-promotion tour is likely to attend.

On-screen, however, it's quite another matter. One cannot cavalierly show the documents in close-up for audiences to read. People do not go to the movies for the opportunity to read printed matter. If they want to read they can stay home and curl up with a fine novel.

Or a book on screenwriting.

We can make the points that need to be made and drop a few clues through a quick glance at the overall shape of the documents. We can combine this with brief snatches of dialogue between Herb and Laura to give the audience some bits of information. For example, while inspecting the documents, Herb could mutter under his breath something on the order of: "Lots of legal mumbo jumbo. Some sort of contract, a travel itinerary, an expense-account ledger."

This would shed light into an otherwise dark corner of the film.

And film requires such illumination. In literature we can exploit language to assert the nature of documents, stating outright precisely what they are. In film, we can only hint at what they might be.

It is a common error for screenwriters—especially inexperienced screenwriters—to linger on the nature of such documents with long, close-up, on-screen examination of them.

Not to belabor the point, but what could be more boring than sitting in a movie theater reading documents projected upon the screen? As a general rule, screenwriters must come to appreciate the differences between what is written on the page in ink and what is projected on the screen in light.

And in that very same light, let us return to Herb and Laura in the hotel room.

Herb sets down the legal documents and author's itinerary and reaches once more into the bag. His fingers fasten upon some object. He withdraws a ream of papers. He examines it and shakes his head in deep, dark dismay. "Oh, no," he says. "Oh, no, no, no, no."

"What?" Laura asks anxiously.

Herb passes her the pages. "It's some sort of typescript," she says, thumbing through them. "A novel, looks like." She lets the pages fall closed and now regards the cover. *"Creature Comforts,"* she says. "The novel is called *Creature Comforts*. There's no author listed."

"That's me," Herb says.

"You? I don't get it."

"I'm *Creature Comforts*," Herb explains. "I mean I wrote it."

"You're a writer?"

"A closet author. I've scribbled several novels over the years. All right, so I haven't sold one yet, but don't count me out. Why do you think I beat my head against the wall as a regional sales rep for a fringe operation like this scientific and technical textbook publisher?" Herb asks her. "Because it's as close to publishing as I can get."

Laura contemplates the typescript. *"Creature Comforts,"* she says. "What's it about?"

Herb takes the script from her, feels its heft. "It's about three hundred and twelve pages," he says.

"Now's hardly the time for wisecracks," Laura reprimands him.

"I agree," Herb says with a nod. "And I'm not joking." He opens the manuscript to the final page. "Just as I suspected," he says. "There are forty pages missing. The whole last act's been lopped off."

"What do you make of it?"

"Beats me."

"What do we do now?"

"One thing seems clear enough."

"What's that?"

"We ought to get the hell out of here. And just as fast as we can."

We can provide Herb with any number of choices here. The sweaty, gooey lovemaking session just recently behind him might provide motivation for a quick shower. I cannot believe, however, given the pressing nature of the circumstances, that he would take the time to shower. According to the Prudent Person Principle, he would be anxious to leave the premises promptly.

A movie is, of course, the most fraudulent enterprise that has ever existed in the history of the universe. I do not exaggerate. What is more jockeyed, juggled, shuffled, choreographed, manipulated, orchestrated, arranged and rearranged than a movie? What art form plays as fast and loose with time and space as do movies?

Nevertheless, movies must appear at the same time to be precisely the opposite of what they are; they must appear to be wholly, naturally, perfectly real.

If an audience cannot believe that Herb would now pause to shower, it could be expected to believe that he might take a few seconds to empty his bladder. Compared with showering, this act carries far greater urgency and requires far less time.

So Herb stations himself in the bathroom before the bowl, at precisely the same moment as a sudden sound of commotion comes from the room: rumbling and crashing, a woman's scream, a couple of gunshots.

Herb stumbles back into the room to find the door ripped from its hinges, dangling precariously from the still connected restraining chain. On the bed lies Laura, limp and crumpled like a rag doll, two dark blue bullet wounds in her forehead, a crimson stain blossoming in the mattress beneath her. Numb with disbelief, Herb sinks to the foot of the bed, where the smoking pistol lies.

Mindlessly he picks up the gun.

At which point the bellhop charges into the room, shouting, "I heard shots!"

The bellhop looks at the still mostly naked Herb—gun in hand, acrid smoke continuing to curl from its muzzle—and at the apparently lifeless Laura, spread nude before him on the bed. He cautiously backs away toward the hall.

"Don't get the wrong idea," Herb pleads.

The bellhop continues to retreat.

"I can see how this must all look suspicious," Herb concedes. The bellhop continues his nervous departure. "Where are you going?" Herb gestures toward the bellhop with the gun. "Wait!"

"Sure," the hop responds, halting in his tracks. "Whatever you say." He trembles in fear for his life.

At this precise moment, from the street below comes the sound of a siren and the screech of brakes. Herb glances over his shoulder through the window, which provides a clear view of the hotel entrance. A nondescript dark brown sedan—magnetic-mount red light on its roof whirling and flashing—sits at a curious angle at the end of dark rubber arcs, four fat commas, skid marks just now inscribed on the pavement. The car doors fly open and several men, apparently plainclothes detectives, leap out and race for the steps to the lobby, drawing their guns mid-sprint.

It ought to be clear to any viewer what is clear enough to Herb: he's got trouble. We do not need to go into his interior mental processes as we might in a novel. What's on the screen ought to provide all the information we need.

Herb brandishes the gun and abruptly orders the bellhop, "Get it off."

"What?"

"The outfit. That monkey suit. Off."

"I don't understand," the hop protests.

"What's to understand? Take off that uniform. Get naked. Now."

The bellhop obediently removes his uniform. As he strips off each garment, Herb frantically pulls it onto his own body.

The bellhop now starts to tug down his boxer shorts.

"Wait," Herb says. "That's not necessary."

Somebody once said of screen story craft that writers need only to set their protagonist in one place, to put his goal in another, and to throw up obstacles all along the way.

But to me this seems a somewhat simplistic view of story structure. It leads to stories that are straight-line instead of rounded, sculpted, shaped, kneaded, finessed, coaxed, coddled, molded, whole. Still, there is something to be said for the desirability in drama of stress, tension and conflict. And indeed, all of these can be enhanced and intensified by throwing in obstacles wherever we can create them.

It might be fun now, therefore, to have a minibattle between Herb and the hop over the issue of the latter's underwear.

"Wait," Herb says to the hop, who is tugging at his shorts' elastic band. "That's not necessary."

The bellhop, continuing to fear for his life, replies, "You said 'Get naked.' "

"I only want the uniform."

"I just want to do whatever you tell me to do. Please don't shoot me, please." He continues to tug at his shorts. "I have young children."

"I told you, keep them on. I changed my mind."

"You ordered me to 'get naked.' If you don't want me to get naked, if you want instead that I leave on my shorts, you have to order me to do so."

"Okay," Herb barks in desperation, "I order you to leave on your shorts."

Dressed now in the hop's ill-fitting uniform, Herb orders the man into the closet and closes the door behind him. He places his shoulder against an armoire and pushes the bulky piece of furniture in front of the closet door, sealing the hop inside.

For the purposes of our story, I need Herb to keep the bags with him throughout the next several scenes. But wouldn't the Prudent Person care not a whit about the bags? Would he not want to flee as quickly as possible? Would he not abandon the bags, which might otherwise slow him down?

I expect that from what we see and hear, Herb's scheme of the moment ought to be abundantly clear: escape from the hotel disguised as a bellhop. To this end, audiences might believe he would stack the bags high on the luggage cart so they might provide something of a barrier behind which to conceal himself.

And that is precisely what he does. He stuffs the various items back in the bags, slams the lids, zips the zippers, snaps the snaps and pops the valises back on the cart, where they form a tall stack. He then wheels the loaded dolly out of the room, into the corridor, and all the way down the hall to the elevator.

No sooner does he press the "down" button than the doors open, disgorging the several apparent plainclothes detectives—guns drawn—whom he'd viewed moments earlier in the unmarked car at the hotel's entrance. These men take no notice whatsoever of a bellhop wheeling luggage through a hotel corridor; why would they? They move right past Herb and down the corridor toward the room from which he has just now fled.

Unchallenged, Herb passes onto the elevator and the doors slide closed behind him.

Herb emerges in the lobby.

Concealed in the luggage's portable shadow, he wheels the cart past the front desk and the bell captain's station, through the front doors and out into the street, where lined-up taxis await passengers. He sweeps aside an elderly couple who are about to board the first cab. He tosses the bags into the taxi, leaps in, slams and locks the door and orders the driver: "Drive!"

And right here arises yet another opportunity to enhance dramatic tension by throwing obstacles in a protagonist's path.

Keep in mind that part of a writer's job is to make decisions. At this point we could decide that the cabdriver simply drives off as commanded. A preferable choice, however, is for the driver to challenge Herb over his discourtesy in pushing to the front of the line. This delay cranks up the dramatic stress and tension.

Added stress and tension are always welcome in drama. In this instance the enhanced pressure is uniquely effective because a dreadfully important event—Herb's escape from the hotel—is delayed by a relatively petty consideration involving his failure to observe everyday courtesies and politeness.

He is, after all, trying to save his life, and that life is now unexpectedly threatened by a lecture from a Noo Yawk cabby, a member of a class hardly celebrated for its command of dignified behavior.

"What da hell ya dink dis is?" the driver could inquire of Herb. "Dis cab's for dem ol' folks ya just now shoved outta da way. It's creeps like you give da Apple its rotten rep."

Perhaps we should note that New York cabdrivers today rarely speak with this once-traditional rich Gotham twang. If one who still drips with that particular drawl could indeed be found, it would be a mistake for the writer to transliterate the dialogue. Writers who spell out particular mispronunciations— as I have here, purely for demonstration's sake—are condescending and patronizing to actors and directors alike.

In fact, nowadays a large percentage of New York taxi drivers are recent immigrants: Sikhs, Pakistanis, Israelis, Arabs, Caribbean Islanders, Russians. Instead of providing the too-familiar Hollywood notion of the Noo Yawk hack, it might be fun here to exploit an opportunity for variety.

So let us make the driver, say, a recent Russian émigré. He confronts Herb, "Pardon to me, my friend, but there is no excusing for such rudeness and I am not to permitting hooliganism inside my taxi motor vehicle. It is precisely such barbarian behavior that gives to Large Apple its unseemly repute. So say I, Slavko Vorkapich."

Note that we've captured in print something resembling a foreign accent without ever transliterating any of the dialogue. We have achieved the effect without spelling out the pronunciation. We leave that, instead, to our collaborators—actor and director.

At this point the stress could be underscored still further by protests from the elderly couple who've been cheated out of their cab. While foul language on screen has long ago achieved full-tilt tedium, some vulgarisms here could be both surprising and funny. The little old lady who has been denied her rightful taxi appears thoroughly proper and prim. We don't expect her to rap the cab's window with her umbrella and squawk at Herb, "Ass-wipe! Fart-face! Dirt-dorking drek-heel! Slime-sucking scumbag!"

It might provide a chuckle.

It might not.

What's clear enough is that Herb has to flee this commotion. How is he going to get the cab moving? He reaches for the gun contained in one of the bags as if he is about to compel the driver in the same manner that he compelled the bellhop only moments earlier.

But perhaps this is one of those taxis that has a Plexiglas security barrier separating the driver from the passenger, rendering the gun essentially useless. In this case, Herb could abandon the gun and reach instead for the cash. He could withdraw a fistful of hundred-dollar bills and thrust them through the fare slot at the driver, who, on sight of such generous remuneration, might promptly drive off as directed.

Frankly, however, for purposes of sharpening characterization, I prefer that the cab not contain any such security barrier. In this case Herb could still reach surreptitiously for the gun, his purpose not clear to the driver but only to himself and the audience. Then he could hesitate, and grab the money instead.

This is visual, graphic expression and, therefore, uniquely suitable to film. It expands character. Without dialogue it reveals the inner workings of a character's mind. It shows us that even though Herb was able to take command of his situation in the previous scene by use of force—brandishing the gun—he is basically a creature of reason, a champion for peace who vastly prefers moral suasion to brute force. Perhaps he also believes that just as you catch more flies with honey, you catch more cab-drivers with money.

So through sight and sound alone, we are able to climb inside Herb's head and view his thinking. The action that he takes— and the action that he does not take—reveals to the viewer Herb's inner struggle.

In any event, one way or another, Herb and his driver, Mr. Slavko Vorkapich, are soon enough clattering through Manhattan's streets in the cab. In transit, Herb strips off the bellhop's

uniform and pulls on a sporty outfit extracted from the luggage.
Perhaps his driver reprimands him: "Just because you are to
giving much moneys to driver does not to suggesting is permitted in taxicab to get naked."

Herb finishes dressing, tossing the hop's outfit through the
window and into the street. Maybe there's a brief flash of a bag
lady standing in the gutter, picking up the discarded jacket from
the pavement, trying it on and calling after the cab, "You got
this in a nine?"

Let's pause here for a consideration of the often-used—
indeed much-abused—term "genre." Some screenwriting educators assert that there are different rules for different kinds of
films. Murder mysteries are held to be structurally distinct from,
say, comedies. And both of these, of course, are altogether different from romance.

Likewise, drama.

At UCLA we dismiss such categorization, as it is by nature
limiting. Creative expression, to the contrary, is expansive. It
does not narrow our perspective but instead broadens it.

In fact, appealing films often blend various genres. Some of
the most terrifying thrillers associated with Alfred Hitchcock,
for example, are from time to time also hilarious—*Rear Window*
(screenplay by John Michael Hayes, from the novel by Cornell
Woolrich) and even *Psycho* (Joseph Stefano, from the novel by
Robert Bloch) spring readily to mind. That is why I strive to
lend our tale, *Creature Comforts*, elements of melodrama and
romance, a dollop of murder mystery/thriller, and substantial
veins of comedy, just for—what else?—laughs.

This suggests yet another principle.

**Principle 9: In screenwriting there are but two genres—1)
good movies and 2) bad movies.**

The cabdriver continues. "It requires not profound insight to
perceive you are fellow on—what is idiom?—the lam. In United

States am humble cabdriver but in former Soviet Republic—to be renamed at a later date—was psychologist. And comes with cabdriver's territory—as with barber or bartender—to practice just little bit psychotherapy. To this end it appears to me you are not criminal type. You have not chance to elude felon-finding apparatus of NYPD. Suggestion: for to face the music."

Herb thinks it through; he nods his head slowly. "Brooklyn Heights," he instructs the driver.

We may recall that earlier in our tale, when Laura first confronted Herb at the booksellers' convention and told him about the breakup of her marriage, she mentioned that she had moved out of "the house in Brooklyn Heights." The repetition of that location here represents integration: something—however seemingly inconsequential—is referred to in one place and then is referred to again later on. I expect audiences will appreciate that the subtext—the underlying meaning—beneath Herb's saying the words "Brooklyn Heights" represents his decision to go to Laura's former residence, to confront her former husband and, as driver Slavko Vorkapich advises, "for to face the music."

What chance has nerdy, geeky, wimpy Herb Castle as a felon in flight? Clearly, his only hope is to go to Laura's residence—the place in Brooklyn Heights—and inform the estranged Carl of her murder and attempt to find support that will somehow lead to a resolution of his seemingly impossible dilemma.

Even if Herb has to confess to adultery, he ruminates, he is certainly no murderer. And even if it comes to a confession of adultery, Carl and Laura are, after all, already separated. Surely this will soften Carl's view of Herb and Laura's sexual liaison. It's likely that Carl can even help Herb retain an attorney.

None of this, of course, is expressed. Instead it is implied. Implication is always preferable to expression—in all formats. The latter tilts toward spoon-feeding, while the former causes the action to take place in the ideal spot: inside the head of the reader or viewer.

And this can be stated as yet one more principle.

Principle 10: **In screenwriting, implication is always superior to expression.**

In such instances viewers do not merely observe the experience but integrate it into their own life. In this way representation of experience becomes experience itself. Art is art and life is life, to be sure, but once a particular life integrates a particular art, the latter is forever part of the former.

Our taxi deposits Herb before a nineteenth-century town house in historic Brooklyn Heights. Herb drags the bags up the several steps leading to the front door. He knocks cautiously and the incompletely closed door swings open in response to the pressure of his knuckles.

He steps into the dim entryway and sets down the bags. In the distance he hears voices in muffled conversation. Herb steps into the living room where the voices are louder, closer. He moves on to the dining room and from his darkened perspective can see, through the slightly ajar kitchen door, several figures engaged in anxious discourse.

There is a middle-aged man who can only be Carl.

And a woman who could only be Herb's wife, Gloria.

Now in literature it is easy to say, as I just now have, that the woman is Herb's wife and that her name is Gloria. But how will this information be rendered to viewers of the scene as it plays out on the screen in a movie theater? From the point of view of a member of that audience, Gloria is merely some unidentified woman. We need to confront the challenge, therefore, of communicating the woman's identity to the audience.

There are any number of ways to do this. We could, for example, have Herb "involuntarily" mutter her name under his breath.

But this technique is heavy-handed and self-conscious. It seems very much to be what it is—the writer narrating information to the audience through the vehicle of a character.

But just for a moment let us suppose that we decide to have

Herb mutter his wife's name. Under his breath he gasps, "Gloria!"

How does the audience know that "Gloria" is the name of his wife? From this particular handling of the challenge—Herb's stating the name aloud to himself—we do not learn that the woman is his wife; we know only that it is some woman who is somehow familiar to him.

And under certain dramatic circumstances that might serve us well enough.

But if we require the audience to realize that the woman is specifically his wife, the muttering would have to include enough information to make that designation clear. Herb would need to say something on the order of, "My God! It's my wife, Gloria!"

Again, I strongly suspect this would strike the audience as the too-brazen voice of the author whispering important story data in their ears. Audiences have every right to expect greater finesse and smoother naturalism in the communication of information.

One way to get around this is to back up the tale's opening just a little bit, and begin the story a trifle earlier. Frankly, I cannot make this recommendation without extreme reluctance. Having read literally thousands of screenplays, I find that for one which starts too late there are sixty that start too early. To suggest that a script ought to start earlier than it actually does is extremely unusual for me.

Perhaps *Creature Comforts* is such a screenplay. (Perhaps it is not.) Instead of starting early in the morning with Herb alighting from the cab in front of the convention center, we could crank backward in time to the previous night when he is dropped off at Los Angeles International Airport by his wife. Perhaps as he steps from the car his salesman's sample case snaps open, as at the entrance to the convention. Perhaps the manuscript of his unpublished novel, *Creature Comforts*, is among the paraphernalia that falls from the case.

Gloria could ask him what *Creature Comforts* is, or she could inquire—perhaps disdainfully—as to why he is taking the type-script with him to New York. That might serve as an integrating force, tying one part of the tale to another.

Having exposed Gloria to the audience's view at this point renders it unnecessary for Herb to identify her in Brooklyn Heights. It sure beats Herb having to gasp "under his breath" something like, "Shucks! It's my wife, Gloria! Did everyone in the audience get that? Are you folks listening? My wife! Gloria!"

Frankly, I believe it's a mistake to fiddle around with our neat, nifty opening at the convention center. The reason I am exploring alternatives here is to underscore yet again the nature of choice-making that lies at the heart of creative expression in general and screenwriting in particular.

Actually, there isn't a single rule which requires that all the information regarding Gloria has to be revealed in a single swoop. Indeed, delay in the revelation provides a bit of a tease and has the desired effect of enhancing dramatic tension.

Besides Carl and Gloria there are a handful of other indi-viduals in the kitchen—perhaps among them one or two of the purported plainclothes detectives seen earlier at the hotel.

Certainly the sight of his wife is sufficient reason for Herb to wonder just a bit about what is transpiring here. Instead of sailing straight ahead—as planned—into the kitchen, as his cab-driver/advisor had indirectly recommended, Herb pauses.

And during this pause there is yet a new commotion: the front door is heard to fly open and smack hard against the suitcases Herb parked there only moments before. There is also the sound of a large body tripping over the bags and then stumbling and crashing to the floor. A shout and a moan follow.

Herb, still lurking in the somber dining room just outside the kitchen door, now backs away and sequesters himself beside a tall piece of furniture—a highboy containing tableware—as the figure who stumbled over the bags in the entryway emerges, rubbing his sore hip. He limps past Herb into the kitchen.

Even in the pale ambient light where Herb lurks it is perfectly clear that this figure is the desk clerk from the hotel, providing another example of integration. A vaguely inconsequential character encountered earlier in the tale suddenly, and unexpectedly, reappears. All by itself this links one part of the picture to another and in doing so shapes the line to lend it the desired roundness. This is a signature of solid tale craft.

Herb watches and hears the scene unfold in the kitchen as the clerk joins Carl, Gloria and the others. "He got away!" the clerk exclaims.

"Tell us something we don't know," Carl barks. "You were supposed to keep him at the hotel."

The clerk responds, "You told us he was a nerdy, geeky, wimpy guy who would just roll over and play dead. Instead he showed some real initiative and managed to skip the joint."

We could now commit a common error. We could have the clerk tell Carl and the others what the audience has already been told: that Herb commandeered the bellhop's uniform and cart, then fled in a cab.

But why give audiences information they already possess? This is a mistake we see in TV show after TV show, in movie after movie. In fact, this calls for a special screenwriting principle.

Principle 11: Do not have one character tell another character what has already been told to the audience.

In the vastly overpraised (in my view) *Scent of a Woman* (Bo Goldman, from the novel by Giovanni Arpino), for example, the character portrayed by Al Pacino sits on a plane beside his youthful caretaker while the latter describes in substantial detail a prank played upon the prep school headmaster. But the audience has already viewed that prank. As I have pointed out, there is no excuse for one character—who is, after all, but a figment of the writer's imagination—to tell another character—yet one more such figment—information already known to the real-life audience.

Even in a film as worthy as *The Crying Game* (Neil Jordan) there is at least one such instance of the squandering of ink and light and time. Near the end of the film the Irish terrorist, now in prison, details for his girlfriend the precise manner in which the hostage came to die.

But we've already viewed all that earlier in the film.

Can it be that the writer wants to expose the girlfriend's reaction to the news? If that is the case, then one must weigh this benefit against the deficit which is inevitably wedded to repetition. The girlfriend is merely a creation of the writer; the audience, on the other hand, truly exists.

My own vote is to exclude the repetition. I always urge writers to err in favor of brevity. Too little information is not as costly as too much information. The former may engender a certain confusion, it is true. But that is not as debilitating as the boredom that accrues upon presentation of data that has already been presented.

Indeed, a certain confusion can even serve as an asset, since it draws audiences closer to the screen; it enhances their attention. Conversely, data that is repetitive causes them to turn away, to pay less attention. And once the writer loses an audience's attention it is an extraordinarily daunting task to recapture it.

Nothing in any film should be merely repetitive without advancing tale and expanding character. We need squander no time, therefore, hearing yet again a description of Herb's escape from the hotel. It is sufficient for the desk clerk merely to tell Carl something on the order of, "At least you've got him here now."

"Here?" Carl shrieks. "Now? What in the world are you talking about?"

"The bags," the clerk explains, "the suitcases you had us prepare—they're here in the house. I practically broke my butt just now tripping over them in the entryway."

"The bags?" Carl asks, incredulous. "Here in the house?"

En masse, the entire group moves to the entryway.

No bags.

They step out onto the stoop and peer up the street. It is deserted. Now they peer in the other direction.

A half-block away, sprinting as best he can at the same time as he lugs the unwieldy bags, Herb approaches the entrance to a subway station. Carl, Gloria, the desk clerk and the "plain-clothes detectives" take off in hot pursuit.

Inside the subway station a half-dozen people wait on line to purchase tokens at the change booth. Herb, frantic, takes his place at the end of the queue for a split second before suddenly rushing to the front. It appears he is about to cut into the line but then thinks better of it, perhaps because the person at the head of the line happens to be six and a half feet tall, weighs three hundred pounds and offers Herb a special New York you-got-a-problem glare.

Herb, desperate, reaches for the gun, but comes up instead with a fistful of cash from the Braniff carry-on bag. "I'll buy your place in line," he says to the heavyset man.

"Sounds good to me," the man responds, impressed with the money clutched in Herb's hand.

But before he can accept the cash, another patron turns to Herb. "Hey, never mind no place in line. I'll sell you my token."

"Quit queering my deal!" the heavy dude reprimands his competitor.

Fierce competition breaks out among the customers. "You want a token that bad?" a woman asks Herb. "Give you my own for ten bucks."

"Nine!"

"Eight-fifty!"

In the turmoil, Herb tosses a handful of bills into the air, seizes a token from the nearest available hand and rushes through the turnstile toward the platform, where a train is just pulling in.

People in the area around the turnstile scramble, flailing for bills fluttering in the air and squabbling over those that have already landed.

At precisely this moment, of course, Carl, Gloria, the desk

clerk and the "plainclothes detectives" rush down the stairs from the sidewalk and arrive at the change booth. Spotting Herb as he boards a car of the waiting train, they leap the turnstiles and hurtle toward the track.

But the doors slide closed in their faces. Panting, huffing, puffing, gasping, they watch Herb glide with the train into the deep, dark recesses of the Metropolitan Transportation Authority's labyrinth.

I normally caution writers against providing any special effects—such decisions belong generally to editors and directors—but a slow FADE-OUT or FADE TO BLACK might be appropriate at the end of this scene.

Right now I need Herb to spend a little bit of time alone with the bags. I could have him check into a hotel, where he will rest up, leisurely explore the bags and come to certain conclusions.

The problem is that watching an actor "rest up" is no fun at all in a movie. There is also little pleasure in seeing a character return yet again to a location as uninspired as a hotel room.

And with regard to leisure, simply stated there should be no leisure in any movie. Leisure is for *after* the movie, when audiences go out for coffee and pastry in order to recover from the delicious tension that the film—if it is any good—has properly created.

Generally, hotel rooms, restaurants, bars, apartments, phone booths and cars are not interesting venues for truly dramatic action. In this instance, consider that we have just departed from a scene in a hotel room, so setting it in a similar location again would be doubly boring.

Granted, in the first instance the room is integrated. We exploit the banter at the front desk during check-in and weave it into the fabric of the tale. And the characters, rather than merely sitting around and chatting in the room, take action—that is, they do things. And what they do is dramatic: they engage in illicit sex.

They also receive and explore the bags, and one of them is apparently murdered.

And that's just for openers.

There is the strong-arming of the bellhop, the comman-
deering of his cart and all of the other events attendant to Herb's
flight. The story is advanced; character is expanded.

Indeed, character is not merely expanded; in Herb's case it is
transmogrified. Herb is changed from the limp, frail pushover
we met at the beginning of the movie into one hell of a take-
charge fellow. If in this scene he does not take command over
his own life, he will surely lose it.

My Westwood colleague Professor Hal Ackerman suggests
that the true Aristotelian beginning of a tale ends at the point at
which the protagonist can no longer retreat to the beginning of
the story. That precise moment arrives for Herb in the hotel
room. But we can hardly have him return now to yet another
hotel room while he routinely recovers from the stress of his
escape and, in unhurried fashion, examines the luggage. Do
writers want characters in our works—and members of our audience—to recover from stress, or do we want rather to expand
and intensify that stress?

Our long FADE-OUT, following the disappearance of the
train into the subway tunnel, is followed now by a slow FADE-
IN. We find the screen dimly aglow in dawn's bleak light. The
pale vista that unfolds is of a vast subway train yard in the north
Bronx.

This is the kind of place they store trains at off-peak hours.
And at this particular moment the place is jammed full of
subway cars.

Now, suddenly we are inside one such car. The car is deserted
save for Herb, who sits upright though clearly fast asleep, his
chin on his chest, the bags balanced precariously in his lap. The
audience can infer that Herb rode from the end of the previous
scene to the end of the subway line, then remained on the train
and spent what must have been a fitful night in relative, albeit
temporary, safety from his pursuers.

This scene, however, prompts a reasonable question: Can one
truly stay the night in a parked New York City subway car?

Even in anarchic, chaotic and often lawless New York City, while it is possible to ride the trains endlessly, it is impossible to spend the night on a car that is taken out of service, as Transit Authority police routinely sweep through these trains and remove any civilians who might still be on them.

One way to get around this is to insert a snippet of a scene showing Herb hiding out somewhere—say, a track-repair worker's safety alcove in the dark tunnel—and then sneaking back onto this or another car. He could be rousted by a uniformed officer, retreat to the shadows of some walkway or alley, and then stealthily make his way back onto the car or onto one of the thousands of other cars idled overnight in the yard.

In fact, however, none of this is necessary. Show Herb riding the subway, then cut directly to him here, and audiences will accept that one way or another he eluded the system and managed to hide all night on the train.

During film's earliest days such fill-in material may have been necessary. Its absence may well have given contemporary audiences a sense of disconnectedness and confusion. Today, however, thanks largely to television's influence, audiences are far more conversant with visual grammar. That is, they are so inured to nonstop blizzards of cascading images that they need far less information to assemble the whole picture in their minds.

This makes it far easier for modern writers to imply instead of express. And as we've indicated earlier, implication is desirable, as it causes the action to play out not on screen but in the viewer's mind.

Implication in this way helps screenwriters exercise the most wonderful sort of economy. For material that is implied, even as it advances story and character, has no heft in time or space. It's a writer's free lunch; it's something for nothing.

In *Parenthood* (Babaloo Mandel, Lowell Ganz, Ron Howard), Steve Martin's wife has been encouraged by a woman friend to believe that her tedious marriage was revitalized by her sudden and unannounced administration of oral sex upon her husband.

Martin's wife decides to try the same thing one evening while they're traveling along the highway in their van. We see her lean down toward her husband's lap.

Instantaneously, we cut directly to the van, now wrecked, at the side of the road. A police officer, pen poised above his writing pad, takes down a report from Martin and his wife. "You folks want to explain that to me again?" the cop asks them.

It earns by far the biggest laugh in the movie. Lesser writers would have crammed in views of the van skidding and swerving and just generally going haywire in traffic. There would have been hair-raising near-collisions with other vehicles, a host of slapstick car stunts.

Such extra footage could appear to offer excellent opportunities for good and grand movie fun. In fact, however, far better than any of these shots is no shot at all. Cutting from the wife's erotic gesture directly to the van crumpled at roadside implies all the other stuff.

And, again, because all of this action is implied rather than expressed, it is vastly superior to anything that could be crafted. For Hollywood's best technicians cannot create on-screen images even the tiniest fraction as palpable and seductive as what even the humblest viewer's mind can conjure, if engagingly provoked.

For the sake of economy, therefore, we are wise to avoid providing unnecessary information.

And it is not economy alone that justifies writers' exclusion of extra material. It is also a demonstration of Aristotle's instruction to favor the "plausible impossibility over the implausible possibility."

What in the world can that mean?

Simply stated: lie through your teeth. Just because something is actually true doesn't mean that it will appear so on screen. It may well appear to be quite the opposite. And writers are foolish to try and prove facts to an audience. Movies are not about fact but fantasy.

Conversely, just because something's untrue does not mean

that it will appear so on screen. In the film *Don't Tell Her It's Me* (Sarah Bird), for example, Steve Guttenberg portrays a formerly gawky fellow who is somehow miraculously transformed into an authentic heartthrob.

In one scene, when he's in his "handsome mode," he rides his macho motorcycle into a gas station. An attractive young woman, dispensing gas to her car, catches sight of him and is so distracted by his virile good looks that she neglects to release the pump handle when the tank is filled and it gushes fuel all over the place.

Now, anyone who has ever dispensed self-service gas knows that the pump clicks off automatically once the tank is full. Yet audiences have no problem whatever with this conceit, even as it plays fast and loose with reality. Again, audiences do not come to movies for reality. Reality is available to them for free in their own lives—they do not need to buy tickets to see it.

We can state this as yet another hard-and-fast screenplay axiom.

Principle 12: **Writers should prefer what *appears* to be true—even if it is not—over that which is actually, verifiably true.**

Back to our protagonist, Herb, who is seen on the subway car in dawn's earliest light, fitfully asleep, the luggage stacked precariously in his lap.

At this point the car suddenly lurches as it is coupled with other cars for the next morning's rush hour. Herb is jolted awake at the same time as the bags fall from his lap to the cold, hard floor of the subway car.

The audiocassette recorder spills out of one of the bags and lands with such a clunk as to trigger it into action. "Harriet went to the door, period," an unfamiliar man's voice says on the tape. "Quote, Who's there, question mark, close quote, she asked, period." The voice sounds very much like that of someone dictating material intended later to be transcribed onto paper.

Perhaps the voice could have certain quirks. It mispronounces "et cetera" as "eck cetera" and says "often" with a hard T: "off-ten."

Later in our tale we'll meet someone who speaks precisely that way. And thanks to the clues contained in the voice's eccentricities, we will know upon meeting him that it is he whose voice is recorded on the tape.

This device also serves to integrate the tale by connecting one thing to another. It connects something early in the picture to something occurring much later, thus sculpting, molding, rounding the interior straight line—or worse, no line—into a picture that is shapely and whole.

Our tumbling tape recorder also presents an example of the "plausible impossibility." Let's face it: one could drop a tape recorder from a lap's distance to a hard floor ten thousand times and it will never, ever be triggered into playing. Indeed, it will turn to puree of tape recorder before it ever reports back any information that has been recorded on it.

Regardless, if the actor drops the device to the floor and it promptly begins to play, the audience—even though intellectually it knows better—will never challenge the action.

I remember, in the very first screenwriting class I ever took, orally detailing a story in which some youthful thieves, wielding a glass cutter, slice out a rectangular pane from within a much larger plateglass window.

"Glass doesn't cut like that," a classmate volunteered.

"In movies it does," someone else responded.

And indeed, the beauty of screenwriting is that many things that cannot happen in life happen quite readily in movies, if only you need them to do so.

I vastly prefer the tape recorder's apparent self-start in our scene because to have Herb deliberately turn it on strikes me as action that renders the hand of the writer visible. The writer needs the tape recorder to play; he orders his character to turn it on. Does it not seem more natural to have the item start up on its own, propelled by action in the picture—its fall to the floor—

than to have the character manipulate it, in brazen and self-conscious service to plot craft and the convenience of the author?

There are few enterprises less "convenient" than a screenplay. Convenience, as I'll underscore in the chapter on rewriting, is not for screenwriters but for audiences.

Herb, sitting aboard the train, listens to the tape, and then spends but a brief moment reviewing some of the bags' other items.

And at last, he appears to come to a moment of decision.

Now, it is easy to talk about things like "moments of decision." And it is quite another matter to communicate such information to folks watching images on a movie screen.

Any and all such directions ought to cause writers to cringe just a little. Whenever we read screenplays in which someone "thinks" or "decides" or "remembers" or "realizes" something, we know we are in the hands of a writer not fully conversant with screenwriting's special nature. Always remember that in film, information can be communicated exclusively via two conventions: 1) sight and 2) sound.

We know, therefore, of Herb's "moment of decision" only because of the material that precedes it, the expression on his face, and the material that follows it.

And what follows Herb's "moment" is an exterior shot of Barry's Bookshop in Manhattan's East Fifties. A large crowd waits on line out front, and there is a substantial number of reporters. Signs in the window boast: IN PERSON TODAY: RECLUSIVE AUTHOR PAGE TURNER GOES PUBLIC!!!

A bookstore, as noted earlier, is the first stop on the author's itinerary that was included among the documents in the luggage.

Inside the shop, mobbed by fans and press, a wary, uneasy Herb signs tall stacks of the boxed set of reissued Page Turner volumes encountered earlier in the tale, when we first toured the booksellers' convention at the Javits center.

Now, viewed from the back, we see a woman make her way through the throng. She maneuvers up close to where Herb is stationed. Herb's eyes widen in shock when he sees her.

As the camera tracks around for a clearer look at the woman, we see that it is nobody other than Laura, whom we left for dead back in the hotel.

In my earlier book about screenwriting, in a section called The God Game, I emphasized the reluctance, and even terror, real writers bring to writing every time they plunk themselves down. I argued that serious, experienced, professional writers actually dread writing, even if they love having written.

One successful screenwriter recently commented that reading that particular section made him feel truly liberated, as he realized that he is not a war criminal simply because he does not leap bright-eyed from his bed each morning to his word processor, eager to confront its yawning, vacant screen.

In that book I also pointed out that whatever pleasure—if any—writing may actually provide to writers lies in the fact that to write is to play God. As God created the universe, writers create the universe of their screenplay. You want rain? Make it rain. You're weary of rain and want the sun to shine? Make the rain stop and have the sun come out. Let it shine all day, if it pleases you.

In movies, come to think of it, you can even let the sun shine all night! (See, for example, the screen adaptation of H. G. Wells's *The Man Who Could Do Anything*.)

In movies writers can even commit murder; and who in his life has never wanted to murder somebody? Moreover, if after murdering somebody in a screenplay the writer feels remorseful, he can even bring his victim back to life.

This, in a sense, is precisely what we do here with Laura. That is, we bring her back to life. I say "in a sense" because it ought to be apparent that Laura was never killed in the first place. She was, instead, part of a complicated scheme in which for some reason—to be revealed later in the tale—Herb was set up to portray best-selling reclusive author Page Turner.

But Laura was not fully informed of all of the scheme's various and nefarious aspects, so that at the same time as she misled Herb, she herself was deceived by Carl, who withheld from her certain aspects of the scheme.

She is similar in many ways to the character portrayed by Eva Marie Saint in the thriller/romance *North by Northwest* (Ernest Lehman), who first deceives Cary Grant but then changes sides, crossing over to join him in love and adventure. There is a similar romantic crossover involving Ingrid Bergman in *Notorious* (Ben Hecht). Likewise, the musical based upon the Faust legend, *Damn Yankees* (George Abbott), contains a story strand wherein Satan's seductress, a femme fatale named Lola, falls in love with her intended victim, becoming in the end his ally instead of his opponent.

The same sort of crossover occurs right here in *Creature Comforts*.

Now, rather than move further through the tale's elaborate twists and turns, let us instead leap to the end and work our way backward. Our purpose is both to articulate a story craft principle and see how identity and theme are related in screenplays—how one informs the other. We'll draw from the central idea of the first chapter, that a sincerely personal, wholly integrated screenplay will succeed in meriting audiences' attention and consideration regardless of its subject.

To that end imagine a prisoner at some correctional institution in, say, upstate New York—Auburn? Attica?—who happens early during his incarceration, some ten years before our movie starts, to join a prison writing workshop. There he writes a romantic thriller. His instructor—an English professor from the local community college—is impressed with the prisoner's talent and discipline.

"This stuff's really good," the instructor tells his prisoner/ student. "Let me send it to a publisher."

"But I can't publish," the writer points out. "Have you never heard of the Berkowitz Law?"

David Berkowitz is a convicted serial murderer imprisoned in New York State. He is more notoriously known as Son of Sam, the nom de crime under which he killed his various victims.

Upon his incarceration, the authorities were afraid he would profit from his dark deeds by publishing a best-seller, capitalizing upon his own notoriety and the grief of his victims' families. To prevent this, a law was passed severely restricting prisoners' rights to market their writing.

Imagine that the incarcerated felon's writing instructor tells him that he can avoid the Berkowitz restrictions by writing under a nom de plume—say, "Page Turner." In that way, the instructor goes on, he will not be able to be accused of trading on his reputation as a criminal, since no one will know who he is. Furthermore, "Turner" will write neither memoirs nor personal accounts of actual crimes.

He will write fiction.

And under such circumstances, if his books sell, the success will be attributed not to profiting from his crimes or trading on his notoriety, but solely to his demonstrated writing prowess.

Indeed, ten years pass and Page Turner, the prisoner, writes perhaps a dozen novels, all of them best-sellers. Some become hit movies, and a handful are wildly successful as television series. What to do about all the money he earns?

It goes to his estate.

And what kind of "estate" can a lowlife convicted felon have? Only his mother, an oppressed cleaning lady living in, say, Rochester, New York. Every six months or so, when she visits her son in prison, he asks her, "Mama, are they sending you the money?"

"Son," she responds, "they send me so much money! Why, last year alone they sent me nearly five thousand dollars!"

Of course, unbeknownst to the prisoner and his mother, five thousand dollars is perhaps but a hundredth portion of what she should have received for the year. She and her son are ignorant of the true value of hot copyrights. And why expect otherwise? Publishing is a fairly sophisticated arena not easily understood even by experienced professionals, never mind lay folk.

In any event, our prisoner is at last released from confinement.

I am not sure how best to craft this particular turn in the

tale. Perhaps "Turner" is found to have been wrongly imprisoned. Frankly, that strikes me as too pat, too familiar. Perhaps, instead, he escapes from prison. But that strikes me as too diverting. This is not a picture about a prison break.

Perhaps he is pardoned. There might be possibilities for dramatic action there, but overall it strikes me as merely an unnecessary complication.

Perhaps he simply serves his time and is released.

When writers in screenwriting workshops—for example, our advanced classes at UCLA—confess to these kinds of uncertainties while recounting their tales, they are often filled with misgivings and even shame. Writers are reluctant to admit they're less than a hundred percent certain regarding their in-progress story's twists and turns.

Personally, I am enormously encouraged to hear writers speak with a certain uncertainty. Writers need to give themselves room to try things out, to experiment with potential and particular paths their plots may take. They need to give themselves breathing room where they can rattle around in their minds and wonder about a story's best route.

They also need, here and there, the freedom to fall flat on their face.

Here, then, is the route *Creature Comforts* takes, at least for now.

The real, true Page Turner leaves prison, learns that his publisher has been ripping him off for a decade and confronts him, demanding the millions that are owed.

The publisher responds by hatching a convoluted scheme in order to avoid paying up. He'll select a bogus Page Turner—the ideal candidate would be some nerdy, geeky, wimpy guy from out of state who is peripherally involved in the publishing business. Next, he'll parade the bogus Turner around in public for a while in order to establish his identity as that of the reclusive writer.

And finally, of course, he'll have him killed.

The schemers intend that the body will be found in an alley—one of a couple of dozen murders that a typical New York day provides—along with the bogus baggage. Police investigators, upon inspecting the luggage, will promptly proclaim that author Page Turner is dead. This, of course, will forever discredit any and all individuals who claim authorship of Turner's work.

And among the discredited will also be, of course, our prisoner/author, the actual Page Turner. He can scream and yell all he wants about how he has been cheated; no one will take him seriously.

Let us say that the publisher orchestrating this scheme is Carl himself, Laura's former husband. And let us assume that after Herb's escape from the hotel, the real Turner, our prisoner, confronts Carl. Carl then shows him TV news footage of Herb signing all those Page Turner boxed sets at Barry's Bookshop— figuring that Turner, a convicted criminal, will himself pursue and even kill Herb once he has seen him on TV claiming credit for the prisoner/author's work.

Somewhere along the way, of course, Turner and Herb and Laura join forces and defeat their oppressors.

Eventually they make their way to the jail where Turner was imprisoned. There, in a conversation with the warden, they recognize the eccentricities of diction on the audiotape. And they understand that the warden is himself one of the conspirators. The last pages of Herb's latest manuscript were ripped off— literally—from the back of the typescript and "dictated" into the tape recorder in an attempt to simulate a work-in-progress, which then became one more item in the luggage of an author on a purported book tour.

Identity: The Only Theme

How, then, does it all add up?

Consider again the law.

During the prosecution of an actual criminal case some several decades ago, the state's attorney routinely asked a witness to state his name for the record.

"Objection!" the defense lawyer barked.

"You object to the witness stating his name?" the judge asked, incredulous.

"Absolutely right, Your Honor."

The judge struggled mightily to remain serene as he inquired, "Do you care to share with the court anything that resembles grounds to support such an objection?"

"Certainly," the lawyer responded. "Hearsay."

Hearsay refers, of course, to testimony that is second or third-hand. Under American evidentiary principles, testimony is permitted only if it is direct. Witnesses can testify to what they actually heard or observed, But they cannot testify as to what they heard other witnesses say they observed. To permit such testimony would be to invite potential error. It would open the door to rumor and innuendo.

"How can the witness testify as to his name," the lawyer said, "except through hearsay? How does he know his name except for the fact that it was told to him by others: his parents, his friends, teachers, employers—all the people around him when he was an infant and through the present day?"

No one will be surprised to learn that the objection was promptly overruled.

Nevertheless, in certain ways the lawyer's point is profound. How do we know who we are? How do we know even our own names? How do we learn who we are except by others reflecting information back to us about ourselves?

Consider dreams.

Who among us does not dream? And who among us does not from time to time experience a dream so vivid, so seemingly real that we are palpably relieved to waken from it and to realize that a dream is all it was?

The obvious question arises: How do I know that what I take to be real, true life is not in fact merely an elaborate hallucination?

How do I know I will not in a moment awaken to discover I am in fact a jackrabbit in Nebraska?

I am old enough to have been an undergraduate—a sophomore—in October of 1962, the moment of the Cuban missile crisis. Rightly or wrongly—wrongly, as it turns out—we believed on that perilous Tuesday night that the world would end in nuclear conflagration sometime the following morning as Soviet and American forces clashed full-bore in the Caribbean.

In the midst of profound, provocative, penetrating, purifying questions, plain as day I recall contemplating one and only one issue: If tomorrow we're all to die in atomic hellfire and brimstone, then why in the world am I studying for the sociology midterm scheduled for Friday?

There was at that moment, as in the best of dramatic expression, a splendid admixture of the profound and the petty, the weighty and the mundane. If in the next moment the world is truly to end, how do I want to spend my last handful of allotted hours? Do I want to listen to the most divine music? Do I want to make love? Do I want to stuff my face with chocolate-covered halvah?

Actually some combination of the above sounds pretty good.

This much is certain: what I do *not* want is to study some subject that does not particularly interest me, and to prepare for some test that will never be given.

Nevertheless, study for the test is precisely what I did.

Films, oddly enough, serve us in precisely the same manner. They reflect to us mirror images of ourselves that are at once recognizable and at the same time thoroughly, wholly alien. And in doing so they encourage us to tolerate the mystery of life even as we fail utterly and absolutely to resolve it. With film's support, we derive the strength to persevere, to carry on despite all the clutter and consternation that confronts us daily.

There is, I believe, in each and every woman and man a schizophrenic sense of who we are. One half of it derives from our own flesh and blood and genes, the meaty, bloody, bony, hairy stuff of our physical substance.

The other half is the result of the picture reflected back to us by those who surround us: family, friends, professional associates and even total strangers.

This is why I've come to regard the movie screen not as a window through which we spy on others' lives but as a mirror in which the images we regard are of ourselves.

A colleague at UCLA, who happens to be one of the most powerful executives in the entertainment business, confided to me that he doesn't know why in the world anyone pays attention to him, let alone entrusts him with hundreds of millions of dollars to run studios and produce movies. Privately he feels like a kid turned loose in a candy store and rues the inevitable day that everyone finds out the truth about him—that they got the wrong guy, that he is in fact not a polished, savvy Hollywood heavy hitter but merely an aardvark in the remotest corner of the Australian outback.

We spend much of our lives trying to reconcile these two halves of our spirit and soul—call it our identity—as we struggle to figure out just what and who it is we genuinely are. The reason we go to movies is precisely to explore these perpetually unanswerable questions regarding our identity.

It's the same reason we go to church, temple, mosque, ashram or meetinghouse: we seek answers to the wonderful and dreadful puzzle of our existence.

The well-structured story, Aristotle argues, contains a beginning, middle and end. But an examination of successful tales reveals that these three parts are not at all equal. Beginnings, for example, are relatively short. Endings are even shorter. It is the middle that occupies the bulk of any well-made tale.

What can this remind us of besides human life itself? Childhood is brief. It is the middle—adulthood—that occupies the majority of our time on earth. And who in the world wants a long, drawn-out ending? Who desires a protracted battle with disease, years of intravenous drips and huffing, wheezing resuscitators?

The ideal death, like the ideal movie ending, comes quickly.

This leads us to one more screenwriting principle:

Principle 13: **Every worthy screen story structurally models the romanticized, idealized human life—short beginning, big middle and even shorter end.**

And that is why all movies at their core treat nothing but identity. Who am I? How do I know what's real and what's not? Why should I cooperate with my neighbors and family and colleagues and tolerate all the bumps and bruises and sorry turmoil that threaten daily to consume me?

That's the reason a truly personal and integrated film's subject matters not a whit. For all movies are merely different treatments of the same subject: the writer.

In *Creature Comforts* Herb finds imposed upon him an identity he views as not his own. At first he resists. Eventually, however, he surrenders to it, exactly as all among us must at long last resign ourselves to our own identities.

Herb has, after all, struggled futilely his whole life to be a best-selling author. Now, suddenly, certain scoundrels attempt to impose precisely that identity upon him. First he resists; but before long he eagerly, earnestly embraces that identity.

It is not unlike what happens in *Dave* (Gary Ross). A humble, easygoing guy has suddenly thrust upon him the identity of President of the United States. At first he resists. But soon enough he eagerly seizes that identity, asserts himself and becomes what his oppressors forced him to be but never in a million years wanted him actually to become.

There cannot be a finer example of this principle than *X* (Arnold Perl, Spike Lee). Here the central dilemma—the main thematic question—is addressed in the very title itself. For what in the world does "X" mean except: Who am I?

The question relates directly, of course, to the unique experience of African-Americans. The oppression of slavery and discrimination has resulted in, among other degradations, the theft of a people's own history. Stolen from them among other things are their very names.

Malcolm X is born Malcolm Little, but from where in the

world does the name "Little" derive? It belonged to some long-dead white guy who raped Malcolm's great-grandmother. Why would Malcolm continue to carry the label of this slave-owning rapist/oppressor?

Malcolm needs to discover and reclaim his real, true name.

But what precisely is Malcolm's true name? Thanks to slavery, that has been lost not only to Malcolm but to history.

Malcolm chooses, therefore, the designation "X" precisely to indicate that he does not know who he is.

But ultimately, as with all meritorious tales, the film's value lies in the way the story transcends its immediate arena and speaks to the hearts and spirits of not African-Americans alone but all humans.

For not only Malcolm but all women and men are in a sense forever strangers to themselves. This enables non-African American viewers to regard *X*'s characters not as alien objects but as reflections of themselves. We are reminded not of what separates us but of what joins us.

And that lends the film its powerful drama.

Write, therefore, a science fiction picture. Write a whacky screwball comedy. Write a soap opera. Write a machismo hair-on-your-chest blood-and-guts action/adventure prison tale. Write a gay coming-of-age story. Write a tale about a woman who builds an addition to her house in the Middle East. For no matter what is written, no matter who writes it, if it is integrated and personal, it treats the same subject.

And it succeeds in saying to all audiences—no matter how diverse—something that is personal to their own experience.

And that is inevitably something worth hearing.

CHAPTER 4

■ ■ ■ ■ ■ ■ ■ ■ ■ ■ ■ ■ ■ ■ ■ ■ ■ ■ ■ ■

Challenges in Story Craft

When I first came to Hollywood I was told that a producer is anyone with ten cents and access to a phone booth. Thanks to inflation, it can now be said that a producer is anyone with twenty cents and access to a phone booth.

As I've mentioned earlier, I receive requests daily not only from agents but also from producers seeking the names of new writers. Most of these producers are legitimate; some are not. Among the latter are those who purport to offer wonderful opportunities for inexperienced writers. Here and there are opportunities to be sure, but too often these are not for the writer but for the wanna-be producer.

Usually such requests are for writers who will work for free.

It's fine for writers to work for free as long as they own a hundred percent of what they write. If they are paid no money to write for someone else, however, that is precisely the value their "employer" will ascribe to their writing. In other words, you get what you pay for.

The easiest thing for me to do would be to ignore all such requests from producers and even agents; but here and there are sincerely worthy people offering real opportunities. Why would

I deny a new writer the chance to connect with a legitimate producer? If I am not familiar with the caller, therefore, I give him a chance to convince me that he is for real.

Not too many years ago, a young man fresh from a leading law school, with close connections to the movie business, showed up at my door. He hoped to commence a career as a producer. He wasn't seeking screenplays to purchase and produce. Instead, he sought them solely as samples of various writers' craft, as measures of their discipline and imagination.

He hoped to find a writer to hire in order to develop an idea of his own. Significantly, unlike the steady contingent of bottom-feeders sniffing around film schools for writers-for-free, the fellow promised to pay some respectable sum to the right writer.

Over several weeks I managed to put him in touch with a number of our best new screenwriting warriors. And one by one he rejected all of them. After some months, and a bit of frustration, I found myself covertly pitching to him a property of my own; it was not even a screenplay, but an unpublished novel, *Deadpan.*

Deadpan is something of a screwball comedy treating bigotry. Call it an homage to Franz Kafka. It is based loosely upon *The Metamorphosis*, in which the protagonist awakens one bright morning to discover that overnight he has been transformed into a beetle or, depending upon the translation, a cockroach.

Art is choice. What besides a bug, I wondered, could a fellow wake up as? What other choices might work? A two-tone swept-wing '63 Chevy Impala? A plant? A planet? Light-to-moderate smog? A plate of pasta primavera with a light cream Béarnaise?

I decided my guy would wake up as a comedian.

And not just any comedian. He would awaken one morning to discover that, inexplicably, he is the world's most popular comedian.

And since so many comedians are Jews, I decided he would be that, too.

This led me, in the interest of lending the tale as much

conflict as I could muster, to create him in his original life as something of an anti-Semite. He's a Buick dealer; it's the gas crisis of the early seventies and nobody is buying big, clunky, gas-guzzling cars. His business is failing and, sorely in need of a scapegoat, he begins to blame the Jews.

One day, while shutting down his teetering dealership for the night, he discovers that the lights he is trying to turn off are instead glowing more brightly. The glare washes away all of his vision and he sees nothing but searing, blinding whiteness.

As his eyesight slowly returns, he finds himself ushered onto the stage of a vast Las Vegas showroom, where a brass band is blaring and five thousand fans are stomping, stamping, and cheering their approval. Wholly bewildered, he attempts to assert who he truly is, and to his horror he finds the audience roaring his lines right along with him, in virtual unison. Apparently he is a hugely successful entertainer whose signature routine is to claim to be the car dealer he actually believes himself to be.

Hollywood, according to critic Pauline Kael, is the one place on earth where you can die of encouragement. Story Department coverage at Paramount Pictures gave *Deadpan* " . . . uniformly high marks . . ." and judged the property to be " . . . worth priority option money." The William Morris Agency, in a confidential internal memorandum, called it " . . . exceptionally well written, extraordinary, unique, phenomenal." It asserted that " . . . a very beautiful and successful movie could develop from this." Columbia requested permission to shop *Deadpan* to several top directors, including Alan Parker and Martin Scorsese.

As I am writing this book, I have yet to squeeze even a nickel out of *Deadpan* twenty years after writing it.

Why did I show *Deadpan* to this fledgling producer? It was not because I wanted to work with him in developing an idea of his. Deep down, I probably fantasized that he would be so bowled over by its towering genius that he would abandon his original scheme and focus instead on purchasing the rights to

Deadpan and win the project both a publishing contract and a megamovie deal.

And so I slipped him the script.

But I was neurotic enough not to put my name on it. I assumed that if he were to praise me, it might very well be because he was fearful of offending me and losing introductions to capable new writers. So I handed him the script under a nom de plume: Ike Warshaw.

Naturally, I had to concoct a credible explanation as to why he could not contact "Warshaw" directly but only through me. I explained that Warshaw—whom I characterized as a scruffy, unkempt wreck of a young New Yorker—had shown up uninvited at my campus office, *Deadpan* in his hot little hand. I claimed that he had arrived only recently from the East Coast, where he'd been unable to win permission to submit the novel to agents. He'd hoped that in Hollywood he could sell it as a movie but had been unable to get anyone to take a look at it.

I told the lawyer/producer that I'd agreed to read "Warshaw's" pages in order to get him out of my hair, but that I'd had no real intention of even glancing at them. It's hard enough, I went on, to keep up with the unsolicited screenplays that arrive at my office day after day after day—but novels? They're even further removed from possibility's realm, I explained.

So, as my fictitious story goes, I pretended that later that same day I began idly to leaf through the early pages, and was immediately hooked. Furthermore, I advised the lawyer/producer not to start reading the pages until he had a sufficient block of time available to read them straight through. Otherwise, I cautioned him, he would become so caught up in the novel that he would have to cancel the rest of the day's obligations.

I also advised him that the work was so excruciatingly controversial, it would require a producer of substantial courage and clout to take it on. I suggested that perhaps this piece was not for him. Of course, the more vigorously I warned him against the work, the more eager he was to read it.

I feigned reluctance but finally allowed myself to be "persuaded" to hand it over to him.

Barely two hours later my phone pealed.

Breathlessly the lawyer/producer related that he was in a phone booth in the UCLA parking lot. He said that when he'd entered his car, he'd glanced, only casually, at the first several sentences of *Deadpan* and had at once become unable to stop reading until he'd reached the conclusion, exactly as I had promised.

"You've got to get me in touch with this guy Warshaw," he pleaded.

"You want to purchase the rights?"

"Absolutely not," the young man said. "You were right about that, too. It's not the kind of project to launch a producing career."

"So why contact the writer?" I asked.

"Because Warshaw's the one I want to work with in developing my own idea."

What writer resents praise? Nevertheless, I did not want to work with this fellow in the way that he proposed.

"How do I reach Warshaw?" the producer asked. "Do you have a phone number?"

"He's crashing with friends in Santa Monica," I lied, moving forward with my well-prepared cover story. "He'll be there a few days until they throw him out. Then he'll move on to some cousin in Mar Vista. There's no reliable way to reach him," I explained, "but he promised to check in with me from time to time."

"Will you please call me the minute you hear from him?"

"Absolutely," I lied yet again. One thing I knew for certain was that I would never hear from the nonexistent Ike Warshaw. I was confident that after some weeks of being put off, he would eventually tire of the game and give up on "Warshaw" and *Deadpan*.

But weeks turned to months and rarely did even a few days

pass without a call from the producer in search of the phantom Warshaw. At last, one day he showed up at my door.

"I know how to find Warshaw," he told me. "Our family corporation sometimes employs private investigators. It's not Sam Spade in some dingy walk-up. It's all upscale, white-collar, I assure you. They'll find Warshaw in a day if I authorize them, but since it is you who initiated all of this, it's not fair for me to proceed without your blessing."

I was confronted with a dilemma.

On one hand, I could fess up and tell the unvarnished truth. This could prove just a touch awkward, as I would expose myself for what I am: a liar. I had, after all, deceived this producer not just once but many times, over a fairly extended period.

On the other hand, I could simply let him go right along and hire his detectives. But I was reluctant to let him squander his money in search of someone I knew could never be found. So after taking a deep breath, I told him the truth: "I'm Warshaw."

He was completely understanding, and soon therafter I found him another writer. For a number of years now we have continued to stay in touch.

It is irresistible, however, to contemplate what might have happened had I chosen the other route. In the interest of examining story, character and theme, let's imagine that I do indeed authorize the producer to hire private investigators to find one "Ike Warshaw," who does not in fact even exist.

Story Craft Challenge #1: Who Is Warshaw?

Imagine that weeks slip by and nobody hears anything of Warshaw. Eventually, inevitably, predictably, everybody forgets about him.

At precisely which time, naturally, our producer calls. "Good news! We've found Warshaw!"

Of course, there has to be a confrontation with this "Warshaw." Who is he? There is substantial challenge in determining the identity of this figure.

For example:

The producer visits my office the next day with "Warshaw." And who is he? A former student who kicked back part of the prize money for an award the professor judged? Or who knows that one of the professor's works is plagiarized? Or that his academic credentials are false?

Over the length of his relationship with the professor the former assistant has acquired a great deal of information about his life, including his life as a writer.

The student knows all about *Deadpan* and the bizarre scheme of creating Warshaw. Like all film students, he is eager to find employment in some corner of the movie industry. In the professor's Warshaw scam, by seizing the Warshaw identity for himself, he sees a way to win a producer's nod. The professor cannot protest, because it could threaten his own academic career.

Challenge: create another possible Warshaw. Then create another and yet another. Who are they? From where do they come? What are the implications of utilizing one or another of them? What is the impact upon other aspects of the tale? How do we resolve the conflict and the mystery that is set up at the top? What do the various treatments tell us about identity? What do they tell us about the ways in which story, character and theme interact?

Story Craft Challenge #2: What's on the Film?

Years ago, when I was a struggling film student, I often found myself on precisely the other end of the referral equation. From time to time I was the one the film faculty referred to producers eagerly seeking writers.

And this is how I came to meet a gent we'll call Vilmos Strowski, a benign and dapper fellow who produced benign and dapper—and ultralow-budget—pictures. They consisted basically of Vilmos himself traipsing from South Sea Isle to South Sea Isle, smiling and nodding, encountering gorgeous bikini-clad women in wretchedly tame settings and situations.

His command of English was strong enough for daily life in Hollywood, but he perceived correctly that his written English—and most especially his screen dialogue—was awkward. He sought in me an inexpensive native ear.

I spent the better part of a week at his side in his penthouse nosebleed-high above the Sunset Strip, hammering out timeless spoken seductions designed to put fluff like "Here's looking at you, kid" to shame. And for this I was paid the princely sum of two hundred and fifty dollars. Lofty aesthetic pronouncements regarding creative expression aside, I can tell you that no experience mellows the spirit like getting paid to write.

Upon completion of the assignment we went our separate ways. Years later—three? four? five?—I spotted a vaguely familiar figure crossing Highland and realized after a moment that it was none other than Vilmos Strowski. We embraced and chatted briefly.

"How did *Love in the South Seas* go?" I inquired.

"The airline!" Strowski said in dismay, his gaze narrowing in ancient and dark recollection. "They lose my footages!"

The film's entire negative, he told me, had vanished in international freight, rendering the entire project null and void.

At least that's the way he told it.

And I haven't a reason in the world to doubt it.

But owning a generally suspicious mind, and having been exposed more than once to Mel Brooks's incomparable *The Producers*, I have a somewhat cynical notion, wholly lacking foundation, as to what really happened to Vilmos Strowski's "footages" for his alleged film, *Love in the South Seas*.

It matters not a whit, of course, whether or not my notion is true. All that matters—as with any movie—is that it is plausible, and that it would make an interesting story, a story a whole lot more interesting than, say, *Love in the South Seas*.

And here it is.

Imagine that as in *The Producers*, Strowski's movie is a total, thorough scam. He plans, in fact, not to produce a movie but instead to make a quick and dirty profit through fraud. He rounds up as many investors as he can among small-time exhibitors and distributors and lowball underwriting syndicates around the globe. Through his old-world charm he acquires substantially more money than is needed to finance the film. Indeed, he sells off perhaps three thousand percent of the movie rights.

He can never be called to account, since no movie will ever be produced. He spends all the money on himself, taking a five-diamond vacation of approximately the same duration as would be required to shoot the movie.

Upon returning to the States, perhaps in concert with some coconspirator at an air freight company who can provide bogus shipping receipts, he claims that the shipper has lost his "footages." He insists, of course, that he spent all the investors' money producing the film, and that there is nothing left, alas, to refund to anyone.

Are the investors angry? Only a little, as each has invested only a little. And whatever frail anger they may summon is more than balanced by their enormous sympathy for the "devastated" Strowski, whose art and craft and soul have been lost, thanks to some lame shipping clerk somewhere in Antwerp or Macau who could care less about film art and creative expression.

Such is the artist's lot, his forgiving investors reassure him.

The months drift away and Vilmos lives comfortably enough on his investors' purloined funds.

But one day there comes a phone call from the airline. Good news! The lost "footages" have been found!

Strowski must, of course, pretend to rejoice. He is now presumably able to edit his masterwork, after all, and also to release it to, no doubt, good and grand acclaim all around the world.

Best of all, he can return to his faithful investors a tidy profit.

Except for the fact, of course, that he never shot any film.

Art, as we observe repeatedly, is choice. And the writer of this film needs to choose.

One choice would be for Strowski to fess up, come clean. But this would tell the audience only what it already knows. And to tell an audience what it already knows is, of course, an unpardonable affront in film.

Furthermore, it would probably mean the end of the movie, and that's not feasible, as the movie has hardly begun.

And so Strowski reluctantly—although in a falsely eager tone—cooperates with the shipping company and agrees to allow them to deliver his "footages" to his cutting room, which is that same apartment high above the Sunset Strip.

The film cans arrive at his door. He thanks the delivery men and women, signs the receipt and is at last alone with his "footages."

He drags the first can to the Moviola, a film editing machine with a small screen. He threads up the first reel and sees . . . what?

I have posed this query to writers in classes at UCLA and in seminars across the world, and have enjoyed a bounty of responses. Some suggest the reels reveal surreptitiously attained images of Strowski himself enjoying poolside frolics at the luxury resorts where he sat out the sham "production" of his film, squandering lavishly his investors' funds. Perhaps there is someone—the former student?—who has been onto him all along and hopes to blackmail him or scam him in reverse.

Others have suggested that the film cans are empty. Perhaps his cohort at the shipping company has double-crossed him. Still others suggest the cans are loaded, but not with film; instead, they are jammed with cocaine and Strowski is being exploited in a drug-smuggling scheme. He cannot go to the police because it would blow—so to speak—his cover on the investment scam.

Frankly, however, as I mention in the What's in the Bags challenge in the previous chapter, I'm sick to tears of drug-smuggling tales.

Of course, the cans could indeed have reels of film in them, exactly as film cans ought, except that when Strowski threads them up we discover that all of the film is blank.

Or they contain footage from classic old movies.

Or from movies unknown to him.

Or pornography.

Perhaps snuff movies in which people are actually murdered purely for the sake of the camera.

Or any number of other possibilities.

Story Craft Challenge #3: Who's the Embezzler?

The universe of creative screenwriting possibilities can be explored again in another examination of a real-life incident, this one involving my neighbors and their joint checking account.

One bright morning not long ago, an envelope from their bank arrived in the mail. It contained a check that had presumably been paid to them. The check had been endorsed—in a crude forgery—over to the bank for deposit. The company on whose account the check was written turned out—need I say—to have long ago gone belly-up, and all its accounts closed.

The check's amount—about two thousand dollars—was deducted from their account, along with penalties and interest.

Of course, no such check had ever been issued. Neither the husband nor wife had ever seen, much less endorsed, any such instrument.

Promptly they called the bank, and just as promptly the bank recognized a too-familiar small-time embezzling caper, closed the account and restored the money to my neighbors.

Here's how the scheme works.

Someone gets ahold of your checking account number. It's easy enough to imagine various ways one might accomplish this. Looking over your shoulder while you fill out a deposit slip? Picking through your garbage seeking discarded canceled checks? Leafing through payroll records at your job?

Next, the culprit obtains a discarded blank check from any closed account. These exist in abundance, alas, in our society. On that nonexistent account he writes you a check for, say, two thousand dollars. He "deposits" it to your account, minus a relatively modest cash-back. That is, he deposits fourteen hundred but takes back, say, six hundred in cash.

Because such transactions have the appearance not of cashing a check but, instead, of making a deposit, bank tellers tend generally to treat them with little attention, little suspicion. Adding money—or at least the appearance of adding money—to an account engenders far less scrutiny than withdrawing funds.

In this manner a plucky embezzler can quickly loot a modest account. Two days—sometimes three—may elapse before the bad check is returned to the account holder, who quickly realizes that no such check was ever written, much less endorsed. During this period it is possible for the perpetrator—depending upon his or her skill—to abscond with perhaps several thousand dollars of the bank's money.

It is important to note that the account holder—in this instance my neighbors—bore no responsibility and suffered no loss. The financial obligation belongs to whoever cashes the check, and that is usually the bank.

Nonetheless, the experience has to be somewhat disconcerting. In addition to everything else, there is the substantial nuisance of changing accounts, filing new signature cards and dealing with various other documents. Still, it's surely got to beat losing thousands of bucks.

The police, no one will be surprised to learn, do not assign top priority to such a crime; they do not unleash their crack SWAT squad in a campaign to bring the perpetrator to justice. A bank eating a couple of its own grand comes somewhere down the list after kidnapping, insurrection and pedophilia. The bank, therefore, conducts its own investigation, but it is a halfhearted one.

For from the bank's perspective, this sort of forgery represents merely one small part of the cost of doing business.

The bank's officer responsible for the investigation interviewed my neighbors, recording various kinds of tedious information. Eventually he said to them, "That's it for now. There's nothing else to do until Friday, when we'll have you come in to look at pictures of the perpetrator."

"You'll have pictures of the perpetrator?" they asked, incredulous.

"Yes. You may very well recognize him. It often turns out to be someone known to the account holder, someone with access to their numbers. A baby-sitter, for instance, or a housekeeper who's gone through your desk while you weren't around. It could be a neighbor, who may have searched through your trash and discovered discarded deposit slips. Your tax preparer. An escrow officer at this very bank. Who knows?"

But how can they precisely pinpoint the particular embezzler? And how in the world do they happen to have such pictures?

Easy.

We may assume those video cameras one sees in banks are triggered into action only upon a teller's activating a silent alarm during a robbery.

Not so.

In fact they operate continually, exposing but a single frame perhaps every few seconds. At this rate one tape can record an entire week's activity. More to the point, bank administrators can easily enough match the video record with the time and date of the transaction stamped onto the bogus check and deposit slip. These are keyed to the particular teller's window where the transaction transpired, and to the precise hour and day.

In this manner they can guarantee a picture of the perpetrator.

My neighbors were more than a little curious to have a look at those printed-out video frames. Would the culprit be Isabel, their beloved and faithful child-care person? Would it be Al, their capable plumber, who had ample time alone in the house the day he searched for leaks in the basement near the file cabinet where the banking records are stored? Would it be Alice Marie, their wacky but lovable neighbor across the street? John, the photographer next door? Sweet, gawky Elizabeth, the adolescent up the street who frequently baby-sat for them?

Indeed, would it be me, their pal and neighbor?

At last Friday arrived, and along with it six black-and-white photos of the person who had forged the signature and looted the account. From the grainy print, and from the imperfect angle, she appeared to be a young Asian woman with long, crimped black hair.

My neighbor thought immediately of Sandy Lee, who works in the payroll office at her job and certainly has access to confidential financial information. She represented a perfect suspect—except that my neighbor could see clearly that it was not Sandy Lee.

From all of this derives, of course, our story craft challenge.

Who's the embezzler?

Is it one of the principles—the husband? The wife?

Is it a brother? A parent? Steve Martin's cat?

A total stranger who reappears later in some other context in their lives?

The perpetrator's image can be shown to the audience, or it can be delayed or even entirely withheld. It is enlightening to contemplate potential story strengths and weaknesses created by our choice.

My own choice involves different reactions from each member of the couple. One member, say the wife, quickly and cavalierly shakes her head, finding the image on the film to represent a total stranger.

The husband nods his head, asserting his apparent agreement. He insists he knows nothing of the individual in the photo. In fact, however, he fidgets anxiously and grows short of breath, perhaps revealing some hidden agenda, some covert information. Is it a current or former lover? Another woman to whom he is also married? A cohort in some embezzlement scheme of his own involving his job?

Take your pick.

And as we pick, we ought to be aware of potential implications and repercussions relative to theme and tale and everything else that is affected by our picking.

Story Craft Challenge #4: *Backdraft*—Who's the Arsonist?

Let us turn now to an existing film, the action/adventure blockbuster *Backdraft*, which just happens to have originated as a class assignment by its writer, Gregory Widen, during his tenure as a screenwriting student at UCLA.

Backdraft is a tale of terror and intrigue in which investigators track a terrifyingly canny arsonist who has been setting fires throughout Chicago. Is the perpetrator Kurt Russell, hard-bitten, hard-luck brother of the protagonist? The writer leaves us many clues to suggest this is the case, but it is merely a skillful tease.

Is it the girlfriend?

Is it some stranger?

A mere stranger who emerges from out of the woodwork is by definition unintegrated, not truly part of the story, simply stuck on at the end and inevitably unsatisfying. Widen's choice is enormously clever and for the most part thoroughly effective. The culprit turns out to be a disgruntled and embittered fireman whom we have come to know quite well by film's end.

It is properly shocking to discover his identity. And it is wonderfully appropriate that it is a fireman, a man trained to put out fires, who is in fact setting them. There are echoes here of Ray Bradbury's timeless *Fahrenheit 451*, a futuristic tale in which firemen do not quench but start fires, burning in particular books, which happen to ignite at precisely 451 degrees Fahrenheit.

If you're going to steal from somebody, let it be from a writer as capable as Bradbury.

Alas, also tied into the scheme is a corrupt Chicago alderman.

I say "alas" because the crooked city councilman, Chicago-bred in particular, has been done to death and represents something of a cliché.

On the other hand, it has to be admitted that clichés get to be clichés because they are so splendidly, dreadfully true.

Nevertheless, it may be instructive to contemplate other possible culprits the writer might have chosen. How significantly would particular choices weigh upon the rest of the film? If they would not make a whole lot of difference, it's likely to signal an ill-structured tale. Keep in mind that a well-turned story should promptly fall apart when even a single item is changed.

Story Craft Challenge #5: *The Hand That Rocks the Cradle*—Who's the Nanny?

For a different example of identity integration, let us look at *The Hand That Rocks the Cradle*, written by Amanda Silver, a student from my own alma mater, UCLA's crosstown rival USC.

A couple seeks a nanny for their daughter. The woman they choose happens to be the enraged, embittered, former wife of a doctor—a doctor who was disgraced and humiliated, and ultimately destroyed, by the girl's parents.

This is surely preferable to the nanny's being somebody who has no other relationship to the tale. Unfortunately, the fact of her identity is revealed far too early. We know right away what's to come. The writer tips her hand, squandering the opportunity for surprise and shock.

Additionally, the nanny is depicted as quirky and mysterious and weird. She ought, in my opinion, to be played in a completely opposite way. She should be the perfect Earth Mother, a model of maternal nourishment, serenity and reassurance. And the fact of her curious, nefarious relationship to the family should be concealed until nearly the end. There could be an unnerving revelation to the family of that special relationship at a point when it is perhaps too late for them to intercede and to rescue their precious offspring.

Consider who else the nanny might turn out to be.

What are the implications of such choices?

The most important aspect of all this artistic choice-making is that regardless of the writer's intent, the choices he makes will be inevitably and invariably personal. It will all represent merely another take on the writer's own psyche. No matter how hard he tries to conceal himself, the work cannot help but reflect the unique personality—the taste, the voice, the style, the sensibility—belonging to an individual artist.

That's why films as apparently diverse as *Babe* (George Miller, Chris Noonan), *Big* (Gary Ross, Anne Spielberg), and *Toy Story* (Joss Whedon, Andrew Stanton, Joel Cohen, Alec Sokolow) are actually different spins on one and the same tale. A pig wishes he had a purpose; a child wishes he were an adult; a toy wishes his powers were real. Each film tells a story in which the central character seeks only to discover his own true identity.

And ultimately, by virtue of choices, writers reveal to us not only their protagonists' natures, but their own.

CHAPTER 5

■ ■ ■ ■ ■ ■ ■ ■ ■ ■ ■ ■ ■ ■ ■ ■ ■ ■ ■

Rewriting: Notes on Notes

As we academics crank up each fall for the new year, many of us greet the season with just a touch of misgiving, if not dread: here we go again, same old thing, year in, year out, semester after semester after semester after semester after semester after semester.

In my case, however, as summer winds down the anticipation and excitement soar.

How could I not be eager to greet our new crop of screenwriting commandos? If past is prologue, in a few years they'll own the film and television industry; in no time at all we professors will be pleading with them for operating funds, scholarships and, God willing, maybe one day even an endowed chair.

At the very least we'll implore them to acknowledge the university in their Oscar acceptance speeches.

Indeed, as so many among them become not only writers but also producers and executives, we'll likely plead with them also for an occasional TV or movie assignment.

Above all else, what thrills me about the new writers I meet both on and off campus is the expansive, open-minded manner in which they respond to criticism.

By "criticism" I do not mean pejorative nitpicking or cynical reprimand. I refer simply to analysis that is not patronizing or destructive, but honest and candid and supportive, commentary offered in a spirit celebrating the courage required of any and all writers to write any and all things. This experience reminds me again and again that art is worth loving and life worth living.

Unlike poets and painters, screenwriters do not operate in isolation. They are part of a vast family of contributors. Given film's collaborative nature, screenwriting involves more hemming and hawing, more bobbing and weaving, more give-and-take, more flat-out compromise than one sees in any other medium of creative expression. It encourages me, therefore, to witness writers eagerly welcoming sincere, supportive criticism and accepting it with gratitude and with dedication to improving their work.

Naturally, here and there is an exception. From time to time, upon citing even the slightest deficit, I have seen curtains drawn shut behind a writer's eyes. The eyes are still physically open but the mind is closed. An attitude like this hurts not the teacher or story editor but only the writer.

Writers should not, of course, mindlessly take notes on ruled yellow legal paper and then promptly execute any and all recommended changes. Instead, they should weigh, consider, examine, evaluate and reevaluate whatever suggestions are offered. If they are like all the writers I've ever worked with, they'll agree with some reactions and disagree with others.

And that is precisely as it ought to be because, after all, it is nobody else but the writer on whose shoulders rests the responsibility for the script and who'll carry whatever credit—or blame—that eventually accrues.

Privately, I admit that from time to time I am dismayed by a writer's earliest draft. In such instances I mask my pessimism and attempt instead to identify and underscore whatever strengths—however sparse—may also reside within those pages. In a worst-case scenario I feel very much like a plastic surgeon working with a burn victim, seeking just a few good cells from which to start a graft. And invariably, upon reading the revision some weeks later, I am astounded by the improvements.

Almost without exception, something clicks inside the writer and at long last he sees exactly what he needs to see. Far more often than not, the revised draft reverses my expectations. The uncanny ability of writers to improve their scripts through rewriting keeps me and my colleagues fresh and alert as we slog it out in the screenwriting education hustle.

Massive experience teaches this much: an inept, all-over-the-place, unwieldy, unfocused early draft can, through the painful but unavoidable process of revision, be rendered whole.

Consults and Insults

Smart writers learn that true success—a career possessing longevity—requires the ability to respond intelligently to criticism and to tolerate sometimes seemingly endless rewrites. With this in mind, writers—from total amateurs to veteran superstars—turn increasingly to professional consultants, women and men who'll read and analyze a script prior to submission, who'll ask the hard questions before the prospective agent or producer or studio executive asks them.

Savvy Hollywood writers have come to appreciate that as difficult as it is to earn money for an original script or to capture a paid screenwriting assignment—known in the trade as a development deal—it is still far more difficult to get that script to the screen. Simply stated: just because they paid for the script does not guarantee they'll shoot the movie.

And getting the script to the screen is what professional screenwriting success is all about.

I have trafficked in the film school community long enough to see writers flare brightly and burn out. I have known writers who were younger than I but who are now, in defiance of fundamental physical and biological principles, older than I. I have witnessed writers win development deal after development deal over a couple of years, earning perhaps a million dollars or more in fees, but never had their scripts actually filmed.

I have known, furthermore, an unfair number of writers who have had their films produced but not released.

The key to success for writers of screenplays is getting the script not only sold but also produced, and not only produced but also released, and not only released but released successfully. This is why, increasingly, writers are learning that the first film professional who views their script ought not be an agent or a producer but a consultant—that is, a capable script analyst.

This is true, as I have indicated, even for writers with development deals. Typically such an arrangement involves what is called "a draft and a set." Everybody knows what a draft is. The "set" refers usually to two revisions. The first is often called just that: a revised draft. The second is often called a polish, presumably because by that stage the script needs merely a bit of last-minute shading and shaping, highlighting and fine-tuning.

Of course, I've never known a writer who was assigned to polish another writers's script who did not believe the job was actually a "page-one rewrite," i.e., a total overhaul amounting, at least in the rewriter's eyes, to an entirely original screenplay.

Often, between various phases of a development deal—perhaps between the first draft and the first revision, or perhaps between the first revision and the polish—prior to turning the script over to the producer the writer will engage a consultant to review it and to prepare notes, all the better to enhance the chances for the writer to stay with the project and for the project to make it to the screen.

I have over the past number of years consulted in this fashion on no small number of screenplays. Sometimes I'm retained directly by the writer (an independent writer or a writer with a commissioned assignment), and sometimes it's the writer's employer (the studio or network) who retains me.

When I consult on a script, I participate in what is by now a rather familiar process.

Once I've decided that a particular writer is one with whom I want to work, and that the script merits encouragement, I don't merely reread the script but study it, blue pencil at the ready, inscribing extensive notes in the margins as I go. It is a painstaking process. Few pages are likely to emerge unscathed. And some pages will have more of my own ink than that of the writer.

I simply do not know how to work with a writer other than to offer criticism that is not generic but specific. I confront concrete, discrete, particular questions regarding a concrete, discrete, particular script. What use is it to a writer to be told to "punch it up" or "tone it down" or "lighten the love angle" or "beef up the antagonist" or "tweak the dialogue"?

When I get to the end of the script, I immediately write a broad overview of the whole picture. I try to identify those places where the protagonist is clearly articulated and where the script's major strengths lie. And I endeavor also to determine precisely where the tale needs to be underscored and undergirded and just generally shored up. I try, likewise, to help the writer focus and refocus with regard to tale assembly and structure, character, dialogue and anything else that is even remotely appropriate.

This commentary is handwritten on the back of the last page and in the margins of the script in an impenetrable chicken-scrawl.

It is necessary for me, therefore, to translate my commentary; I do so in a written report usually running twenty to thirty single-spaced typed pages or more. There are two reasons this report is needed. First, there is the aforementioned illegibility (I blame my fourth-grade teacher at P.S. 112 in Queens, Miss Desdemona Pickerel). Second, I have invented a homemade, freeze-dried shorthand, my own personal stenographic code. I have created this system not with the purpose of being coy, cute or cryptic but simply because it helps me move more quickly through the script analysis.

What follows is an inventory of the kinds of notes that I inscribe upon scripts. It catalogues the notes I write and, therefore, the sorts of errors—and strengths—I most commonly encounter.

Notes on Notes

hwk? *or* see/hear *or* ink v. light

"Hwk" simply stands for "How [do] we know?"

"See/hear" simply asks of the writer: "Precisely what is it that we see; precisely what is it that we hear?"

Recently I analyzed a script containing a passage meriting the notation "hwk?" or "see/hear." The screenwriter had included the following description: "Charlene is wounded by this revelation; she is reminded of the many years of neglect—and even outright abuse—she suffered at the hands of her mother."

It is, of course, easy enough to impart such information to the reader of the script. But how in the world is the viewer of the film, seated in the theater, made privy to the same data? Writers need ask themselves: What do we *see* and *hear* that renders meaningful whatever it is that occurs in the head of the viewer?

Screenwriters need to remind themselves constantly that a screenplay represents only two kinds of information: sight and sound. All other aspects of a screenplay—story, character and everything else—derive from these two kinds of information alone.

This is one of those screenwriting facts that is so obvious that—like Edgar Allan Poe's *Purloined Letter*—it is all too easy to overlook. "Hwk" or "see/hear" may seem on the surface to indicate a petty, technical criticism of a script, but in fact it points out a fundamental misunderstanding of the art and craft of screenwriting.

ess. det. only *or* SIFYN

These designations stand for "essential details only" and "save it for your novel."

I read a screenplay containing a passage describing a delicatessen in which a particular scene plays out. All sorts of colorful but unnecessary details are included: the clanking of plates and silverware, the din of the dishwashers, waiters calling orders to the chefs, the harsh fluorescent lighting, the plateglass window looking out onto the street.

Astonishingly enough, the writer provided even the following information: "The air is thick with the rich, sweet smell of pastrami."

This is a movie. It's true enough that movies do from time to time smell, but only metaphorically, and never of pastrami. The incorporation of all these details violates the requirement that all data must be essential. In addition, it violates the sight/sound principle.

A screenplay should contain no information that can be excised without materially affecting the reader's impression of what is on the screen and what is in the sound track. Tolerable details are integrated. They move the story forward and expand our appreciation of the characters. "Integrated" in this sense is synonymous with "essential."

If the movie plays just as well without the information or extra language, that information or language is not essential and, therefore, has no reason to be in the script.

As I urge my students, writers need to embrace a rule belonging to espionage. Spies, it is said, operate on a "need-to-know" basis. This means they are given only as much information as is necessary to accomplish their task. If they are captured and subjected to torture, they cannot reveal information they never possessed in the first place.

Writers ought to reveal only essential information because otherwise their readers will feel tortured by having to endure too much data. Readers of such material quickly realize—

sometimes consciously, often subliminally—that a writer who offers too much information does not require readers to pay close attention, as much of the material is mere window dressing that fails to deliver tale and character freight.

Writers ought to imagine that the ink in their pens or the dye in their typewriter ribbons or the toner in their ink-jet printer cartridges costs a million-billion-trillion-zillion dollars per ounce. This will encourage them to use it sparingly. It is not, of course, the ink that has such value; rather it is the time and attention and consideration of the reader.

One splendid screenplay currently slated for production describes a scene at a vast country estate in the Hudson Valley of upstate New York. On a summer afternoon, an elegant banquet takes place on the grassy riverbank sloping down to the water's edge.

If writers were paid by the word, they could grow quite rich composing the description of this scene. They could describe the weather, the way the puffy, white clouds billow in the bright summer sky, the way the sun dapples the grass as it filters through the willows that shudder and tremble in the breeze. They could add to their fortune by spending time—and ink—detailing the costumes of the guests and the staff, the cuisine, the festive decorations, the hairstyles.

Bash Hollywood as much as you like, but everybody agrees that the mainstream American film community gives great wardrobe, hair, lighting, set and scenic design, and art direction. If the screenwriter throws in all sorts of extra-added information, he not only renders the script that much more difficult to read, but worse, he intrudes upon the territory of his various collaborators.

In our Hudson Valley tale, therefore, the writer can effectively condense the description to the following: "A lavish lawn party is in progress."

Seven words.

And aren't these words enough to evoke the precisely desired

image? A most curious aspect of creative expression—
especially in screenwriting—is that the fewer the words, the
clearer the meaning. Less language allows for a greater appreciation of the scene, setting, story and characters. In other
words: less is more.

drekt/akt

This designation is closely related to the previous one, as it
comments upon necessary details in a script. Specifically, it
refers to extraneous directions and cues offered to the actors.
Usually these are instructions to "pause" or, worse, to "pause
thoughtfully" or "meaningfully." A weak writer may offer
expression on the order of: "Alice hesitates for a moment. She
looks to the sea, then to the shore, then to the barn and the distant hayloft. She settles down onto the overturned wheelbarrow
and contemplates her life."

I can't imagine an audience that would be excited by the
image of an actor "contemplating" anything at all, much less her
so-called life.

"Drekt" and "akt" stand for "direct" and "act." The note
simply advises the writer not to direct the picture or to act out
the parts, but "merely" to write it. I place the word "merely" in
quotation marks because that word should never be used in the
same sentence as—much less adjacent to—the word "write."

There's nothing "mere" about writing. Ask anyone who's
tried it.

$?

A dollar sign residing next to a question mark usually sits in
the margin beside some sort of inconsequential action or dialogue. The everyday polite exchanges—greetings, salutations—
that saturate life are fine in the real world but in the reel world
are boring.

This little icon simply poses the question: Is this particular line of dialogue, or bit of action, sufficiently special as to warrant an audience's hard-earned money? It usually accompanies dialogue along the lines of: "Say, would you like a cup of coffee?" Or it may be placed in the margin alongside a bit of business such as: "Gladys enters the apartment, removes her hat and coat and hangs them in the closet. She goes to the kitchen and boils a pot of water for tea."

Let the apartment teem with terrorists!

Let the closet contain goblins and ghosts!

Let the water turn out to be industrial-strength hydrofluoric acid!

Let the screen broil with action that is saturated with conflict, that engenders sweet stress and tension, that is worth paying money to see. Audiences most surely prefer this over mundane, ordinary occurrences that might replicate real life but fail to advance character and to expand story.

s. or n.

This simply stands for "something or nothing."

It suggests that if writers provide a character with a line to speak, it really ought to be a line to speak. In other words, no groans, no moans, no gasps, no wheezes, no mere sounds, no stammering or stuttering.

Typical places that might win the "s. or n." notation are lines of "dialogue" such as:

MARY
Arrrgghhhhhh!

I place the word "dialogue" between quotation marks because such a line is not dialogue at all. Actors simply cannot pronounce the writer's idea of a transliterated—spelled-out—gasp of pain, pleasure, confusion, satisfaction or anything else. Such noises are going to be produced by the actor in the unique manner that he or she produces them. Additionally, they will grow out of the scene and setting and situation, not out of a last-minute decision by a writer to toss in some spelled-out intake of breath, or cough, sniffle or sneeze.

Another typical spot for the "s. or n." notation is in the margin beside a fragment of a line in which a character says, effectively, nothing.

For example:

>MARY
>But . . . I . . . I . . . only wanted to . . . you . . .
>I . . .

"S. or n." simply means: give an actor a line or don't give an actor a line. Don't give him a fragment of a line. Don't give him a mere noise to make.

3 strikes

Baseball is tough, but screenwriting is tougher.

In baseball you're allowed three strikes before you're out. In screenwriting, however, you need three hits before you're permitted to get to first base.

What in the world can this mean?

Simply this: not one or two but three questions regarding information in a screenplay—be it character, action or dialogue—need positively to be answered before that information should be tolerated in the script. The questions are: Is there a purpose for including the information? If so, is it a worthy purpose? And again, if so, is this the best way to achieve that purpose?

This is just another way of underscoring the primacy of integration. Humbly stated, everything in a script—indeed, everything in any work of creative expression—needs to have a purpose in order to be truly a part of the whole picture. All too frequently I encounter writers who, upon being asked to explain the purpose of a specific item in a script, respond that there was none. A writer may contend, for example, that there was an amorphous "feeling," a generalized sense that it would be nice, or cool, or charming or groovy to include whatever it is that is included.

In fact, however, there can be only one legitimate purpose that justifies including anything at all in any script, and that is integration. Bits of description or dialogue are worthy if they move the story forward and expand character, palpably and unmistakably. If the asserted "purpose" is merely to satisfy a whim on the part of the writer, that is the same as no purpose at all. This sort of information ought to be promptly deleted.

Even if there is, in fact, a purpose for the information, that does not necessarily justify its placement in the screenplay. Rather, it leads only to the second question: Is this a purpose that is truly worthy?

Once again, a purpose that is worthy is one that affects, steers, expands and enhances both story and character.

For example, if a writer's purpose is to set the scene's mood, I will urge against it. Mood, I frequently point out to writers, is "doom" spelled backward. It's easy enough to smear oodles of moody descriptions upon a screenplay, but it hardly replaces story and character.

Where in the world does Shakespeare describe the "mood" at, say, the opening of *Hamlet*?

Nowhere.

The mood arises as it ought to—naturally, out of the unique configuration of scene and setting and character and dialogue and action that all together add up to *Hamlet*. If the action opens on a castle wall at night with a prince confronting the ghost of his murdered father, the mood is not exactly party time. The writer does not need to assert that it is dark, grim, somber, as all that is plainly self-evident.

Setting the mood, therefore, is in my own view not a legitimate purpose worthy of a writer's time, talent and toil.

A final way to make sure that the purpose of including certain information is ultimately justified is to ask the following question: Is this particular line of dialogue or bit of action the best way to achieve that purpose?

At a crucial turn in *The Lion King* (Irene Mecchi, Jonathan Roberts, Linda Wolverton), for example, Simba's father is killed, trampled to death by a stampede of rampaging wildebeests. Is there a purpose to the scene? Absolutely. The father needs to die so that, first of all, Simba can eventually assume his place. Every bit as pertinent, in keeping with antagonist Scar's scheme, Simba needs to be made to hold himself responsible—however falsely—for his father's death.

There is, therefore, not only a purpose but one that is clear and necessary. But is the stampede of wildebeests the best way to achieve that purpose?

Again, yes.

Surely we can concoct a host of other ways to kill the father. He could become ill; he could become trapped in a deep excavation into which he stumbles; he could fall off a steep cliff. There is no end to the manner and method by which his demise could be contrived.

But a stampede of wildebeests contains such exquisite drama. And it is all so splendidly in keeping with the setting, so neatly integrated into Scar's sophisticated scheme, which entails not only the lion's death but the need to instill in Simba a sense that he is responsible for his father's death.

Three hits.

The writer can go to first base.

The wildebeests can trample Simba's father into lion marmalade.

The important thing to remember about this particular rule is that if only one or even two of the criteria are met it is the same as if none have been. Only when all three questions are satisfactorily addressed is the material deemed worthy to reside in the screenplay.

notnot

I am constantly bemused and befuddled to read material in screenplays that instead of telling me what happens—what is seen and what is heard—informs me of what is *not* seen and what is *not* heard.

This most commonly occurs in language describing a character's failure to respond to a particular line of dialogue. Remember, no response is just another kind of response.

Imagine that a character in a script is asked a question but fails or refuses to answer. Writers will too often write: "Sharon does not answer."

Isn't it obvious that if Sharon answers, she answers? If she answers, that answer will be contained in the next line of dialogue with Sharon's name above it. The "notnot" notation simply means that writers should write what happens and what is spoken, not what does *not* happen and what is *not* spoken.

I read a script years ago containing a scene in which one character grills another and the latter refuses to respond in any way other than through silence.

On the page, the scene reads like this:

> HARVEY
>
> Answer me!
>
> JACK
>
> No response.
>
> HARVEY
>
> I demand that you answer!
>
> JACK
>
> No response.

I asked the writer if he intended for the character named Jack actually to say, "No response."

The writer asserted that, of course, this was not his intent. He simply meant to indicate that in the onslaught of Harvey's questions, Jack remains silent.

But if Jack doesn't answer, I argued, then he doesn't answer. The writer simply gives him nothing to say, leaves the space blank.

"You mean the character's name with nothing under it?" the writer asked me.

No, I explained. No character's name, no dialogue.

"But how does the reader know that Jack does not respond?" the writer asked.

But how, I countered, does the reader know that Jack does not sprout wings and fly? How does he know that Jack does not on the spot have a sex-change operation and win election as President of the United States and, on top of all that, just for fun, sing the chorus from *Carmen*?

The business between Harvey and Jack ought to appear on the page as follows:

HARVEY
Answer me. I demand that you answer.

Note that no "beats" or "pauses" or parentheticals (for example, "angrily") or other directing or acting cues are necessary.

Remember, anything that is not in the script is not in the script. Writers only need to provide information as to what dialogue *is* spoken and what action *is* taken, not what dialogue is *not* spoken or what action *not* taken.

This may seem stunningly self-evident, yet it is, like so many other obvious matters, commonly overlooked.

And it is a problem that infects not only dialogue but also action. For example, in the above-mentioned script, a writer may have the impulse to include a descriptive sentence like "Jack does nothing" or "Jack sits perfectly still."

If Jack does something, tell us precisely what it is that he does.

Do not tell us what it is precisely—or even generally—that Jack does not do.

Do not tell us that Jack does nothing.

Readers ought to be credited with the ability to understand that what's in the script is what's in the script. What's not in the script is all the rest of God's creation.

too straight-line

Not long ago, when I was testifying in court as an expert witness in a case involving copyright infringement, the opposing attorney asked me what precisely I meant when I used the word "story."

Why, everybody knows what a story is, I responded. You don't need to be a senior, tenured member of the faculty at a world center of higher learning to know what the word "story" means, I stated in court. This happens, that happens, something happens after that and so on. That's the story.

Certainly there is no denying that the nature of story is one thing following another after another and another until its end. Nevertheless, there is much more to story than simply that. Stories ideally want to appear shaped, sculpted, finessed, molded. Their final shape should be round, not a plain and simple straight line.

Stories start to look this way when cause follows too hard upon effect, when dramatic tension is heightened and then immediately resolved, a question asked and promptly answered.

Dave is a movie in which screenwriter Gary Ross avoids a too-straight-line look in any number of ways. There is a scene in the presidential limousine, for example, where Dave, attempting to pass as the President, enjoys a lusty glance at the First Lady's thigh. Quite some time later in the picture she reveals to him that it was at that moment she realized he was not her husband but an imposter. Her husband, she explains, has not regarded her with lust in a long, long time.

An effective technique to avoid the "too-straight-line" designation is to connect one piece of plot to another by distancing them along the story line. A less skillful writer than Ross would have shown the First Lady responding to Dave's glance in the very next scene, perhaps even in the very next moment, confronting him with the truth of the situation. "You regarded my thigh with lust," she might have said to him. "I know, therefore, that you are not who you claim to be."

There's drama there, to be sure. It's not dreadful, not wretched, not awful, but it's also not nearly as good or as stirring as it potentially could be. By mixing and remixing the incidents and anecdotes that make up the tale, the writer can tease and seduce the audience, while configuring and reconfiguring the arousals and resolutions.

checkerboarding

"Checkerboarding" is just another way of saying "too-straight-line." A checkerboard has a much more effectively integrated shape than, say, a Monopoly board. In the former, chessmen or checkers swarm and move up and back and across the field in any and all directions. In the latter, all the pieces move in the same direction and follow an identical path.

The well-turned plot starts somewhere, goes somewhere else and then somewhere else before finally returning to a point it had been earlier. The overall effect could be said in a roundabout way to resemble a checkerboard.

l.f.

Baseball provides useful parallels to screenwriting. The abbreviation of "l.f." stands simply for "left field." The designation indicates that a tale has taken so rude a twist that it has come to resemble a movie entirely different from the one we'd been watching.

A film producer told me once of an otherwise commendable

script submitted to him telling the story of a young man's struggle against cruel disadvantage to win an advanced professional education. He overcomes various obstacles that are personal, emotional, social and situational. Add then, practically at the end of the script, he becomes involved, quite unexpectedly, in a dreadful automobile accident that leaves him paralyzed.

Such a highly charged incident cannot be tacked onto the end of a tale like the cardboard appendage in Pin the Tail on the Donkey. All of a sudden, the film will seem to be some other film. Imagine, for example, a movie in which an adopted daughter seeks her birth mother. At the last moment, an hour and a half into the picture, Martians land in her backyard and take her through a time warp to Brooklyn in October of 1955, where Johnny Podres is shutting out the Yankees two-zip in the last game of the World Series.

I'm not saying you could not have a wonderful film depicting a woman kidnapped by Martians. But that is one story; the adoption/search tale is another. Solidly crafted narratives seek a sense of connection, each thing linked with everything else. Too much "l.f." material leads, on the other hand, to stories with elbows sticking out at odd and awkward angles, in dark, confusing, lost corners.

conk

"Conk" stands for "concrete."

A couple of years ago I came across an excellent definition of concreteness in Thomas S. Kane's *Oxford Guide to Writing* (Oxford University Press, 1983, New York, Oxford).

In it, Kane asserts that the best writing is not abstract or generic or general, but concrete.

An example Kane offers reads more or less as follows: "The lake was surrounded by various structures." He compares this inferior description with the following, more concrete one: "Surrounding the lake were a rickety clapboard boathouse, a dock and a log cabin."

It may not strike anyone as poetry from Shakespeare, but surely the latter example is plainly superior to the former, just because it is concrete.

In screenwriting—as in any and all writing—concreteness is one of the most essential elements. For example, rather than setting a film, or a scene in a film, in, say, "a midwestern town," try "Springfield, Ohio." Writing generally about a vague town dilutes a screenplay's effect. Even if there is no such place as the writer presents, the reader senses that the opposite is the case, and enjoys the feeling that he is reading about something that is actual rather than an invention of some writer's imagination.

Instead of saying that a character is dressed in expensive clothes, identify the particular label. Or even create a label of your own. No one will ever challenge you. A depiction of a man wearing "a broad-breasted chocolate-brown Armani suit and alligator Ferragamo shoes" is far more effective than the vague description of "modern, tasteful, costly clothes."

The trick is, of course, not to go too crazy smearing on extra language. The beauty of concreteness is that with precious few words, writers can pack a lot of wallop and create descriptions that are fleshy and fulfilling.

This rule also applies to the description of actions performed by characters in the script. In a second-grade classroom, for example, instead of having the schoolchildren "engaged in various activities," have them "gluing Popsicle sticks, fingerpainting, cutting colored paper into magic lanterns."

mstrso

"Mstrso" is short for "master scenes only."

If one reads a great many screenplays—as I heartily urge writers to do—he ought to be aware that there is a substantial possibility that the script he is reading is in fact not an early draft but a shooting script. Shooting scripts are the ones distributed most widely, since numerous copies need to be made available to all the artists and craftsmen and the various studio departments:

props, casting, editorial, sound, camera, advertising and more. Once a film is released and exhibited and, eventually, consigned to foreign distribution, video release, cable and the like, the production company will discard its scripts. Those that survive end up in bookshops and catalogues of mail-order script suppliers.

Keep in mind that there is a vast difference between a draft written with the purpose of selling it and a final shooting draft. The latter inevitably contains information that may be necessary for the technicians—camera angles and other sorts of data—that would only impede the pace at which the reader could absorb the tale.

When a film is actually produced, the typical scene is shot several ways at various angles with various numbers of players contained in each shot. Ultimately the editor arranges the image in an appropriate series of quick cuts including close-ups, long shots, wide angles, medium shots, full shots, two-shots and other technical designations that have pertinence where the cinematographer, editor, script supervisor and director are concerned but otherwise make for difficult reading.

If I see a lot of "two-shot" and "wide" and "close-up" in a script, I'm likely to scrawl "mstrso" in the margin in an attempt to encourage the writer to include only the overview, the broad image of the whole scene, without interfering with the reader's ability to scan the pages. I discourage the writer from trespassing upon territory that belongs not to writers but to our collaborators.

prez

All action and description must be told in the present tense, even if it's set in the past or in the future. For example, *2001: A Space Odyssey* is a film that starts thousands of years in the past and moves into the not-too-distant future. Nevertheless, the whole picture unfolds on the screen in the here and now.

Writers should attempt not to describe what is about to happen or what has just happened but only what happens. This may strike some readers as a relatively minor issue but, in fact, it represents a most fundamental screenwriting principle.

Some writers insist that there is no way to describe a particular facet of a particular action without stating it past tense. A common example is the return to a scene that was previously jam-packed with characters but is now empty. How do you describe the second leg of that pair without saying that "everyone has left"—which is, of course, a past-tense construction?

The movie *Dave* provides a good example of this dilemma. The antagonist, portrayed by Frank Langella, is an underhanded political czar. He stands in a room filled with people, all of them watching Dave's speech on television. We cut away to Dave delivering the speech "live" before Congress. It becomes clear enough that he is blowing the whistle on the political power broker, exposing his crimes.

We cut back to this character. He is in the same setting but it is now completely devoid of people, except for himself. The writer does not need to say, "Everyone has left the room." Attempting to discover a present-tense way to impart this information, he need write merely: "The room is empty," or "The character is alone." Instead of telling what has happened, we are telling instead what is happening. We are not whispering in the reader's ear and betraying the particular form in which we write. Instead, we do precisely what we must do: tell the reader of the script exactly what it is that the viewer of the movie in the theater sees.

This kind of change executed throughout the whole picture represents not a minuscule but an enormous—and enormously beneficial—improvement. It brings the writing into closer focus and conveys to the reader the sense that he is in the hands of an experienced professional. Additionally, it picks up the narrative's pace.

novry

This smashed-together mash of letters stands for "no very." What I mean is that there is virtually never any excuse for including the word "very" in the descriptive passages of a screenplay. There may arise an occasion to use the word in the context of dialogue, but even this is most exceptional.

Almost any word when combined with "very" can become another, more precise, more appropriate and effective word. If someone in the film runs, for example, "very fast," we can say instead that he sprints, hurries, rushes, scrambles, races, breezes. If someone is "very scared" we can say he is terrified, terrorized, petrified, shaky, shaken, trembling, quaking, rattled, sweating, numb, paralyzed, frozen.

As far as I am concerned, a writer is welcome to set her word processor on Global Search and Replace to delete every appearance of the word "very."

xpltlang

This designation stands for "exploit language," a phrase that encapsulates all the tools the writer has to tell his tale, to depict characters, to describe their actions—in short, to write the screenplay.

When I scrawl "xpltlang" in the margin I refer specifically to the selection of particular words. That is, writers ought to be selective about the words they write. I am fed up, for example, with the wretched abandon with which writers abuse the word "incredible." The sight is incredible, the reaction is incredible, the sound is incredible, the heat is incredible, this is incredible, that is incredible, the other thing is, well, incredible.

What about astounding, amazing, preposterous, wonderful, wondrous, extraordinary, splendid, stunning, shocking, paralyzing, mesmerizing, profound, deep, marked, remarkable? If we writers do not exploit the English language to its best effect, if we do not deliberately and purposefully protect it, who will?

drma/do

As I mentioned earlier, the word "drama" comes from the Greek word meaning "to do." It does not mean "to talk."

Turn on the TV, surf through the channels; in series episodes and in televised reruns of feature films alike, you are guaranteed to come upon too, too much talk.

Of course film is a visual medium and it is far better, therefore, to show rather than tell. Writers need merely to get their characters out of the same, lame, drab locations—restaurants, bars, cars, living rooms, dining rooms—that are prone to recitation and conversation and to place them in newly invented settings that present opportunities for action.

This does not mean that all scenes must play out in collapsing skyscrapers during earthquakes or among squadrons of soldiers on battlefields; nor does it require that all the actions be heroic. Simple, ordinary, everyday actions will work quite effectively, if wielded by writers with discipline and craft.

A writer at UCLA created a film that depicts the meeting, romance and eventual marriage of two people who at the beginning of the story work together in the same office. When they first confront each other, the scene is not set around the water cooler or in some conference room or behind some desk.

It is set instead in the underground parking garage.

The woman is on her way to an important meeting but discovers she has a flat tire. The man comes upon her as she is struggling to change the tire and he offers to help.

She is deeply offended by his offer. Does a man think that a woman cannot change a tire?

"Is that what the woman's movement is all about?" he asks. "Have women struggled so that their sister, dressed to the nines in preparation for an important business meeting, needs to break her perfectly manicured nails and tear her hose in the service of removing lug nuts from the rear right wheel of her steel-blue Camaro?"

In what is otherwise an ordinary setting—a parking garage—

actors do not merely talk out their conflicts and their emotions, but they actually play them out, act them out. They wrestle not only emotionally but also physically as together they jack up the vehicle, pry off the hubcap, struggle with the hex nuts, haul the spare from the trunk.

Can anyone fail to see how vastly superior a location the underground parking garage is to, say, the upstairs reception area? Cannot anyone see that the latter is a location that encourages talk, while the former invites action?

moomPIX

This designation is closely related to the previous "drma/do."

Growing up in New York City, "moving pictures" was pronounced "moom pitches." For economy, I've shortened the "pitches" part to "pix." It means simply that film is an enterprise requiring eyes more than ears. And it suggests, also, that whatever those pictures are, they ought not be static but dynamic; instead of lying there still and flaccid, they ought to bounce, pop, sizzle, crackle and roll right along.

In *Shoot the Moon* (Bo Goldman) we are treated to the image of an actor sitting quietly at the beach contemplating his fate. For seven and a half or eight dollars, an audience is entitled to something more exciting than watching a guy ruminate or contemplate, even if the guy happens to be portrayed by as capable and distinguished an actor as Albert Finney.

In too many films we watch actors sit and talk and recite the tale. But movies, when fully realized, are mainly things that are looked at, not listened to. And the images that are looked at are supposed to be not static, still, limp and wan but supercharged with action, tension and the scintillating, sparkling stress necessarily at the heart of any and all dramatic expression.

That's what makes it dramatic.

People do not exit a movie whistling the cinematography. Pretty pictures alone won't do. They need to be integrated with the action and the dialogue; like everything else in the movie, they need perpetually to advance tale and character.

I love a good slide show as much as the next guy.

But a movie is not a slide show.

cue the pigeon!

For all that movies have to do with dreams, fantasy and imagination, they are in fact also a relentlessly practical enterprise. They need not only be dreamed up and written down but also physically crafted.

The late director Frank Capra, in his biography *The Name Above the Title*, tells of working as an assistant director during the silent era. His director demanded that the sky in a scene at the seashore be filled with birds. Cleverly scattering fishermen's bait on the sea, Capra was able to attract a vast flock of gulls. He was proud of his achievement.

But this was not good enough for his boss, who, after peering through the viewfinder, demanded that the birds be brought in "one at a time."

The point is that everything in a film script must actually be capable of being filmed. Nothing should be thrown in that is not truly expected to appear in the final film.

I read a screenplay once where, in a scene in a park, the writer designates that "a pigeon settles onto a bench." If this film is *The Attack of the Killer Pigeons*, a tale of terror involving a plague of rabid fowl bent on destroying civilization, then it is certainly appropriate to expect special effects involving pigeons.

But a writer cannot just for fun throw a living pigeon into his film, any more than he can throw one into the washing machine along with his underwear and socks. You want a pigeon in your picture? You've got to have a pigeon wrangler to train and control the wee beastie, to get him to do the things he's supposed to do and not to do the things he's not supposed to do. Moreover, a representative of the Society for the Prevention of Cruelty to Animals must be present on the set.

This takes a lot of time.

And costs a lot of money.

If, on the other hand, the writer's intent was to include the pigeon merely for color, solely to lend effect to the reading of the script, the effect may not be the one he intended. Chances are, readers of such a script will conclude that they are dealing with a writer who is loose with details, who does not intend for all the paraphernalia in the script actually to appear in the film.

What possible result can this have other than to communicate to the reader that she need not pay close attention to what she reads? Is that the effect writers seek? Most certainly not. Indeed, smart writers desire the contrary. They want the reader to believe that each and every item in the script is important, that it counts for something, that it moves tale and character and is fast and funny and sad and dazzling.

Is it possible to achieve such a result?

Yes. Make the script brilliant.

Easy to say; hard to do. But at the very least, be certain that each and every detail occupying the script, each item of aural and visual information, is integrated. This means simply that it is there because it has to be there. By taking this approach, writers can hope to captivate the reader and create the impression that will, in the long run, lead to representation, sale, and career longevity.

fmpmt!

This acronym may read like a stifled sneeze or an exhalation of disapproval, but in fact it represents the following: find and make your point and move your tale!

This notation generally accompanies a lengthy description or block of dialogue that is overwritten and unwieldy and wants desperately to be pruned. For instance:

LINDA
I've been thinking about this for quite a long

time, Harry, and it has finally occurred to me
that in the end there's truly no hope for us.
Why, all you ever do is think of yourself.
You have no room in your life for any other
person. How can you ever expect to be
happy? I don't know how you can stand to
look at your own face in the mirror each
morning when you shave. All I know is that
I'm sick to tears of this marriage and can't
stand even another minute of it.

This speech just rambles on and on and on. Depending upon
the picture's context, the writer may well have decided that the
central point is contained mid-speech in the sentence: "You
have no room in your life for any other person." Or perhaps it's:
"How can you ever expect to be happy?" Or: "I'm sick to tears
of this marriage and can't stand even another minute of it."

The point is that the writer needs to find the point! She has
to make that point and move the tale forward. She has to lose
all the stuff that surrounds the point. Otherwise, good dialogue
is smothered by unnecessary chatter. Cutting, excising, trim-
ming, deleting enhance drama and all other forms of creative
expression.

"Fmpmt!" applies not only to dialogue but also to descriptions of settings and actions. I frequently read material of
this sort:

Harry places his hand on the doorknob, hesitates, now slowly
turns it. He takes a deep breath, looks at Linda, now at the
door as he pulls it slowly open. He steps through the portal
first with his left foot, then his right. And now, with a ringing
finality, gradually he pulls the door closed behind him,
leaving Linda and the house and his past life where it
belongs, in his own, personal history, in that special part of
his former existence that exists for him and for all the people
in his previous life no more.

The writer is using almost a hundred words to say what could easily be communicated through only two: 1) Harry; 2) leaves.

Moreover, it may not be necessary to say even that much.

Almost invariably, violations of good-writing rules that win a screenwriter the "fmpmt!" note in the margin conjure up violations of the "drekt/akt" notation advising writers not to direct or act the picture but instead merely to write it.

payoff?/aha!

This particular designation relates generally to questions involving integration. We have already asserted that the healthy screenplay is the integrated screenplay, where every item fits, every element possesses a useful purpose that is effectively and economically achieved, and one that consistently advances story and character.

That is why when I see a particular item of dialogue or description in a script, contained usually in the early pages, I will write beside it the first part of the above designation: "payoff?" I simply mean to take note of the item and remind myself, and the writer, that eventually this item needs to be touched upon again, and some special meaning has to be made apparent so that it is justified as a piece of plot and character craft. Language in screenplays does not exist for its own sake but for the sake of the tale, the character, the reader of the script and the viewer of the movie. Make a special effort, therefore, to eliminate all superfluous, whimsical, unnecessary, word-squandering, attention-debauching language in the script.

When the item is in fact paid off—if indeed it is paid off at all—I will rejoice in that payoff by writing "Aha!" in the margin, recognizing that the writer has managed to meet this difficult requirement. It is, after all, hard enough to set up anything that is worthy, harder still to keep track of it and harder yet to maintain it in one's own mind and in the mind of the reader or viewer.

At the beginning of the excellent screenplay *Phenomenon*

(Gerald DiPego), protagonist George, portrayed by John Travolta, rises from his bed early one morning and crashes into a handcrafted willow chair. We quickly see that his house is cluttered with an oversupply of such chairs.

This might very well call for a "payoff?" in the margin.

Later on, we will learn that a woman, Lace, whom George finds thoroughly attractive, manufactures the chairs and that George has covertly been purchasing them. This would win a bold, blue "Aha!" The writer managed to set something up, then paid it off. Character expands; story advances.

Later in the film, George finds himself suddenly dizzy, queasy and nauseous while walking through a field. The feeling quickly passes. Again, this would earn the writer a "payoff?". Later, DiPego will reveal that this ill feeling is associated with a seismic fault in the earth and reflects George's ability to predict earthquakes.

Again, an "Aha!" for the writer.

When the "payoff?" meets the "Aha!" not immediately but some distance down the story line, the writer demonstrates an ability to "checkerboard," which also helps to avoid writing material that is "too straight-line." Once again, we see that nothing stands alone but is instead part of the whole picture.

clue/hands

Writers just generally love to gripe, most especially regarding ways in which idiot story editors screwed up their precious poetry.

Nevertheless, I must say that in my own experience I have enjoyed generous and attentive consideration from studio executives and story editors, with whom I have struggled in the service of good screenwriting.

At Warner Brothers many years ago, for example, I worked with a particular story editor on the screen adaptation of my first book, a novel. From time to time I would write within the dialogue words like "anyway" or "besides" or "by the way."

Whenever I would do so, the story editor would reprimand me in the marginal notes with a jocular remark on the order of: "Besides, since Richie has apparently forgotten that we're paying him five thousand dollars a week to mold, shape, sculpt, plane, carve and whittle dialogue so that it flows naturally, he's going to fall down on the job and cop to crude locutions like 'anyway' or 'by the way' or 'besides.' "

When I see one of those words in the context of an otherwise worthy piece of dialogue, I inevitably scrawl "clue/hands" in the margin to indicate that there is evidence—a clue—that the writer is setting up a bit of information that needs to be established through the character's speech, smashing it together with another necessary bit of information, then connecting the two with a "besides" or similar bit of language. In other words, I see the writer's hands showing, steering and forcing the dialogue into shape.

I have a writer pal with whom I go to the movies sometimes. Whenever he hears such dialogue he'll start to type in the air, as if to suggest that he can actually hear the writer flailing away at his word processor just beyond the frame.

Great film art and craft is supposed to be, at the top and the bottom of it, invisible. The dialogue should appear to have been created naturally and effortlessly. And it should appear also to have been created not by writers months and years earlier, but by the characters in the movie here and now as they recite the lines. When we hear "by the way" or "besides," we are reminded that the movie was written by a writer.

too on-the-nose

When something is too much what it is, it can be said to be "too on-the-nose." In other words, what is sought is not text alone but subtext, not expression alone but implication.

In the vastly overpraised *Leaving Las Vegas* (Mike Figgis, from the novel by John O'Brien), in order to show that the protagonist, a disgraced and discredited—guess what?—screenwriter, suffers from alcoholism, he is viewed prancing through a supermarket filling his cart with bottles of booze. Throughout the film he is seen repeatedly guzzling liquor straight from the bottle, puking his guts out, then collapsing unconscious. This represents a perfectly clear example of business that is too on-the-nose. The organizing principle of the protagonist's character—his drunkenness—is revealed not subtly but brazenly, not subtextually but superficially.

Compare this with the far more effective treatment of alcoholism in the classic *Lost Weekend* (Charles Brackett, Billy Wilder), in which protagonist Ray Milland's addiction is revealed not by his imbibing fluid from a hip flask but, instead, by his sneaking to the window, opening it and pulling up a string dangling from below, revealing, finally, a hidden booze bottle.

We do not even need to see him take a nip.

This represents superior writing.

I found another example where the writer has skillfully avoided scripting scenes that are too on-the-nose in a splendid script involving a prison riot at San Quentin. (This is a screenplay sent to me by the incarcerated writer whom I talked about earlier in the book.) At one point midway through the tale the protagonist flies into a rage, wrecks his cell and is slammed into solitary confinement. In order to depict his loneliness after several weeks in the hole, the writer could have had him recite an eloquent soliloquy commenting upon his fragmented, disconnected existence. But this would have been entirely too on-the-nose, too much what it is, too flat-out obvious.

Instead, the writer crafts a scene in which the same character is discovered to have befriended a rat. He rolls his crusts of bread into tiny pea-sized balls and tosses them to the rat. This is his only contact with another warm-blooded creature. Is that not a whole lot more articulate, more artistic, more emotional, more dramatic, than the guy delivering a speech, no matter how poetic, regarding his sad and sorry and isolated plight?

Eventually another prisoner, serving on the food detail, delivers bread-and-water rations to the solitary-confinement cells. He rattles on the door and whispers through the grate, "Nasty, it's me, Noodles. You okay in there?" Nasty does not say that he is not okay, that he is in fact miserable. What he says instead is, "Sure, great. Never better. It's Club Med in here."

This represents understatement, overstatement, irony and sarcasm all rolled into one. By stating not the case but in fact the polar opposite of the case, the character's loneliness is rendered most understandable, most poignant, both for the reader of the screenplay and the viewer of the film.

Generally speaking, as indicated earlier, writers are well advised to imply rather than express. What is expressed hangs there full and whole in front of the audience for their observation and comprehension. But what is implied plays out where all worthy art ought to play: in the mind of the observer. And that is the most effective kind of creative expression, because it involves the audience not as a dispassionate observer but as a participant, a collaborator.

6v.4

The numbers here represent approximations and the "v." stands for "versus."

As I review screenplays, I often find so much overwriting that in an attempt to illuminate the problem I'll actually number the necessary and unnecessary words and then express them in a kind of ratio separated by the v. The ratio can refer to overwriting in dialogue or in description.

Earlier we addressed the problem of a writer inserting into his script an example of overwriting on the order of: "Harry slowly, quietly turns, opens the door, and at long last leaves, letting the door drift closed behind him." All that is truly needed are the words 1) Harry and 2) leaves. The additional seventeen words have absolutely no purpose at all other than to squander the time, attention and consideration of the reader.

In the given instance I'll write "2v.17" in order to indicate that of nineteen words there are only two that have any rightful place in the script, and seventeen that do not. This is, of course, a fairly exaggerated example. Contemplate instead that merely four words were wasted out of a sentence of, say, ten. That would result in a notation of "6v.4."

Someone might well protest that this is a relatively petty criticism. Four words have been wasted; so what? So this: at this rate of cutting, a script of 110 pages will be reduced by 56 whole pages.

Once again it is demonstrated that if all by itself a particular miscue in a screenplay appears to be petty, in fact these sorts of errors are never alone but are part of the context of the whole picture. A small change—of language and of attitude—can cut a wide swath across a screenplay, rendering it more economical, helping it to sizzle and dazzle.

noFX

In technical movie talk "FX" stands simply for "effects."

Here, however, the designation refers not to film effects—shimmer dissolves, spiral wipes, morphing, blue screen and the like—but, rather, computer/printer effects such as centering, right margin justification, italics, boldface and related word-processing capabilities. The "noFX" designation stands actually as a reprimand. While the benefits of the computer age can provide screenwriters with some help, they also create vast new opportunities for errors.

For many film professionals, it is actually easier to use the new technology than not to use it. Give an inexperienced film-maker a zoom lens, for example, and you can count on it: he's going to zoom.

Writers need struggle to avoid being dominated by the new technologies, whereas it ought to be the new technologies that are dominated by the writers.

Right-margin justification, as an example, refers to the condition of printing where the right-hand margins of the pages all line up evenly, just as in published, typeset works. It may seem perfectly logical that text printed with right-margin justification ought to present a more orderly, neater appearance and ought to enhance pages' readability.

In practice, however, precisely the opposite is the case. Studies reveal that the same material written with right-margin justification reads more slowly than when printed ragged right.

All that aside, there are far better reasons for writers to eschew any kind of printer effects. Their scripts should simply appear to have been typed on a typewriter. This does not mean that they must not use computers and the fanciest laser printers; it requires simply that the appearance of the script be such as to suggest it was typed.

Why all the fuss?

Fancy computer graphics in a script—like boldface—carry the same burden as artwork. I have viewed screenplays that were magnificently illustrated with full-color paintings, drawings and photographs. Alas, for all of the gorgeous imagery, the net effect of the graphics is a screaming, wailing siren alerting readers that the writer is an amateur.

Subliminally, if not consciously, fancy graphics suggest to the reader that the words alone are somehow not enough to tell the story, depict the characters and create the dialogue, and that they need extra attractions—new-age electronic doodads and add-ons—to expand and enhance their meaning.

If a writer needs to italicize a description or a dialogue fragment, rather than exploiting printer functions, she should simply underline the text to achieve the desired effect.

Truly dazzling tales need no help from graphics. They should emerge whole from the plain and simple use of language. Look how much Shakespeare accomplished centuries before the advent of gigobytes. The single most amazing aspect of screenwriting has to be that from the properly astute configuration of ink on paper an artist is able to fire up the imagination of a reader, producing a Technicolor blaze of image and emotion.

clok?

Movies move.

If a motion picture has no motion, the clock still continues to move.

"Clok?" (sometimes depicted as a little circle with a pair of hands in it—a crude icon representing a clockface—with a question mark beside it) poses the question: How much time will this particular bit of business in the script actually occupy on-screen?

It confounds and saddens me that so many writers seem unaware of this most fundamental screenwriting principle. So many screenplays are replete with do-nothing, hang-around material in which people and events effectively just stand—or lie—there, apparently for their own purpose rather than to advance plot and expand character.

We have already described screenplay passages in which a woman enters her apartment, hangs up her coat, fixes herself a drink or prepares a pot of tea, changes into more comfortable shoes and, at long, long last, dials someone on the phone. Why include all this lame, nondramatic material in the script? "I merely wanted to set the tone," a writer may explain. "I wanted to give the audience a breather."

Breathers are for after the movie. During the movie it's not breathers but breathlessness we seek.

In such instances I am certain to inquire: Precisely how much time will be expended to depict this so-called breather?

The writer will typically respond, "Why, only a couple of minutes."

I'll invite the writer to sit quietly with me—not looking at a watch—and experience the feeling not of two minutes, but of one. In truth, we'll sit not even for a minute but only for fifteen seconds; that's not half a minute but half of a half. It is, however, ample time to feel preposterously awkward. Writers will squirm and fidget, sweat and just generally die from the discomfort attendant upon sitting quietly for even fifteen seconds with nothing to do.

When the quarter minute expires I'll ask, "Are you surprised to discover how heavily even a mere minute weighs in the absence of drama?" Inevitably, the writer is astonished to contemplate that a minute could represent such an unendurable period of time. When I tell him that the period was not a minute but merely a fraction of a minute, the writer realizes that this time ought to be used more wisely.

100min18mos

Speaking of minutes, the ideal film occupies approximately one hundred of them.

And eighteen months from script to released picture is just about the shortest amount of time in which a movie can be produced.

In recent years, I've observed that too many movies run on too, too long—well beyond two hours, never mind a hundred minutes. This is testimony to the (self-)destructive power of directors. Neither Scorsese, nor Coppola, nor Streisand, nor Oliver Stone, nor Terry Gilliam, nor Spike Lee, and certainly not Akira Kurosawa or Chen Kaige or Bernardo Bertolucci, are above making films that run way beyond their true, proper, Aristotelian ending—that is, the point after which nothing happens.

In too many movies the director simply refuses to get off the stage.

Movies are often awash with inconsequential events that squander precious time but fail to exploit character and story. When an ending runs on too long, or when pointless, ordinary, everyday action occupies and preoccupies a script, I am likely to scrawl "100min18mos" beside it in the margin.

If the writer is the luckiest screen scribe who ever breathed, if his script wins representation the day after it is written, if a producer is so swept away that he damns the torpedoes and produces the picture forthwith, it may actually appear on screens eighteen months later. This represents, of course, the highest, most desirable, most favorable set of circumstances.

Call it a best-case scenario.

The obvious question, therefore, that the writer of every script must ask himself when writing every detail and line of dialogue is this: If eighteen months from now I finally win a hundred minutes of an audience's time, is this how I want to spend even a fraction of one of those minutes? Do I want to have them view a woman getting into comfortable shoes after fixing herself a pot of tea? Do I want them to hear characters trading inconsequential chitchat?

To paraphrase Tennessee Williams: "Do something. Anything. Stand on your head. Pull down your pants. Instead of nothing, do something."

Though fixing a pot of tea and hanging up a coat in a closet are, in their own way, "something," in dramatic terms they're nothing, since they pack no emotional wallop, expand no story and advance no character.

Unless the teakettle boils over and severely scalds someone or the closet contains the rotting, flesh-shredded remains of a serial killer's latest victim, the action is merely a waste of time, effort, ink and film.

eye/eye

This is sometimes inscribed as two eyeballs. Effectively it suggests to writers that at this point in the script they should be heightening a particular conflict, that the competing interests of the characters in the scene need to be underscored or rendered with sufficient intensity to suggest that they are eyeball-to-eyeball in conflict.

There is a scene, for example, in Chazz Palminteri's *A Bronx Tale* where a gang of motorcycle hoodlums bursts rudely into a neighborhood bar that happens to serve as the unofficial community social center. It happens also to be run by the local crime boss, who politely requests that the bikers leave.

The lead biker responds without particular hostility that he and his buddies merely seek a couple of beers, after which they'll happily depart. Since his request has been made in a manner that is respectful, the don acquiesces, instructing the bartender to serve the fellows.

If the scene went on much longer in this manner, I might have drawn double eyeballs in the margin, suggesting that there's no fun in movies where folks congenially come to serene and reasonable agreement, and that the writer would be better advised to craft some eyeball-to-eyeball conflict into the moment.

Chazz Palminteri, however, is too skillful a writer to require such advice. In an instant he informs the setting with truly original physical and emotional conflict, ending with the Hell's Angels being chastened and chastised. Beer sprays, feet and fists fly, heads are bopped and motorcycles parked outside are reduced to scattered nuts and bolts and twisted metal.

The writer of another film, enormously overrated in my view, could take a cue from Palminteri. In *Field of Dreams*, Phil Alden Robinson has his protagonist, portrayed by Kevin Costner, choose, upon hearing mystic voices in his head, to tear up the cornfield in front of his country home and build a baseball stadium in its place. When he confronts his wife with his scheme, she speaks dialogue that takes the following tack: "Honey, I know your plan sounds crazy, but we love you, and we'll stand behind whatever you want, no matter how zany it seems."

That's precisely the kind of passage that would get an "eye/eye" from me. Would not the scene create more tension if instead of blindly, blandly acquiescing, the wife angrily protested? And would not the engendered conflict render the picture far more dramatic?

Instead of her saying, "Hey, it sounds wacky, but if it's what you want we'll support you," she might argue, "Are you out of your mind? You dragged us out of the big city to this lost, remote outpost. And now that our lives are finally beginning to work out, you decide suddenly, on the basis of some infantile, macho, adolescent wet-dream fantasy about having a catch with your dad, to wreck it all again, tear up the cornfield, disrupt and sully and destroy our lives. Count us out! We won't stand for another moment of your selfishness."

I'm not about to argue that the suggested dialogue is poetry. But isn't the attitude expressed likely to create greater dramatic tension and stress than did the actual dialogue? A wife blithely consenting to her husband's wishes, deferring not to her own but to his dreams, may fulfill the male author's idealized, romanticized notion of what a marriage ought to be—especially with regard to the subservience of the wife—but does it represent the highest, most effective drama?

I say Robinson wins a pair of eyeballs in the margins for this scene.

1 or o.

The designation "1 or o." stands for "one or the other." It usually applies to the tiniest fragment of a screenplay—for example, a line of dialogue—but in certain instances it can refer to an entire scene.

Let us say the dialogue is as follows: "No. Absolutely not." In the margin beside such a line I might very well write, "1 or o." This means, of course, that either of those brief sentences is sufficient; why include both? How is character expanded and plot enhanced through the repetition of the same notion in different words? All that a writer wins through redundancy is squandered time, wasted attention, spilled ink.

"No" means "absolutely not."

"Absolutely not" means "no."

Why in the world say the same thing twice, or worse, three times? Sometimes I see information repeated many more times than that; in such instances I may inscribe actual numbers beside each instance—1, 2, 3, 4, etc.—recording a tally in order to help the writer see precisely how many times he repeats himself.

As with virtually all criticism of screenplays, the vast majority of writers are grateful to have such repetition pointed out to them. They would rather be alerted to deficits by their teacher, or by their fellow writers, than by agents or producers or executives they hope will facilitate the making of a deal and, God willing, a movie.

Nevertheless, from time to time a writer receiving a "1 or o." protests that the repetition was included in order to lend emphasis. "No, absolutely not," the writer may argue, is stronger, more vigorous, more adamant, than merely one or the other of those minisentences.

But the effect is in fact precisely the opposite. Repetition that fails simultaneously to expand character and move story—repetition that merely replicates what has already been stated—does not add but diminishes dramatic impact.

In my first book on screenwriting I compare the well-integrated screenplay to the intelligently designed automobile dashboard. I point out that every switch, every knob, every lever has to fulfill a necessary function. A switch performing no such purpose, a lever that is simply there for the look or the feel or the sound it produces—for example, a bright, crisp click—is evidence only of poor design.

But this same reasoning operates from the other side of the table as well. That is to say, two switches performing the same function are just as bad as one switch performing no function. Senselessly duplicated controls represent poor design, because each renders the other pointless.

The same can be said for the abundant paraphernalia that constitute a screenplay, be it a line of dialogue or, as we suggest above, an entire scene. Even the briefest survey demonstrates that this sort of repetition is all too common, not only among bad films but among worthy ones as well. Steven Zaillian's masterful screenplay for *Schindler's List*, for example, is not above rating a "1 or o." in its margin.

In this movie there is a scene in which a young woman prisoner is executed with a shot to the head. It succinctly establishes the lethal nature of Nazi cruelty, perversion and persecution. Not long after the scene, however, we are treated to the specter of the concentration camp's commandant wielding a rifle and, from his balcony overlooking the camp, gunning down prisoners.

It is, of course, all by itself a horrible image and ought to evoke an emotional response from viewers. But it is not all by itself; it is part of the whole picture. And when placed in the context of similar scenes that have imparted the same sort of information, scenes like this make a point that has already been made, and rather than sensitizing viewers it numbs them. The horror of Nazism is not that deranged maniacs murdered people but that otherwise sane, common, rational, ordinary citizens— millions of them—coolly, blithely tolerated it and, still worse, eagerly supported it.

In the overlong and ponderous *Prince of Tides* (Pat Conroy, Becky Johnston) there is a scene early in the picture when a suicidal daughter witnesses the degrading spectacle of her father refusing to pause even briefly from his television show in order to acknowledge his child's birthday. The scene descends into substantial violence involving, among other things, a son destroying the TV by shooting it with a shotgun.

In a later scene, the same character is raped by a trio of marauding criminals.

Is the latter dramatic? Again, all by itself it is very much so. But in the broader context of similar scenes saying similar things, the impact is dissipated. Tension, instead of being heightened, is reduced. And reduced tension is, of course, precisely the opposite of what we seek in the worthy, healthy, integrated screenplay.

As indicated earlier, there is simply no reason for a character in a movie to tell another character something that the writer has already communicated to the audience.

Choose one.

Or choose the other.

But don't choose both.

The superior choice, of course, is that in which action occurs and events transpire. This is preferable to having a character detail the situation through the recitation of mere dialogue.

Again, film is a medium whose center resides in movement, not of lips but of pictures.

'veen

" 'Veen" is a crude abbreviation for "convenient."

I often read scripts in which one or another aspect of the plot occurs apparently for the convenience of the writer alone. Regardless of the often solitary nature of screenwriting, successful writers of movies are never alone; in a sense they collaborate not only with the other members of the creative family of artists and craftsmen who make the movie but also with the audience viewing the finished product. And it is for the convenience of this latter group, not the writer, that the movie is ultimately created.

In a comedy of a few seasons ago, a man desperate for money "rents" his bride to a wealthy character for the weekend. Surprisingly, the bride falls in love with the fellow. Why? Because he is attractive? Because he's rich?

As far as I could tell, the only reason for her to fall in love is that the script requires her to do so. Certainly this serves the convenience of the writer, who, without this particular turn in the plot, would not have much of a story.

Always keep in mind that screenplays are written for the convenience not of the writer but of the audience. Even if events do not flow smoothly, they must appear to do just exactly that. The anecdotal, incidental material that constitutes the story cannot appear to have been set up like ducks in a row to suit the purposes of the writer. They need to seem to unfold seamlessly, spontaneously, naturally.

And this is true even if—upon close analysis and inspection—there is nothing about a movie that is seamless, spontaneous or natural.

"Bw!Cyc!"

This unpronounceable designation stands for a line ranted by King Lear during a storm: "Blow, wind! Crack your cheeks!"

I write this in the margins next to dialogue that is lame, flat, pedestrian or otherwise inconsequential. Frequently this is dialogue that is merely time-passing, the sort of swapped courtesies and politenesses that saturate real life but have no place in the movies: "Hi! How you doing?" "Pretty good, you?" "Great! How about a cup of coffee?"

Pedestrian passages may move a smidgen of tale data, but they always fail to expand character. In such dialogue like this writers have their characters narrate the story instead of acting it out. "I went to the parking lot to look for Janet but she wasn't there. I waited for a while, then walked around the neighborhood to see whether or not I could spot her. Finally I just gave up and went home."

This will definitely earn a "Bw!Cyc!" to indicate that even if the writer cannot equal Shakespeare, at the very least she ought to try. Loud, proud, poetic dialogue has got to be preferred to that which lies there frail and flaccid like a slice of smoked salmon.

A simpler way to express this principle: movie dialogue should be worth listening to. It should pop and sizzle and crackle and sparkle and dazzle, make us laugh, make us cry, scare us half to death, even repel and offend us, but never bore us.

And, of course, it must also expand character and advance story.

It is, I know, easy for a teacher or consultant or agent or producer to demand that dialogue meet these high standards, and quite another for writers to achieve them. But that's why writers are paid so well—when they are paid at all.

2bxpo

Every screen story has what is called its "back" story, information regarding the characters and their lives implied to have occurred prior to the commencement of the film itself. For example, the earliest images in the film *Midnight Cowboy* (Waldo Salt) feature the Texas dishwasher Joe Buck shedding his apron and preparing to make his way by bus to mean old New York City.

Clearly Joe had a life before this point. He was born, he suffered whatever privations had led him to the lowly job of dishwasher, he might have received a stunted sort of education that convinced him that New York City pulses with sexually starved women who are eagerly waiting to couple with a masculine, leather-clad dude like him.

Sometimes it is necessary to reveal some of this information to the audience concretely; often it is not. In the former instance, it is wise to dispense with the facts quickly.

We do not need, for example, the big, long speech spoken by the scientist portrayed by Richard Attenborough in *Jurassic Park* (Michael Crichton and David Koepp, from the former's novel) wherein he explains what he has accomplished on his island of dinosaurs. The same point could be made by a scene that shows characters arriving on the island and being astounded by their discovery of prehistoric creatures that are very much alive.

Even *Casablanca* (Philip and Julius Epstein, Howard Koch) could stand to lose the little introduction—the too-brazen exposition at the front of the film—in which, just in case anybody failed to have heard of World War II, a short lecture summarizes the state of hostility among nations.

"2Bxpo," therefore, stands for "too-brazen exposition." It can apply not only to back-story data that may need to be revealed at the beginning of the movie, but also to scenes occurring later.

And now for the real thing. Here are the first few pages of the earliest draft of the screenplay that became *River's Edge*, written as an assignment in a UCLA screenwriting class. The notes are those actually provided for the writer, Neal Jimenez. They provide a concrete example of notes in action and their place in the process of rewriting.

THE RIVER
Neal Jimenez

EXT   RIVER   BARELY DAWN

TIM, twelve, stands on a footbridge overlooking the river. ~~braving the cold, dark morning.~~ He holds a <u>doll</u> in his hand. [~~and stares at the water rushing by below him.~~] 7 V.9

AKT/DREKT

SIFYN! ~~The dim, lonely light of dawn casts a languid, dreamlike spell over the scene, further enhanced by Tim's icy stance.~~

He drops the doll off the bridge. ~~and we see it slowly fall, fall through the air. We hear a distant, human sound over the ambience of the rushing water, and~~ Tim casts his eyes to a faraway cliff at the river's edge.

Two <u>human</u> <u>forms</u> can be made out on the cliff, one lying, one sitting. The prone figure ^{is}~~appears to be~~ nude. ~~Again we experience the languid spell, only this time it's caused by more than just the light: [time itself has been slowed,] obvious from the graceful flutter of the leaves on the trees and the hypnotic stirring of the dust.~~ The Seated Figure lets out a distant WHOOP. ~~which echoes and dissipates just as~~

PRES.

THE DOLL hits the water with a [~~very~~] ~~pronounced~~ SPLASH. ~~which carries into~~   *noisy*

INT   KIM'S ROOM   EARLY DAWN

KIM, six, opens her eyes, as if awakened by the splash.~~ing sound. only half-awake, and we see her room from within~~

~~her lingering nightmare: dark spaces stretch infinitely, curtains hang ominously, shadows move with menace.~~

hunk?
see/hear? A DARK FIGURE appears at the door. The figure slowly approaches. ~~but~~ Kim [~~cannot move, she's paralyzed.~~] She screams ~~louder and louder~~ and the figure ~~keeps coming and~~ finally grabs her. ~~and we are snapped out of the nightmare because it's~~

MATT, Kim's 17-year-old "stoner" brother, comes to comfort her. ~~Were it not for the immediate calming effect he has on the hysterical Kim, we might be worried about his presence in her room. After a moment~~ <u>Madeleine</u>, Kim's 35-year-old mother, appears at the door, dressed in a tattered robe as faded as the light in her eyes.

                          MATT
          Settle down, Kim, everything's okay.

                          KIM
          She's dead, she's dead⟨·⟩

EXT   RIVER

THE DOLL floats downstream at normal speed and in the background [~~we see~~] TIM climbs on his bike and rides off.

"merely" [~~The camera follows the doll in a closer shot for a ways before we~~

~~PAN UP to~~ the cliff, ~~seen earlier.~~ SAMSON TOULETTE, a large, muscular teenager, sits at cliff's edge, smoking a *everything* joint. He lets out another WHOOP.
in the wide   *lies*
margins "we Behind him [~~we see~~] ₍the NUDE FIGURE. She is dead
see" and covered with handfuls of leaves and twigs and dirt. ~~Her eyes open wide, she seems to stare at Samson as he finishes his joint.~~

EXT   SACRAMENTO STREET

SAMSON cruises the barren streets in a dinosaur of a car. Occasionally a nine-to-fiver flashes past him.

INT   7-ELEVEN

TIM plays a video game in the corner of the store. SAMSON enters, pulls a single <u>beer</u> from the rack and sets it on the counter. The two acknowledge each other with a glance.

The CHECKER looks skeptically at Samson, then points to a sign that says: IDENTIFICATION REQUIRED FOR PURCHASE OF ALCOHOL.

                    SAMSON
     I left it at home.

                    CHECKER
     Sorry.

The checker ~~goes to~~ grabs the beer, but Samson has a hand on it. ~~first.~~ Tim~~, from the corner of the store, watches. the mild conflict. He~~ moves to the drink section.

                    CHECKER
     I'll take that, thank you.

                    SAMSON
     Don't be tight.

                    CHECKER
     Let go of the beer.

Tim pulls a second beer from the rack. At that moment he
lurk? [~~notices~~] the STORE CAMERA ~~set just above him. He~~
looks into the lens and ~~[we see] him~~ stares straight out of
the MONITOR right over the checker's shoulder.
                       AKT/DREKT "MERELY"
Tim's ~~looks to make sure he isn't being watched~~ his back
is now to us on the monitor. He puts the beer in his coat
pocket and walks out of the store.

~~Samson and the checker are still in a stand-off. Finally~~
Samson ~~gives in and~~ turns to leave.

EXT   7-ELEVEN

~~TIM~~ [Tim] waits by Samson's car. Samson comes out of the
store and climbs into his car, noticing immediately the beer
sitting on the passenger seat. ~~He looks to Tim.~~ [AKT/DREKT "MERELY"]

> TIM
>
> Don't mention it.

Samson ~~doesn't mention it. He~~ [NOT/NOT] opens the beer.

> TIM (CONT.)
>
> I saw you this morning.

> SAMSON
>
> Yeah?

~~He takes a swallow of the beer. There is a pause.~~ [AKT/DREKT]

> TIM
>
> Got any dope?

> SAMSON
>
> No.

~~Another pause. Tim is beginning to get uncomfortable. He~~
~~is not impressing Samson, as he had hoped.~~ [SEE?HEAR? AKT/DREKT "MERELY"] Samson
reaches over and opens the passenger door.

> SAMSON
>
> ~~Get in.~~ I know where to get some.

Tim ~~hesitates, then starts~~ [DREKT/AKT] loading his bike into the back
seat.

INT   SAMSON'S CAR   MORNING

~~SAMSON~~ [Samson] cruises the empty streets as ~~TIM~~ [Tim] watches him
drive. ~~a reverence in his gaze.~~ [AKT/DREKT]

PART TWO

BUSINESS

CHAPTER 6

∎ ∎ ∎ ∎ ∎ ∎ ∎ ∎ ∎ ∎ ∎ ∎ ∎ ∎ ∎ ∎ ∎ ∎

Gratitude Versus Attitude

The first part of this book argues that writing is a wondrous—if often painful—journey of self-discovery. Understanding the importance of identity is crucial for writers. Since they write ultimately only of themselves, it follows that a clearer, stronger sense of self helps produce clearer, stronger screenplays.

However, writers need contemplate not one but two identities.

First, there is the artistic, creative self who writes the scripts and also "acts" in them, portraying not only the protagonist but all the other characters as well.

Second, there is the professional self. This is the writer/ entrepreneur, the responsible working screenwriter who embraces the uniquely daunting, cruelly competitive dream-trafficking dodge with intelligence, circumspection and toleration. He confronts with serenity the maw and muck and mayhem that mark the professional film and TV community.

A writer's job is, after all, to place himself inside the minds and bodies of other people and to think and act as they do. This is true, of course, for every character in every script a writer writes. And it is every bit as true for the professional writer dealing with "characters" in the show business community:

agents, producers, story editors, development executives, attorneys, studio and network vice presidents.

Film is, of course, not about fact but feeling. And writers—like all artists—are souls who feel deeply and passionately. If from time to time they soar and rejoice, every bit as often they wallow in depression and despair.

Frustration and dark emotion come with the territory and have got to be accepted by every writer. Moreover, they have to be exploited as part of a writer's arsenal for expression.

But obsession with disappointment and anger to the exclusion of affirmation can encumber an otherwise successful writing life. Indeed, it can bring a promising career to a screaming, grinding halt. Too often it causes writers to be their own worst enemies. Hollywood does not have to destroy writers; writers are perfectly capable of destroying themselves, and often with remarkable style and aplomb. And this happens not only among inexperienced writers, but among the highest-paid, most widely celebrated professionals as well.

Rather than squander the energy derived from the dissonance and frustration that inevitably accompany creative expression in any medium or format, writers need to channel that power, to exploit it in the interest of charging their work so that it pops and buzzes and crackles and sizzles and dazzles and sparkles right along, more powerfully than they ever imagined it might.

Save the Rage for the Page

At UCLA's film school and all around the world—at screenwriting seminars, conferences, lectures, panels and workshops—I am asked every imaginable question on every screenwriting subject: dialogue, story, character, agents, packaging, contracts, options and more. Sometimes the queries address scripts I have read. Whatever the question, I always try my best—with uneven success—to answer as precisely as I can.

There are two questions in particular, however, I steadfastly refuse to answer. In fact, they are broad and narrow versions of the same question:

1) Do I have what it takes to be a writer?
2) Is this script worth revising or should I just abandon it?

It is not up to anybody but the writer himself to decide whether or not he has what it takes to be a writer. I have met writers who showed no early promise but over time achieved a creative critical mass that exploded into a stunning career.

And sometimes I read scripts that appear to be hopeless but upon revision suddenly crystallize and achieve vast success.

It is so easy for one writer (or writer/educator) to tell another that his script is going nowhere and he ought to abandon it. Why throw good effort after bad? he might glibly advise. Cut your losses and pull the plug. Chalk it up to drill; chalk it up to experience.

On the other hand, a writer may have some substantial amount of time, toil and talent invested in a particular script, to say nothing of the soul and the spirit of the artist that resides in any work of creative expression. It may all come together in that next draft.

Conversely, a writer may actually be wasting his time, poring over work that ought truly to be let go. It can be a dreadful mistake for a writer to keep rehashing the same old material. I know writers who've rewritten one script over and over again dozens of times over dozens of years.

Thus, as easy as it is for one writer to tell another to abandon a script, he can just as cavalierly tell him to stick with it. And advising him to stick with it might be every bit as faithless as telling him to quit.

Who's to decide?

Clearly, the awesome responsibility for such a choice resides solely with the one who must bear the burden of its consequences: the writer. It is he, after all, who ends up doing the arduous rewriting of a script that ought to be cut loose or heavy-heartedly cutting loose a script that ought to be rewritten. For success, to say nothing of sanity, writers need to learn not merely to tolerate but to embrace the struggle. I have met a handful who were so embittered, so crazed with anger, so bloated with pessimism and contempt for themselves and for everyone around them, that I strenuously had to resist advising them to sprint as far away from the movie business as it is possible to travel.

I remember one writer who was where every new writer wishes to be. He had a respectable agent eager to represent a script he had written. The problem was that in its earliest version he had collaborated on the story with another writer. The two had a falling-out and a residue of ill will remained between them. Moving ahead with this project required the consent of the other writer, as he still had legitimate claims to some portion of the copyright. "The greedy bastard wants twenty-five percent plus shared story credit," the writer complained to me.

I asked him what he thought was fair.

"I don't doubt he's entitled to shared story credit," he allowed, "but as far as the points are concerned, I don't believe he ought to get more than fifteen."

"That's the dispute?" I asked. "You think he should get fifteen and he wants twenty-five? What's the problem? Offer him twenty and if he balks, let him have the whole twenty-five. It's only five points worse than what you yourself agree is reasonable. And it happens to be five points of what may well turn out to be nothing. In the meantime you've got an agent eager to circulate your script. Even if you don't sell it, you begin to create a reputation and launch a career."

"It's rape!" the writer protested. "I'd rather have the whole project scuttled, his reputation blackened."

First, I ordered the writer never again to use the word "rape," and thus avoid trivializing a serious and dreadful issue. I went on to explain to him as patiently as I could that I thought he was acting like a damned, bloody fool. For lack of agreement over five phantom points of a purported deal that didn't even exist, he was willing to settle comfortably into the warm, soothing marinade of his anger.

Anger has its place in our lives. There are some excellent causes for anger, and if we never get mad we are brain-dead. Anger is a natural, wholly human and in some instances even a useful, productive enterprise. It can motivate a writer to do what needs to be done. It can be part of the emotional engine that drives a screenplay. But what anger must never be is the organizing principle of a personality. That needs instead to derive— especially for an artist—from quite the opposite: affirmation, healing and love.

Writers need to save their passion for their scripts. Energy devoted to hating agents, reviling directors, loathing actors, producers, executives and every other manner of collaborator should instead be directed to tale and character and the rest of the art and craft of screenwriting.

I once recommended a truly excellent script to a producer, who returned it to the writer with a basically benign rejection letter that included an innocuous and misguided comment characterizing some of the dialogue as ". . . occasionally stilted." But so what?

Whether the producer was right or wrong is a matter of opinion, but the writer chose to respond with an incendiary letter decrying the insult, denouncing the commentary and its creator and consigning him and his company to the bowels of existence.

What useful purpose was served by this tantrum? How does this writer expect to succeed in an arena as difficult and competitive as screenwriting if he assigns strangers such vast authority over his work and his self-perception?

I can tell you one result of the angry response: I never again recommended this writer to another producer. If he doesn't receive precisely the reaction he seeks, I reasoned, he flies into a rage and presents a dreadful impression. In the end, he reflects poorly not only upon himself but also upon me, a person merely trying, however feebly, to support him.

Greg Widen, a friend and former student, now a hugely successful writer, has said quite aptly that there is an ocean of difference between the merely solid spec writer—a writer capable of turning out a crafty original speculative draft all by himself—and one who can work with producers. He pities writers who create a promising script but then fly into paroxysms of vein-popping rage when someone suggests that the girl's dress should be green when the script indicates quite clearly that it is yellow.

He calls this "the green-dress syndrome."

"Green? Are you an idiot? That's the stupidest thing I ever heard of! Green! Quit tampering with my vision! Quit marching roughshod across the broad, shining terrain of my creativity with your mud-caked, blood-splotched jackboots!"

Writers like this burn themselves out before they have a chance to burn out everyone around them. They burn themselves out before they even catch fire. They cannot see beyond the horizon of their own heartache. They do not understand that the professional film and television community is actually quite small and that if you burn your bridges you also burn your britches.

Now and again I've had the good fortune to work as a producer, supervising the development of scripts. I recall winning a generous development deal for a writer of a family comedy. The executives entrusted me to serve as the project's den mother, alternately coddling and scolding the writer as appropriate, generally shepherding the project through the maze of big-studio script development.

The studio executives were ready to turn the writer loose to write a full draft—which was exactly his desire—except that they first needed, if only to satisfy their egos, to "approve" the outline. This way they could do what studio executives do best: pretend to be creatively involved in ways that they are not. It is common among experienced writers to collude with producers in this harmless ruse, then down the line perhaps trade it in for a modicum of clout on an issue that sincerely concerns them.

The meeting opened with the usual banter and repartee and

mindless sports chatter ("How about that game!") until at last the so-called discussion came around to the script. "Now remember," the executives said to the writer, "make certain that the protagonist is strong."

Clearly they wanted a simple nod, a generic reassurance, and they would have then been happy to approve the writing of the draft. All the writer had to do was tilt his head forward and pretend to understand. One minute later these executives would not even remember that we'd had the meeting, much less what had been discussed.

Instead of nodding, however, instead of murmuring a benevolent, inconsequential consent, with beads of sweat forming on his forehead the writer squawked, "Strong? What do you mean?"

"You don't know what 'strong' means?" they asked him. "Forceful. Willful. Adamant. Firm. Uncompromising. Committed. A fellow with a point of view that radiates conviction. A man who doesn't waffle. A guy who's not easily swayed. A fellow who doesn't flit from this to that. Ballsy. Hairy-chested. Vigorous. Get it?"

Instead of nodding sagely and asserting that he understood perfectly, the writer stammered, "Not really."

The meeting dragged on and on, with the guys in suits growing nervous about the writer and the project. I practically had to carry him out of the room with a promise to the executives that we'd be back for another meeting soon.

And at that meeting, of course, we promptly won the go-ahead. This is because, under the threat of death, I'd gotten the writer to agree to nod and say yes whenever I looked at him, and otherwise not to speak at all unless I tugged on my left earlobe.

The Writer as Victim

Not long ago a spry, elderly, energetic writer—an Oscar winner—complained bitterly to me about his inability to win assignments in television or film. Why? Ageism, he claimed. Nobody will hire a writer over forty, he told me. I contemplated the plight of all those unemployed writers who had yet to reach forty. Here were scribes who could boast that they were truly ahead of their time. Instead of waiting till they were forty to be jobless, they were jobless now.

My older writer pal had decided to write a book.

Well, not write it, exactly.

And not a book, exactly.

Eventually it would be a book that he would write, he assured me, but for now he had written merely a letter describing the future book. The letter—not quite one whole page—was directed to a prominent New York literary agent. All the writer sought was a commitment from a publisher to print the book when it was written and a nominal (in his eyes) advance against royalties of, say, merely fifty thousand dollars.

The agent wrote back a most respectful letter saying that he would be delighted to work with such a splendid writer but that the realities of the publishing business required that, notwithstanding the writer's film experience, he would need to see a sample portion of the book, a middle chapter for example, plus a two-page outline.

He also cautioned him that even if fifty thousand was chump change by Hollywood standards, it was an uncommonly hefty advance for almost any author, let alone one like himself who was unpublished.

The writer almost had a stroke.

He lamented: what a sad commentary on the state of American letters that a writer with a quarter-century-old Oscar and a host of TV sitcom episodes couldn't get a token advance plus a guarantee to publish! To say nothing of a twelve-city promotional tour including London, Paris and Rome.

His next course of action was clear: get drunk.

He would do what he did virtually every day: go to the golf course, maybe even stumble through nine holes. Then, he would head for the clubhouse, toss back whisky all afternoon and bitch and gripe and carp and complain with his writer buddies at the bar about the mindlessness of an American cultural scene so vacant, so hollow, so blind as to be unable to appreciate the useful purpose in sending him money.

So much complaining by so many (purportedly) oppressed writers! The new-age movie moguls won't hire us, they lament. All of the studio executives are kindergarten kids whose nannies wait, prams and pacifiers at the ready, outside their offices.

In fact, however, the so-called baby moguls of ten and fifteen and twenty years ago are—guess what?—ten and fifteen and twenty years older now, which is to say that they are gentlemen and ladies in their late forties and mid-fifties. They'll go with good material if it's on the page. Alfred Uhry was a youngster of fifty-three when he wrote his first play, *Driving Miss Daisy*. All that it won him is an Oscar and a Pulitzer.

Too many writers who win success in television or film come to believe they have a birthright to employment; they expect it to continue into eternity. They come to depend on guaranteed money and too, too often cease doing what every writer must do: continue to speculate, continue to take chances, continue to create without guarantee of sale. Writers need to learn that when action—screenwriting—is married irrevocably to expected outcome—dollars—frustration and disappointment are the inevitable result.

I recently had a conversation with a writer of substantial repute. He is the author of one of the all-time box office successes; there are precious few people in the world who have not at the very least heard of his film.

Nevertheless, for nearly twenty years he has not worked at all. He confessed to me with rare and splendid candor about the two reasons his career had gone cold. First, after his monumental success, he got too big for his britches, fired the independent agent who had faithfully struggled for him during his scuffling days, and succumbed to the siren song of one of the star-studded superhuge firms, where promptly after signing him they put him on Ignore.

Even worse than that, he simply lost the will to speculate. He had grown fat—metaphorically and actually—on TV deals, where the money is always delivered in advance of any actual writing, and rich feature development deals, where a writer may win a sizable advance before he is required to apply butt to chair and fingers to keys.

A former student of mine who has achieved astonishing success with a wildly acclaimed comedy tells me that his greatest struggle now is to avoid the distractions—rich rewrite assignments and plush development deals that are not likely to lead to actual pictures—and churn out his goal of three daily pages of speculative draft.

And this is precisely what all writers—experienced and not—must do. They must write a script. With no promise of remuneration, writers must nonetheless write. They cannot sit around and wait for somebody else to tell them what to do. They cannot become slaves to a studio or a network or even a university. They must assert themselves in their own lives as their own masters. And the clearest way to do this is to continue to create material, no matter what. These are the writers who succeed and who continue to succeed.

I have seen writers flare brightly and promptly burn out. Truly successful long-term writers write.

And when they're busy with their writing, they simply have no time to bemoan their fate, to feel so wretchedly sorry for themselves, to wallow in self-pity, to contemplate self-destruction, to contemplate destruction of studios and studio bosses and studio bosses' nannies.

A winning writer's winning attitude is Write on!

If a writer is fortunate enough to earn money in the screenplay racket, he should save the bulk of that money to buy time against those periods that he is "between assignments." And he should use that time to do essentially three things: write, write and write.

And he should be grateful for the privilege of being mistreated in this business. Far worse than mistreatment is no treatment at all—that is to say, the gnawing, hollow horror of being left quite completely undisturbed.

Frankly, writers should be grateful for the opportunity to suffer, because suffering is at the heart of creative expression's nature on every level and in every medium and format. Writers should be grateful that they have found the courage to reach and stretch and attempt something different, something new. They should be pleased that they're actually doing what so many others merely talk about: writing.

Satisfaction

Another thing to keep in mind is that writers should never seek sweet, serene satisfaction.

Consider an incident reported not many years ago in the *New York Times*. A vigorous, elderly gent—shock of snow-white hair—entered the Museum of Modern Art carrying an attaché case. He rode the elevator to the second floor and made his way along the corridor until he stood before a vast abstract canvas, part of the museum's permanent collection, a work that had hung in that same spot for the better part of forty years.

He set the attaché case upon the floor, snapped it open and withdrew a vial of turpentine, another of linseed oil, various tubes of paint, several paintbrushes, an artist's palette. From the tubes he squeezed upon the palette multicolored dollops of pigment.

By this time, of course, the museum's security officers had been summoned. Unobtrusively a pair of uniformed guards assembled behind the man in the rear of the gallery. Upon observing him lift a brush toward the canvas, they sprang into action, slapping handcuffs on him. They informed him, first, that he was under arrest and, second, that he had the right to remain silent and, third, that if he should nonetheless choose to speak, anything he said could and would be used against him in a court of law.

All the while he protested, claiming to be the very same internationally renowned artist who scores of years earlier had painted the very same canvas hanging now in front of them. The following part of the exchange was not reported in the *Times*, but given that this was New York City, I bet one of the guards responded, "Really? Well how about that! I happen to be Albert Schweitzer, and this gentlemen here," he likely went on, pointing toward his comrade, "is Arturo Toscanini."

Amidst their prisoner's energetic but futile remonstrations, the security officers carted him off to the local precinct house, where after an hour or so he was able to summon an associate who could vouch for the fact that he was indeed the artist he claimed to be.

It seems he had visited the museum a week or so earlier, had taken a look at his painting and had decided that it needed a bit of a brushup in one corner.

Now here is a true artist!

Celebrated worldwide, wealthy beyond any artist's wildest dreams, he is still not satisfied. He still wants to rewrite—or in this instance repaint—a vastly respected work created almost a lifetime ago.

Screenwriters, painters and all purveyors of creative expression are well advised to quit seeking satisfaction. If they hope to maintain even a semblance of sanity, they need to learn how to live with dissonance, discord and a generally unsettled opinion of themselves and their work.

Not only that, but they should be grateful that the luck of the draw brought them the strength to welcome risk. And what precisely do they risk? Failure, for one thing. Humiliation, for another. But remember that failure and humiliation and disappointment reside in our own eyes rather than in the eyes of others.

And should an artist fail, it is not nearly so dreadful as never having tried, never having afforded himself the chance.

All who struggle to be creative, in the most important sense, cannot fail, because it is creativity above all other traits that renders us human.

Fall on your face if you must, but rejoice that it is your own face and nobody else's upon which you fall. And be grateful that you have the energy and spirit to soar high enough to crash once again most gloriously.

■ ■

CHAPTER 7

Agents

Why do so many writers perpetuate the myth that agents will not read material by new writers?

Two accomplished writers whom I first came to know through our program at UCLA recently told me that aspiring writers actually become angry with them when they insist that they won their first jobs as staff writers on a long running comedy on television not through some fancy political ploy, but simply by writing speculative episodes and then penning quick, smart letters to agents.

Mail Manners

One screenwriting educator, however, complains that it is absurd for me to suggest that writers can win an agent's consideration by simply writing a smart query letter. He argues that what really count are elaborate, sophisticated alliances, interlocking matrices of relationships developed by schmoozing it up at seminars and panels and in chic, trendy showbiz restaurants, and getting to know the right people. He asserts that the reason I tell this dreadful lie is because it's what writers want to hear.

Ironically, the last thing writers want to hear is that it is easy to get an agent to consider a screenplay. This is because it is far more soothing to contemplate that there is something wrong with the agent than to confront the sorry reality that there's something wrong with the query letter or, worse, the script.

Instead of worrying about clever schemes for winning an agent's agreement to represent a screenplay, writers should worry about writing a screenplay that is genuinely worthy of a good agent's representation. In fact, agents eagerly and urgently seek scripts. My office at UCLA receives dozens of requests every week for new material from new writers. Callers and correspondents actually get mad at me if I fail to supply them.

If agents are hard to reach, if they are reluctant to consider new writers, how can one explain all of the telephone traffic, letters, faxes, E-mail and even messengers showing up in the flesh, refusing to leave until they are handed a screenplay for delivery to their bosses?

On one occasion no fewer than six agents from what is arguably the most prestigious agency in town showed up in person at my office to stage a full-fledged commando raid (I could have sworn I saw hand grenades strapped to their belts) in demand of screenplays by new writers. I have seen agents appear uninvited at screenwriting award ceremonies, clipboards at the ready, signing new writers as they strut through the door.

What counts, again, is the writing. To reach an agent a writer need merely write a sharp, short, smart, savvy query letter. In my previous book, *Screenwriting*, I provide an example of such a letter, the actual query that won consideration for the then-unknown writer of the screenplay that became the film *Highlander* and the basis for all of its sequels.

If the query letter is properly written it will lead to an invitation to submit the screenplay. In this way it is possible to turn an unsolicited script into one that an agent will truly plead to read.

From time to time writers complain that they have tried this technique and failed. They assert that they wrote to any number of agents and received no solicitations to submit their script; their requests were either outright refused or, more typically, ignored.

When I hear such stories I invariably ask the writers to read me their query letter. In virtually every instance the problem becomes plain as day: the letter is a train wreck. More than likely it contains too much information about both the writer and, even more often, the script.

One of these writers, however, read me his letter and, frankly, it struck me as perfect. I could not for the life of me imagine how any agent—much less dozens upon dozens of agents—could have refused the opportunity to consider the script. After a long silence during which we collectively pondered his dilemma, the writer muttered under his breath, "Maybe it's the synopsis."

"The what?" I asked.

"The synopsis," he said again.

"You sent a synopsis along with your letter?" If a writer encloses a synopsis in his letter, that is what the agent will read.

But don't some agents and agencies insist upon seeing a synopsis?

If they do, keep it short. Treat the synopsis as a tease, a mini-Previews of Coming Attractions dedicated to seducing the agent into wanting to know more about the project. In this regard, the more information you provide, the less likely that the agent will want to read the script.

If an agent insists on a synopsis, double-space it and limit it to a fraction of a single page. Don't try to cram each and every tidbit of story and character into the synopsis. The purpose is to coax the agent into making those discoveries in the script itself.

This query-letter "system" was recently tested and confirmed to work quite well. A screenwriting instructor in a major cosmopolitan center—thousands of miles from Hollywood—conducted a survey at two different university film departments. Students in four screenwriting classes wrote query letters and sent them cold to a sampling of agents gleaned from the Writers Guild Franchised Agencies list.

Before the letters were mailed, however, they had to be approved both by the instructor and all the students in the class. The letters were painstakingly studied, with an eye toward economy and seduction. They went out to agents only after winning approval in the classes.

The reported "take" rate (the proportion of favorable responses—that is, invitations to submit the scripts): ninety-six percent! When the query letters were adjudged to be properly, effectively written, ninety-six of a hundred agents agreed to consider the scripts. Moreover, a substantial number among them were agents who designate on the Writers Guild list that they do not accept unsolicited scripts.

Remember, they did not agree to represent the scripts but merely to consider them. Once an agent agrees to consider a script, it is the script's merit—or lack thereof—that will persuade him to represent it or, conversely, to pass.

If writers are reluctant to believe that agents want to consider their scripts, they find it even more improbable that agents actually want to like those scripts. Should that come as a surprise? Does not anybody reading material prefer to like it than not? And would not any agent covet the prestige of launching a new writer, to say nothing of garnering a hefty commission on the sale of his script?

This is one of those truths that is so obvious it is difficult to see. It obliterates the myth that agents are generally cynics whose greatest pleasure is to dash writers' dreams, break their hearts, bust their chops. On the contrary, agents want to respect what they read. Writers need to recognize that the relationship between artist and representative—like that among all members of the creative film family—is not adversarial but collaborative. Writers and agents are not at odds with one another. Both need the same thing: a script that is marketable.

Once again, the simplest, most effective, most straightforward way to win an agent's consideration is simply to write him a standard query letter. I stand behind that proposition today more firmly than ever.

Do not send the letter, or the script, return-receipt requested. Sometimes these parcels result in a notice being left by the carrier instructing the addressee to report to the post office. It's damned frustrating for an agent to schlepp there and stand on line only to discover that what awaits her is a letter from a writer seeking permission to submit a script, or the script itself. It creates an impression, all right, but not the kind that any smart writer seeks.

It is a wise idea, also, to avoid any fancy tricks or stunts when submitting scripts. Within days of the birth of my son, for example, I received a package, brightly gift-wrapped, with the inscription "It's a Boy!!!" emblazoned upon it. I figured it was a present for the baby. But it was a screenplay. To the writers who had collaborated on its creation it represented their metaphorical "child." Their hope was to attract special attention.

They attracted special attention, to be sure, but not of the kind they had sought.

More recently I received a huge box. Inside was nothing but packing foam. Amidst all the foam I finally found a single fortune cookie. The "fortune" was the news (presumably lucky for me) that a new script by a new writer was on its way.

I admit it: I was annoyed at having squandered even a little bit of time searching through the packing material to see if there was anything in there, wondering whether or not something had been lost. And I was doubly disturbed having to trek down the hall to the waste bin in order to ditch all that trash. Did this take up a great deal of time? No. But all of the time it did take up— every split second of it—was wasted; it achieved absolutely no purpose other than to create an unfavorable impression upon a potential reader.

The single most preposterous script-submission stunt I ever heard of involved a huge package arriving by special messenger at an agent's office. Inside was a birdcage containing a screenplay and a live bird.

The hapless creature turned out to be a homing pigeon.

Attached to its leg was a small leather pouch. A note contained instructions: upon reading the script, the agent was to check "yes" or "no" on a scrap of paper, insert it in the pouch and release the bird at the window. Presumably, the bird would carry the notice to its sender.

But alas, as the script lay at the bottom of the cage, it already contained commentary from the bird; commentary that was at once fowl and foul.

Telephone Etiquette

Screenwriters use the telephone entirely too much.

They use it in movie after movie wherein characters narrate the tale via telephone conversations rather than act it out. Writers need instead to invent action to carry the main burden of tale assembly. That's why the players are called "actors" and not "talkers." That's why the medium is called "motion pictures" instead of "radio."

But there is another way writers abuse the telephone.

And that is when they call agents. There is simply too much telephone traffic for even the most devoted agent to handle. He can, on the other hand, handle his mail. And that is why writers should write letters to agents instead of punching up their telephone numbers.

On those rare occasions, however, where it is appropriate to telephone an agent or producer, certain simple rules of procedure should be followed. I am astounded by the number of otherwise intelligent writers who act as dumb as a sack of sand when it comes to telephone etiquette.

Never call merely to find out if a script was received.

I've already mentioned that it's a mistake to send material return-receipt requested. Alternatively, the writer can provide a self-addressed, stamped postcard for the agent to pop in the mail, but I regard this to be an error as well. It just looks bush-league; it carries the rank air of amateurism.

How can one know if a script has been received?

First, make certain you get the mailing address exactly right. And while you're at it, spell your correspondent's name correctly. You cannot imagine how many letters are addressed to me with my name misspelled. My name is surely easy enough to spell, but in a running count I kept this past year I tallied fifty-four correspondents seeking my support who did not take the trouble to find out how to spell my name.

Do I care a whole lot if my name is misspelled?

No.

Others, however, may take substantial offense, and see the misspelling as a probable indication of the care—or careless-ness—that went into the errant writer's script.

If the address is current and correct in all its details and speci-fications, and if it is clearly typed, the likelihood that it has arrived is overwhelming. There are, of course, exceptions, but they are just that: exceptions.

Additionally, be mindful that in Hollywood your first impres-sion is your only impression with any particular script. So be certain that the proffered screenplay is truly ready.

Never call in order to tell someone <ins>not</ins> to read a script recently submitted because the draft has subsequently been revised.

If the script needed to be revised it should not have been sent in the first place.

These days, no doubt thanks to the capabilities of word processors, there are no discrete first, second and third drafts but instead just one wriggling, writhing, endlessly evolving draft. Writers hand me a script at ten in the morning and have a revised version at two o'clock that same afternoon.

I sometimes receive phone calls from writers advising me that

I am about to receive a package with revised pages 8, 18, 22 through 25, 61, 73 through 78 and 109. Accompanying the new pages is a request, naturally, that I re-collate the script.

I do not doubt that the day is near when a writer will request that in addition to re-collating his script I also come to his house to vacuum his carpet. Who knows? Maybe, just once, if it's a truly promising writer, I'll oblige.

But I don't do windows.

About the only legitimate reason to utilize the telephone to intrude upon an agent or producer is to return a call he made to you.

Begin every message with your name and telephone number.

Does that not seem obvious? Nevertheless, scores of people telephone without doing so. I receive messages from strangers like the following: "This is Joyce in North Carolina. Please call me back."

Can you see me calling Directory Assistance? "Please give me the number for Joyce in North Carolina. What? Well, all right, let's start with just the first six thousand."

Make it your practice to leave your number even if you are absolutely certain the party already has it.

If this strikes you as petty, remember that underneath it lies a mature appreciation for the receiver of the message, the person you hope will return your call. For one thing, he may be calling in for his messages from afar and not have his ten-pound Rolodex handy.

Writers should get into the habit of opening all of their messages with their name and number. Even when I do not desire a call to be returned—for example, when I am merely imparting some requested information—I will announce my name, then state something like the following: "There's no need to call me back but, for your convenience, if you have any questions or comments, my number is (555) 555-5555."

When you have to leave a message, keep it short.

It communicates a great deal about the respect and considera-tion the writer possesses for his listener's attention and time when the information he leaves is cogent and useful instead of rambling and incoherent.

Be certain that the outgoing message on your own voice mail, i.e., your own greeting to callers, is straightforward and to-the-point.

A complex production with horns blaring and hooves beating, accompanied by a dramatized voice-of-doom narration, might be funny the first time—if at all—but every time thereafter it is just a pain in the neck, a waste of the caller's time.

Some people are reluctant to include their name in their voice mail's outgoing greeting, and that is just fine. Nevertheless, it is useful to let callers know that they have reached the correct number.

In your outgoing greeting, be certain to report the name or phone number of the party that has been reached, including the area code.

There are so many area codes now that in my town, as in so many others, even local calls require at least eleven digits: 1, plus the area code, plus the seven-digit number. Many people—myself, for example—are calling through switchboards that require yet another code to be dialed in order to access an outside line.

That could all add up to fourteen digits merely to call across the street. Under such circumstances, cannot everyone under-stand how easy it is to misdial?

It is useful, therefore, to let callers know precisely what number they have reached. It is frustrating, indeed downright maddening, in attempting to return someone's call—someone I am inevitably trying to help—to reach voice mail containing no clue as to the identity of the party that has been reached.

Bear in mind also that voice mail is now very much a part of our culture. There is no longer any need to indicate in an outgoing greeting that it is an answering machine that has been reached, that we're either on another line or away from the phone, that your call is important to us, that we'll be back shortly, or any of that now all-too-familiar fluff. Nor is there any purpose in instructing callers to wait for the beep.

Of course, all this discussion regarding answering machines and voice mail presupposes that the writer possesses such service. Personally, if I attempt to return a call and reach a line that rings without answer, I will not call again. The same applies to a busy signal. A writer who wishes his calls to be returned needs to be available even when he's unavailable. He requires, therefore, not only voice mail but also Call Waiting. What the savvy writer desires is to make it not difficult but easy to be reached.

But above all else, remember that the finest telephone etiquette is not nearly as effective, as considerate or as smart as writing a simple, old-fashioned letter.

To sum up all of the above in the form of a screenwriting principle:

Principle 14: If you want others to treat you as a professional, you must treat yourself as a professional.

A Foolproof, Shockproof, Waterproof, Tamper-resistant Method for Reaching and Acquiring an Agent

While query letters may work for writers seeking representation for feature-length film scripts, it is somewhat trickier in television, particularly for writers seeking to write episodes of existing series.

Too many writers—like too many civilians—are snobs about television. In certain corners of institutions of higher learning, television is referred to only in whispers and even then often as "the T word."

But television is like all other creative expression—film, theater, dance, music, painting, sculpture, literature—in that most of it fails and some small portion of it is truly excellent. Still, even experienced television writers who ought to know better will tell you the real glamour is in film, and that they're merely biding their time in TV until they make their breakthrough into theatrical features.

When the Writers Guild went on strike some years ago, I was assigned picket duty at a studio gate, where I ran into an old film school classmate from the University of Southern California, action/adventure *meister* John Milius (*Apocalypse Now*, etc., etc.). Wielding bright Day-Glo STRIKE! signs, we tramped up and back before the entrance to NBC's massive facility in Burbank.

Spotting our signs, several tourists approached us. "You guys writers?"

We nodded.

"How do you get into TV?" one asked.

"What you really should ask," John quipped, "is how do you get *out* of TV?"

But the truth is that television is the arena where writers are treated and paid most generously. If a top screenplay price is, say, four million dollars, consider that for creating and writing the TV series *Family Ties*, Gary David Goldberg earned more than forty million dollars.

The greatest show business fortunes consist of trillions of nickels and dimes: record and publishing royalties and, especially, television residuals. In a typical season, for example, an episode of a TV series will rerun in prime time at least once and almost certainly twice. Each rerun under such circumstances pays the writer a hundred percent in residuals; that is to say, each time the show is rerun he is paid all over again the whole amount he was paid for writing the piece in the first place. If he got twenty-five thousand dollars for a half-hour sitcom script, in that first season alone he will likely take home three times that much for that one episode.

If that were the end of it, it would still be generous compensation by any standard. But it is not the end; it is merely the beginning. In subsequent seasons the writer will continue to earn residuals, albeit on a declining scale. If, however, the show goes to syndication, even as the individual airings pay less and less, there are more and more of them, so that the overall amount of money that accrues actually soars.

And perhaps best of all, to earn all of these payments the writer has to do exactly this: nothing! The residuals that flow to him during his lifetime—and thereafter to his heirs—are payments for work he has already done.

Generally speaking, therefore, financial compensation in television is far greater than in film. The various collaborators in a television series that produces a sufficient number of episodes to qualify for syndication may well share more than a billion dollars among them.

A hit television series is like *Star Wars, E.T.* and *Jurassic Park* all rolled up in one.

And you can probably toss in *Batman, Home Alone* and *Independence Day,* too.

As dizzying as such remuneration may be, writers in television are also treated better than feature film writers, in a host of ways. This ought to come as no surprise, as it is television writers who make up the majority of working Writers Guild members and it is natural to assume, therefore, that the rules and regulations would be designed to favor them.

Note, for example, that a writer at a pitch meeting for a film may be asked to return for further discussions regarding a particular proposal. Indeed, he can be invited back again and again without limit.

And without compensation.

Some writers may consider the many meetings to be encouraging and flattering, but the experience quickly comes to resemble free brain-picking.

In television, on the other hand, after an initial pitch meeting, if a producer wants to discuss the matter further, he must pay at least Writers Guild scale for a story. These days that's something like four, five or six thousand dollars minimum—and that for only a two- or three-page double-spaced outline.

No wonder the television market is tight; no wonder it's uniquely difficult to reach agents handling writers in that arena. Exacerbating this situation is the fact that over the past decade the freelance market in television has largely evaporated. Writers who break through and enjoy sustained success almost invariably are those who, after selling a handful of episodes, end up on staff at a particular show. This causes the availability of freelance work to shrink still further as staff writers consume more and more of the assignments.

Good news: there is a solution.

Upon encountering resistance from television agents, writers can take another tack altogether: write to the writers. Which writers? The writers of the shows they hope to crack.

How can one find out the names of these writers? Copy them from the tube. Watch the credits as they flit past; if they move too quickly, record the show on your VCR and exploit your freeze-frame capability so that there's ample time to read the name (and, let us repeat, to spell it correctly).

Once one has the name of the writer, how can one find out his address?

All film and television writers have the same address.

Here it is: c/o The Writers Guild of America, West, Inc., 7000 West Third Street, Los Angeles, CA 90048.

What should these letters say? First of all, they should praise the writer. You'll never go wrong praising talent. You need to invent some breezy, respectful, affirmative opening gambit. For example:

Dear [writer's name],

Likely I watch more television than anyone ought to, but every once in a while a show comes along that makes it all worthwhile. Your episode [episode title] of [series title] changed my life forever.

Next, praise some specific aspect of the writer's work.

I recall in particular the way [character] confronted [character] over the question of [issue]. When she tells him [line of dialogue] and he responds [line of dialogue] I just about fell out of my La-Z-Boy recliner.

I even dropped the channel zapper (which my schnauzer promptly ate).

In what might otherwise have been but a mildly diverting half hour you were able keenly and precisely to articulate extraordinary insights into the human condition. I'll never view the question of [issue] in quite the same way again.

Do *not* state that you are yourself a writer, and that you are willing to commit unnatural acts upon him if he'll only read your work and recommend it to his own agent. Instead, self-effacingly wonder aloud about some arbitrary and mundane aspect of the writer's work habits.

I've always wondered about the day-to-day methods of talented, disciplined artists such as yourself. I am curious to know, for example, whether you write with pencil and ruled yellow legal pad or utilize a word processor.

Of course, I have no right to presume you will respond to such questions; I recognize they're none of my business and, moreover, that you are undoubtedly too busy creating still more dazzling fare.

Therefore, I won't squander another moment of your time. Please know that I am forever grateful for your having touched my life. I offer you congratulations and thanks for sharing your considerable gift with me and millions of viewers all around the nation and the world.

Sincerely,

[your name]

I offer two promises. One: the sun will set in the west. Two: the writer will answer your letter.

There are two reasons you can count on a reply. The second reason derives from an important screenwriting principle alluded to earlier in this book.

Principle 15: Every single successful professional writer—without exception—was once totally unknown.

Lingering in the memory of even the hardest-bitten steel-tempered veteran is the recollection of his scuffling days; he'll be eager to provide support to a fledgling scribe who approaches him in a clever and sincere and, most important of all, respectful manner.

But before all else, you can count on this:

Principle 16: Every writer will do anything, will seek any excuse, to avoid working upon the particular assignment in front of him at any given moment.

What could be more odious, more flat-out frightening, than to confront the endless task of filling blank paper—or glowing phosphor—with language worthy of an audience's time and attention?

That is why any writer will seize upon the opportunity to reply. It is the perfect outlet for him to avoid his own work. It offers him a double whammy: he gets to put off his own work and he also wins the chance (not without justification) to feel like a good guy, a caring, generous soul.

Ask yourself: If you were a successful writer and received such an inquiry, would you not reply?

Of course you would.

A friend of mine who is now an enormously successful writer tells me that when he was completely unknown, fresh out of college and working a grim day job, he wrote a letter of appreciation—really nothing more than fan mail—to none other than renowned novelist, essayist, poet and critic John Updike, complimenting him on his latest book.

He mailed the letter on a Monday. Thursday of that same week, there was a handwritten nine-page reply from Updike. No doubt there is solid testimony here to Updike's generosity. But you can also be certain that even John Updike wants to avoid whatever it is that's in front of him on his desk at any given moment.

In the proposed sample letter I suggest that after praising the writer you ask not about profound literary issues but, instead, about the writer's personal work habits. Are writers willing to discuss this subject with perfect strangers?

Just try to stop them!

Just try to get them to shut up!

Writers crave the opportunity to wax prolific, to rant and rave about their particular and peculiar quirks: what level of rag-content they seek in their writing bond, how soft the lead in their pencil, which blend of coffee roast they favor in order to stay awake while slogging through their tedium.

In the movie *The Front* (Walter Bernstein), Woody Allen portrays a bartender who fronts for blacklisted writers, writers who cannot sell under their own names because they are politically out of favor. Woody thus receives screen credit for stories he did not write, then secretly passes the remuneration to the actual writers.

His girlfriend quizzes him about his writing but he is always reticent. He asserts that he simply does not like to discuss it. "I don't get it," the girlfriend complains. "Generally you can't get writers to cease prattling on and on about their writing."

Amen to that!

Once the writer has replied to your letter, write back to him, thank him and perhaps ask yet another innocuous question or two. Eventually you will have established enough of a relationship gingerly and delicately to presume to ask the guy to read your script. Perhaps you'll write something like this:

> . . . and finally, I want to let you know that you have so inspired me that I've myself actually written an episode. I do not tell you this in order to solicit your consideration of my wretchedly amateurish effort with an eye toward a recommendation to an agent (yours, for example) but merely to share with you how affirmatively your creativity has affected one particular member of your vast, adoring audience.

I promise two things. One: the sun will rise in the east. Two: the writer will volunteer to show your script to his agent or, at the very least, to recommend it to another agent or even a producer.

He may well do this even if he thinks the script stinks. Perhaps he wants to demonstrate to you—and to himself—that he has the power to get a script read. But whatever his motivation, it will finally all come down to one and only one thing: the script.

Let it, therefore, be worthy.

PART THREE

THE END OF ADVERSITY

CHAPTER 8

■ ■ ■ ■ ■ ■ ■ ■ ■ ■ ■ ■ ■ ■ ■ ■ ■ ■

Cooperation and Collaboration

Except for photographs proving it actually happened, I would expect I'd hallucinated the entire episode in a mescaline-addled late-sixties flashback. But the fact is that in the fall of 1967, when I was a film student at the University of Southern California, I served as teaching assistant to the nuttiest professor of them all, Jerry Lewis.

He taught a course in directing.

The details of my warm and curious relationship with Jerry Lewis are sufficient to constitute an entire other book. For our purposes here, let me simply say that after a couple of years he made me an offer I could not refuse. He needed a dialogue director on what would turn out to be his last big-studio picture.

Because Jerry Lewis enjoys rubbing elbows with star athletes, he cast as actors in the picture several members of the Los Angeles Dodgers. Foremost among them was center fielder and team captain Willie Davis.

Davis was in the full flush of his prime. Twenty-nine years old, he had enjoyed the strongest season of his career, and was arguably the best player on the team.

He was also a contract holdout.

This was the era before free agency, and players were severely limited in their options; they had largely to go along with whatever deal management chose to dole out. They could not jump to another team. Their sole bargaining chip was the threat to sit out the season.

And indeed, during the winter of the picture's production, that is precisely what Willie Davis threatened to do. One morning, while driving to the studio, I heard on the news that he had finally signed his contract. When I encountered him on the set, I asked, "How much?"

He answered, "Fifty thousand dollars."

Even with his salary adjusted for inflation, this superstar and leading hitter and fielder for one of the most profitable franchises in baseball agreed to an amount representing but a tiny fraction the commission pays to a modern player's agent.

The movie's property master took home that much in a year. By any measure, for a fellow at the top of his game in so cruelly competitive an arena, here was compensation that was scandalously paltry.

It will be asserted by many, of course, that fifty thousand dollars is a whole lot of money for a fellow to earn for playing ball. I disagree most vigorously. I have little patience for those critics who over the years said that Johnny Carson, for example, was paid too much money for "merely" hosting a TV talk show.

That same inconsequential little talk show has earned hundreds upon hundreds of millions of dollars for the National Broadcasting Company over several decades. The total worldwide syndication value of its episodes surely reaches well into the billions.

Did Johnny Carson personally contribute to the show's phenomenal success? Certainly the folks at NBC thought so, as they soon agreed contractually to marry Johnny's name to that of the show. It was no longer *The Tonight Show* starring Johnny Carson but *The Tonight Show Starring Johnny Carson*. Even when Johnny took a night off and a guest host (occasionally

Jerry Lewis) replaced him for an evening or a week, it was still *The Tonight Show Starring Johnny Carson*.

Carson had become, in effect, not an employee of the network but a co-owner of the show, not a hired hand but a partner sharing appropriately in the profits. He no longer worked for "The Man" in exchange for wages, however generous; he was instead The Man himself.

The same applies to professional athletes.

Thanks to free agency, star athletes no longer toil as field hands for their masters; instead they subcontract their services and are paid not a salary but something much more closely resembling a portion of the proceeds they generate for the overall enterprise. At the outset owners complained that such arrangements would bankrupt the sport, and painful public battles have been waged over this issue. In truth, however, team profits have generally soared. It has turned out to be an arrangement beneficial to all parties.

At this point, a reasonable reader may ask why in the world a book about screenwriting is even touching upon this subject. The answer: because it provides solid evidence of a wider and encouraging trend that characterizes a healthy development not only in film but in television and other entertainment enterprises in the new millennium.

For as we sprint toward that millennium, the boundaries between once clearly delineated areas of conflict—these people against those people, this country against that country, master versus slave, labor versus management, North versus South, East versus West, landlord versus tenant, capitalism versus communism, commerce versus art—blur, blend, overlap and merge. Formerly clear territories bleed around the edges, seep into one another and eventually their borders disappear altogether.

Old, familiar, comfortable, trusted distinctions no longer obtain, but give way to a new singularity that finds its most creative embodiment in nothing less than the moving picture.

Labor/Management

We have already seen that in professional sports there is a substantial erasure of the line dividing owner and player, and this is increasingly true for corporations in general. Workers associated with, say, United Airlines are now characterized as worker-owners. Indeed, the notion of employees becoming shareholders in the company for which they work represents a phenomenon that is increasingly familiar.

An attorney does not merely work for the firm; if he passes muster after a decent interval as an associate he becomes a partner, with full rights and responsibilities. University professors do not simply work for the campus; once they survive the rigors of tenure review they participate actively in its governance, determining and executing its principles, policies and procedures.

But in no world is the marriage of labor and management more abundantly clear than in show business. For in movies— and in some ways even more so in television—labor *is* management. Increasingly, writers produce the shows they write.

A common misconception among writers—and among the general public—is that to protect their writing, writers must also direct. I have known a number of writers, however, who acquired sufficient clout to win the right to direct their own screenplays, only to have those scripts wrecked and devastated beyond description. Worst of all, with the writer at the helm of his own picture, there is no one else around to blame when schedules and budgets go awry.

The only thing worse than having some idiot director wreck your script is wrecking your own script.

Perhaps at long last the overappreciation of directing is diminishing. George Lucas, for example, has had no directing credit since the original leg of the *Star Wars* trilogy approximately twenty years ago. But who can doubt that Lucas has placed his creative stamp on a host of films that are unique to him, to his special style, to his singular aesthetic and personality?

I am often asked whether I'm bothered by the high prices—

millions upon millions of dollars—now paid to leading screen-writers for a single script. My answer is always no! I am, after all, a writer and a writing educator. Why would I object to writers receiving oodles of money for their services?

Others may ask: Does not all this attention to money obscure the basic principles that inspire writers to write in the first place? And does it not sully the bright spirit that brings audiences to movie theaters? What about art, creativity, dreams, invention, imagination, fascination and fantasy? Doesn't all that get lost in the flurry of dollar signs?

I'll say it again: I'm not a bit bothered by writers getting paid lots of money. I firmly believe we ought to get as much as we can persuade—or even compel—movie companies to pay us.

But what I like best about the newly elevated compensation for writers is that it serves as testimony to the truth of the proposition that it is not the director but the writer who is truly film's first artist. Writers have always appreciated this fact. The high prices articulate a new screenwriting principle:

Principle 17: **Screenwriting is not about the movie business; the movie business is about screenwriting.**

The dollars announce that at long last even Hollywood gets the message. And the message is this: a movie can't make money without a solid story.

And story is the domain of the writer.

Writers, therefore, instead of working for the producer, find themselves increasingly to be the producer's partner.

Reality/Illusion

If former adversaries such as labor and management can now be seen for what they truly are—partners—the same can be said for reality and illusion.

We live, after all, in a constant firestorm of signs and symbols; in our modern, technological society an information hurricane rages, illusions rain down perpetually upon us, competing ceaselessly for our time and attention.

It distracts us, attacks us, provokes us and just generally annoys us.

And we love it.

Studies demonstrate that people typically enter their homes and hotel rooms and promptly turn on the TV, then leave it on, even if they're not watching any particular program. The TV set is the equivalent of another person—or group of people—being present in the room. Indeed, many people leave the TV on even when they're not at home.

In the perpetual battle for even the tiniest sliver of people's attention, we are endlessly bombarded with images. Not reality itself but representations of reality crop up everywhere. A man in a public lavatory standing at a urinal, for example, is likely these days to find himself staring at an advertisement perched eye-level directly above the porcelain. Why squander even this minute? the ad seems to suggest.

Is it not to be expected that as the number of images burgeons in time and space, and as the technology necessary to transmit these images expands and improves, there arises ever-greater confusion in differentiating between the images and whatever it is they purport to represent? Is it not increasingly difficult to distinguish between what is real and what is reel?

A story is told of an impoverished family living hand-to-mouth, struggling daily to survive in their wretched tenement apartment. Whatever humble tranquillity they have been able to muster is disrupted one day by the presence of a rodent who comes to plague the premises. While they are able to scrape together enough money to purchase a mousetrap, they cannot afford even a nickel more for a bit of food to serve as bait. In desperation, they clip a full-color picture of a big, ripe, yellow hunk of cheese from an advertisement in an old magazine.

They bait their trap with the picture of the cheese.

The next morning, sure enough, they find in the trap a picture of a mouse.

Consider now an example not from an imagined story but from life itself in which reality becomes irrevocably confused with illusion.

Los Angeles County recently passed laws prohibiting the possession of "look-alike" guns. These are models of weapons, primarily handguns, that so faithfully replicate the original—except for the fact that they cannot fire a bullet—that they are virtually indistinguishable from the real thing. It ought to come as no surprise that such items are from time to time utilized in crimes. A victim confronted with an authentic replica of a handgun wisely assumes the weapon is real and cooperates with the felon who wields it.

Real guns, however, that can actually fire bullets and maim and kill remain perfectly acceptable, wholly legal. As long as the gun is real, as long as it can actually blow away your head, the law cannot touch it.

Is this not splendid, dreadful evidence of the increasing difficulty in differentiating between reality and illusion? The perfectly harmless representation is prohibited while the lethal reality is routinely, cavalierly tolerated, even licensed.

Consider another example.

I recently received a telephone call from the management team steering the career of a major prizefighter. As his boxing days head inevitably toward a conclusion, his handlers see him moving into the entertainment industry as an actor. Because I am someone who reads a lot of screenplays by new writers, they asked me to keep an eye out for an action/adventure tale that would represent a suitable vehicle to launch this new phase of their client's career.

Moments later, however, they called again. They wanted to add one condition: in keeping with his deep-seated commitment to religious and social responsibility, and his desire to present American youth with an affirmative role model, the fighter was unwilling to be seen hurting anybody on-screen.

Even though I have repeatedly argued that it is in real life, not movies, that we need to exercise social responsibility, I was impressed by our fighter's sincere devotion to the world around him. But there is no escaping the irony here. The only reason the guy even has a management team to telephone me in the first place is that he became famous for having punched real men's faces with his real fists in a sincere attempt to bludgeon them into real unconsciousness.

He draws the line, however, at merely *simulating* such activity.

Such apparent confusion between reality and illusion, it seems to me, is at the heart of the current hysteria regarding violence in the media. We're so frustrated by our apparent inability to suppress crime in the streets that we try instead to limit representation of crime on television and in film.

Alas, not only in movies and TV but in our real day-to-day lives, we marinate in murder and mayhem. In our desperation to confront violent crime we enact ever more stringent laws, we arrest greater numbers of criminals, we build bigger, stronger prisons.

And the bloodbath, instead of abating, grows ever worse.

And in our frustration over our inability to ameliorate the problem we decide instead to control not the problem but the representation of the problem, not real crime and violence but simulations of them in film and on television.

Of course, such pretense serves no useful purpose. On the contrary, it merely underscores our failure and our pain. Worse still, it encourages the kinds of limitations upon creative expression that inevitably pollute art at its core, that do not solve but only exacerbate the dilemmas that confound us.

Make no mistake about it: free thought is married to free expression. The most extreme authoritarian/totalitarian government cannot prevent people from thinking whatever it is they may choose to think. It is merely the expression of those thoughts that can be controlled. This is why censorship is in fact nothing less than thought control.

Of course, the individuals seeking censorship will not parade in the streets bearing signs reading THOUGHT CONTROL NOW!!! They will call instead for "intelligent, reasonable, enlightened, expanded, responsible limitations upon only those sorts of expression 'proven' to be destructive."

Writers, whose stock-in-trade is expression, should reject such seemingly high-minded notions, however well-intentioned some of their proponents may be.

Perhaps the clearest example of society's broad-based confusion between illusion and reality is embodied in a single phenomenon: Ronald Reagan. When I arrived in California in the summer of 1966, Reagan was engaged in his first campaign for the governorship. There was something resembling consternation over the fact that a man whose training was in acting would seek political office.

By the time he'd finished his second term as President, it had become clear that acting was absolutely the perfect preparation for politics. Clearly, people today are sick to tears of reality. Polls reveal that whatever Reagan did or did not accomplish in office matters not nearly so much as the fact that here was a fellow who appeared just exactly as the President of the United States would appear in a movie, a fellow delivered quite literally from Central Casting.

People will take illusion over reality any day of the week. In an era of images, where it is increasingly difficult to tell the difference between appearance and substance, mobs stand atop freeway overpasses cheering a real-life fugitive from justice fleeing real police in a real white Ford Bronco. Routinely they regard the actuality playing out before their eyes as some sort of readout on a computer screen or image on a television monitor.

What's crazy about all this is that it is not crazy at all, but all at once woefully and wonderfully logical.

Chaos/Order

Many years ago, when I was a graduate student at Syracuse University's Newhouse School of Public Communications, students conducted an audience survey of the local television market for a class assignment. Specifically, we replicated the Arbitron method of assessing television ratings in a particular market on a particular evening.

In the survey's first stage, a computer generated a scientifically random sample of addresses and telephone numbers of Syracuse homes.

What concerns us here is the sample's random nature. There are, after all, virtually endless configurations of households, limitless statistical principles that could have determined the sample's underlying order.

Why, first of all, have any sample at all? Why not simply call every home in Syracuse?

A child could figure out that this was not remotely feasible. Since even in this merely midsized market there were approximately a hundred thousand homes, it might have taken several years to make all those calls. This would have been impossible under any circumstances, but particularly so in an experiment that required contemporaneous reporting of viewership over one hour.

How many calls could reasonably be made? Let's postulate that all the students in the class—approximately fifty—calling different households could make perhaps twenty calls each during the targeted hour, for a total of one thousand such inquiries. You don't need an advanced degree in math to know that a thousand calls in an area of a hundred thousand homes would represent precisely one percent of the market.

That may seem like a minuscule sample, with each individual home representing not itself alone but an additional nine hundred and ninety-nine other homes. But in the Neilsen rating system—the industry's standard over scores of years—eleven hundred homes represent not a single market such as Syracuse, but the entire nation, and an individual home represents nearly a million homes.

Can such findings be accurate?

What interests us here is not the accuracy or inaccuracy of the findings but, again, the nature of the sample. One can imagine any number of methods for selecting the sample. If one out of a thousand homes is to be called, why not simply scan the list alphabetically and call every thousandth home? Or, alternatively, why not break up the town into a geographical grid and distribute the calls by territory?

Such methodologies might well seem reasonable. A key proviso of statistical analysis holds, however, that samples be truly random. That is to say, taking the case at hand as an example, there must be absolutely no connection between one household and another. Choosing one particular home should reveal absolutely no clues as to which home will be chosen next.

If one were to summon on a computer screen a menu of orders, a catalogue of methods or systems by which to arrange and order phenomena, there would be virtually no end to the potential listings. Among our Syracuse households, for instance, it could be odd-numbered addresses, or even-numbered ones. It could be every fifth home, or fifteenth, or five hundredth or thousandth or whatever. The sampling could be done by street name, or by family name, or by virtually any criteria the mind can conjure.

And among all those various orders would be included the one that statisticians require for accuracy in such samplings: perfect, scientific randomness.

In other words, in the final analysis, total disorder is merely one more style of order.

During the 1920s, Albert Einstein, confronting inherent randomness in the then-new field of quantum mechanics, protested, "God does not play dice."

But today scientists assert that the playing of dice—that is, total, random disorder; call it chaos—is not merely another kind of order but the ultimate, most whole, most complete, most perfect order of all. Indeed, perfect disorder is now closely integrated into modern cosmological theory.

The earliest humans surely looked at the stars and saw nothing but chaos, an arbitrary sprinkling of light across the heavens. But thousands of years ago Druids, Egyptians, Greeks, Mayans and others saw quite the opposite, not merely a suggestion of order lurking in the apparent chaos but wholly perfect, completely reliable order bound by rules that are dependable, predictable and quite thoroughly unbreakable.

Are not solidly constructed screenplays more than a little bit that way? In movies, indeed in all story-oriented expression, we seek disorder's apparent naturalness. Audiences surely do not want to see the hands of the creator—the writer—shoving and steering all the incidents and anecdotes and events around and around, shaping them, sculpting them, molding them into some sort of design that makes sense, stirring them into some sort of stew that tastes just right.

Viewers demand instead that the tale appear to unfold naturally, spontaneously, without conscious design on the part of any Master Designer.

Other Assorted Adversities

There appears to be virtually no end to the list of ancient opposites whose borders and boundaries have now blended and even vanished.

Criminals—for example, the Menendez brothers—are now often viewed as victims. Formerly clear distinctions between liberals and conservatives seem similarly smudged. Previously neat distinctions between communism and capitalism whose struggle dominated global affairs throughout the century have evaporated suddenly and blown away like so much dust.

And not only the narrower division between communism and capitalism, but even the broader separation of East and West, is increasingly blurred. It is difficult to tell upon arrival at any airport—without checking your ticket—whether you are in Paris, Buenos Aires, Beijing or Newark. Moreover, in all of these places it is increasingly likely that one and the same language prevails: English.

Even the boundaries separating life and death are not what they were. There is precious little agreement as to the precise point at which human life begins. Conception? Quickening? Birth?

And death is no less controversial. Does it occur when brain waves read flat on an oscilloscope? The moment an individual forever loses consciousness? Upon cessation of breathing?

Such phenomena are no longer viewed as clear entities in and of themselves so much as stations on an existential continuum. Their significance lies not in how they break apart but in how they come together.

Most pertinent for screenwriters is the mounting difficulty of separating truth from falsehood. Even apparently straightforward physical questions—the day, date, hour—cannot be determined without considering the observer's position, place and politics.

The search for truth leads not to answers but only to further questions. Whose truth? As viewed from where?

And what in the world can this mean for screenwriters?

Simply that they should not get all tangled up in some grandiose notion regarding what they believe to be "the truth." I have seen fine screenplays brought to ruination by writers' highfalutin, misguided mission to deliver their notion of what is really, truly true. If we cannot agree even in real life as to precisely what it is that is "real," how can we ever come to anything resembling agreement in art?

Instead of embracing Truth, writers should stick to their responsibility as film artists to provide a worthy movie for a paying audience.

When I challenge writers as to why they put a particularly ineffective scene or line of dialogue in a script, invariably they say to me, "That's the way it actually happened," or "That's the way people really talk." But a writer's wrongheaded devotion to "the way it really is" can suffocate an otherwise brilliant screenplay.

What audiences want, what they are entitled to, is not "truth" but that which is most dramatic. What is truly true in film is not facts but feeling. Even if the incidents and anecdotes are fanciful, the emotions should be authentic. Tears wept by an audience viewing a young mother die of cancer, as in *Terms of Endearment* (James L. Brooks), are chemically indistinguishable from those shed by people at a real funeral.

In film, the facts are usually phony but the emotions must always be real.

I met a writer in Austin, Texas, who told me that when he heard me instruct him "to lie through his teeth" while writing the story of his father, he felt as if he had finally set down a duffel bag stuffed with bowling balls that he had been carrying for eleven years. He realized that the significance—the dramatic truth—of his father's story lay not in the data surrounding his eccentric, tragic life but in the emotions he evoked, both in those who loved him and those who did not.

The writer thus had to fudge on the so-called facts—shuffle them around a bit, eliminate some and embellish others—in order truthfully and faithfully to replicate the special struggle his father endured.

Competition/Cooperation

What often appears on the surface to be competition is actually just another version of cooperation and collaboration.

Consider the Olympic games.

Here is a universe of apparent conflict and confrontation. Are not athletic games even called "competitions"? Are they not models of one side's attempting to triumph over the other? Are there not clear winners and losers in the end?

In truth, however, the winner who achieves a lopsided victory is not admired so much as he who scores a close win over a capable competitor. What a capable competitor requires above all else is another such competitor, for it is skillful, disciplined opposition that makes us strong. The opposing sides, therefore, most desperately need each other. Once again, what separates them is petty compared with the traits, designs and goals they share.

Muscles do not become strong from lifting weights that are light and airy. If opposition makes us strong, strong opposition makes us stronger. The heavier the weight, the greater the growth in the muscle that strains against it.

I view creative expression as an enterprise that is among other things athletic, requiring keen spirit, sharp reflexes and a body strong enough and healthy enough to support whatever talent may reside within it. I encourage writers to get off their sedentary butts and every once in a while flex something, perhaps even a muscle. Jog, bike, row, jump rope, swim.

At least shoot some hoops or go bowling.

Would it be such a tragedy if you played a little tennis or golf?

I am an addicted swimmer who cannot write—or sleep or breathe—without his daily freestyle fix. As such, of all the Olympic events I take the greatest interest in aquatics.

While viewing the swimming competition in Barcelona during the summer of 1992, it occurred to me that the event—swimmers panting, gasping, sprinting up and back, side by side, separated by the necklace of floats that formed the lane lines—was not competition so much as cooperation and collaboration.

After all, it requires a staggering number of individuals even just to stage the Olympic events. A site has to be chosen. Facilities need to be constructed, and in a timely fashion. There are officials and judges and administrators, timers, coaches, referees and assistants of every stripe who need to be recruited, trained and appointed.

To say nothing of the athletes themselves.

Competition, again, can be seen as but another kind of cooperation.

The Whole Picture

Film represents the noblest, most elegant model of affirmative, creative, cooperative competition.

Where else besides film does so diverse a family of artists and craftspeople—and don't forget the business folks: accountants, attorneys, executives, distributors, exhibitors—combine in such great numbers and so progressively and productively in a common cause and purpose? Ideally, each participant rejoices not in his own but in the collective ego that represents the whole picture.

Simply stated, film is not an adversarial enterprise. Indeed, more than any other entity, it provides women and men with a vehicle emphasizing not separation but symbiosis, not drudgery but creativity.

What, in practical terms, does this mean for screenwriters?

It means that they should not act or direct or photograph or edit the movie. They should not art-direct it; they should not scenic-design it. They should not cast it or sound-record it.

They should merely write it.

Unnecessary language renders a script just that much more difficult to read. Worse, it intrudes upon the creative territory of other artists and craftspeople collaborating in the creation of the whole picture.

Writers ought not restrict and restrain but invite and encourage the active, vigorous participation of their creative partners, the whole family contributing to the production and exhibition of the movie. True, the players may wreck the film. But there's also every possibility they will cause it to soar beyond the writer's most rapturously imagined ideal.

This leads us to yet another screenwriting rule.

Principle 18: **Smart screenwriters first show the way, then they get out of the way.**

My earlier book on screenwriting established three broad, somewhat unseemly principles that have provoked controversy and even anger. And here they are:

Principle 19: **Reach as many people as you can.**

Films are made, first and foremost, for audiences. They are not made to please the artists who create them. They do not need to reach a blockbuster audience, though there is no scandal in doing so. But they must at least reach more than merely the immediate friends and family of the filmmakers.

Principle 20: **Sex and violence occupy a proper place in film and television.**

They have been at the heart of dramatic expression since the earliest recorded drama in ancient Greece. While armies need not beat each other's brains out, more often than not worthy drama covers precisely such terrain and conflict.

Principle 21: **Lie through your teeth.**

What is real, what is important, is not the data but the emotion, not what is factual but what is dramatic.

To these precepts I should now like to add two more.

Principle 22: **Bourgeois, middle-class values are the hope of the world.**

There simply is no opportunity for art, for creativity, when one is forced to obsess about the struggle for food, clothing and shelter for oneself and one's family. All other human questions are luxuries and distractions, however glorious, until the most elemental requirements of daily—hourly—life are met. Lives organized around scarcity are not likely to resonate in creative expression.

Principle 23: The wisest course, the most enlightened route for any person or people, is not separation but assimilation.

People complain that it is virtually impossible, for example, to buy a wholly American-made car today. Each and every automobile contains components built in a host of countries on various continents.

May we not be allowed to rejoice in this?

It's great to know your roots, but this cannot take the place of interacting with all the diversity around us. Current trends that compartmentalize the human experience, that re-legitimize apartheid, that lend currency to the old, discredited institution of segregation, that balkanize our daily existence, represent but a blip on the landscape. The whole picture of the future is the assimilation and, for better and for worse, the homogenization of world population, culture and experience.

Is that wonderful or dreadful?

Yes, it is wonderful or dreadful, depending upon who views it, from where and at what particular time. There's an undeniable sadness in bidding adieu to that which is familiar. And uncharted territory is always fraught with fear and danger.

Nevertheless, the Irish cannot save Gaelic. Jews cannot save Yiddish. It is one thing to study, to protect and to preserve phenomena that form such a cherished part of a people's legacy. But it is quite another to turn history around and run it in reverse, as if with some sort of celestial VCR we could freeze-frame our existence at that precise moment we ideally, romantically consider it to be its absolute prettiest.

Marshall McLuhan proposed years ago that the invention of the printing press made mass production possible. The shattering of experience into bits and pieces of representational information brought us the assembly line and the whole industrial revolution. And printed books, themselves products of that revolution, became the first mass-produced items.

There are echoes of this process in film. Film makes possible the worldwide sharing of experience that renders inevitable the resurrection of the global village. And every bit as important, at the same time as film is the instrument of such change, it is also itself the embodiment of that change.

For nowhere else is there more collaboration among diverse parties in the creation of something whole, something wondrously common, than in the motion picture.

And those among us lucky enough, crazy enough, to participate in creating the plan—the screenplay—fulfill a charge that is placed upon us not by any mere studio chief but by the Force that is with us and that drives not only movies but life itself.

CHAPTER 9

■ ■ ■ ■ ■ ■ ■ ■ ■ ■ ■ ■ ■ ■ ■ ■ ■ ■

Crazy Art: A Word on Authority from an Authority on Words

I am now in my third decade of teaching.

Counting all the way back to kindergarten, however, I have logged more time as a student than as an instructor.

I recall with uncanny clarity the very first hour, the inaugural morning of my formal education at P.S. 11 in Sunnyside, Queens, just across the river from Manhattan. For it was on that particular late-summer Monday in 1950 that I learned screen-writing's single most important lesson.

Our kindergarten teacher, the overfed and underloved Miss Crimmons, was every bit as decrepit as the Benjamin Harrison–era building in which she plied her trade. Scanning the roster, mispronouncing virtually every name, she inquired of each of the forty or so five-year-olds what it was our fathers did for a living.

There was not a modicum of interest, of course, in whatever our mothers might have done. Mothers during that period generally did not work outside the home. So, we reeled off our fathers' professions. This provided the opportunity not only to learn about our classmates but also to consider appropriate subjects for further study. One kid's father, for example, was an electrician, and this sparked a discussion regarding the miracle of electricity, that curious and splendid phenomenon that boils our Maypo even as it freezes our Popsicles. Another pupil's father was a plumber, and from this there flowed conversation regarding water and waste in urban America.

At long last came my turn. I volunteered that my father was a musician.

"No, no," Miss Crimmons said somewhat too patiently, suppressing a grimace. "We're not talking about hobbies. We're not talking about what our fathers do for fun, for sport, for recreation in the evenings or on weekends. We're talking about professions. Do you understand what we mean when we say 'profession'?"

"It means you get paid," Artie D'Agostino called out. He owned a perpetual off-kilter half-grin—symptomatic, possibly, of premature Bell's palsy—that would lead swiftly to his designation among his classmates as Crazy Art.

"No calling out!" Miss Crimmons called out. She asked me again, "Do you understand what we mean when we say 'profession'?"

"It means you get paid," I said.

"That's right," Miss Crimmons said, nodding approvingly. "So tell us then," she instructed, "what is your father's profession?"

Musician, I responded again.

"He's paid money to play music?" she scoffed in a tone affecting mock toleration. I don't doubt she was ruminating that there would always be students incapable of embracing certain fundamental principles, no matter how painstakingly articulated; such was an educator's lot. "He's paid money to play music?" she asked me again.

"That's right," I said.

Now, ever so gradually, enlightenment seemed to encroach upon her. "You mean a musician? A professional musician? Your dad performs at weddings and dances and bar mitzvahs?"

"I expect he played such gigs when he was working his way through college," I allowed. Growing up in a musician's home I was amply conversant with the lingo, even if I did not consider it to be lingo at all but plain, everyday English.

"And what precisely does he do now?" Miss Crimmons asked, leaning far too heavily upon the "now," extruding it and then sectioning it into several distinct syllables.

"He performs with Arturo Toscanini and the N.B.C. Symphony Orchestra," I told her.

Her eyes widened only slightly. "That is impressive," Miss Crimmons conceded, however grudgingly. And then and there, on my first day of kindergarten during a sultry mid-century New York City September, she posited the most profound interrogatory it has ever been my experience to hear.

Granted, on the surface it may not sound like a whole lot.

Her gaze narrowing, our teacher inquired: "What instrument does he play?"

"Bass," I answered.

"What?" she said, recoiling, squinting, her nose wrinkling as if someone had just cut a ripe, wet, buzzing, mustard-colored fart. "He plays what?"

"Bass," I said again.

"What's that? What in the world do you mean?"

"Bass," I said with a shrug. "Sometimes it's called string bass or contrabass, sometimes double bass. I've even heard it called bull fiddle. But musicians call it bass. It's like a great big violin. It's so big, in fact, that the player can't hope to tuck it under his chin like a violin. Instead it stands on the floor; the performer positions himself behind it."

"Now hold on just one moment, young man," Miss Crimmons said, brightening. "It's like a big violin?"

I nodded.

"And it stands on the floor?"

"Right."

"The musician behind it?"

"Correct."

Teacher seemed now to overflow with satisfaction. With serene conviction she announced, "That's called a cello." To be certain that I had it right, she repeated herself, enunciating each syllable as if it were a whole and separate word. "Chell," she said. And after a decent interval she added, "Oh."

"It's like a cello," I allowed. "Certainly the bass is closer to the cello than it is to the violin," I said, nodding eagerly.

"Stands on the floor?" Miss Crimmons said.

"Yes."

"Musician behind it?"

"Right."

Our instructor regarded me with impatience dissolving to anger. "That instrument," she pronounced ever so slowly, "is called a cello." Even a five-year-old could see that Truth and Reason were not likely to prevail on that particular Monday morning.

I chose a new tack and said the smartest thing I have ever said in my entire life.

I looked her in the eye and said, "Okay, it's a cello."

I spoke the words with neither sarcasm nor hesitation. Never did I doubt, however, that I was right and she was wrong. Never did I suspect that my own dear daddy was mistaken about his life's work. It simply did not occur to me that Colleen Crimmons alone might know the truth regarding the appropriate nomenclature for the several brownish-red, curved, carved, sculpted wooden behemoths that graced nearly every corner of our home.

That day I learned a most fundamental principle regarding life, art and screenwriting.

Principle 24: People in positions of authority do not know what they're talking about. Worse, they do not *want* to know.

Offered the opportunity for expansion, given the chance to learn the truth, instead of welcoming enlightenment, authorities are likely instead to reject it. And if pressed on the matter, their scorn turns rapidly to rage.

What a sweet and sour irony it is, therefore, that in light of my lifelong disdain for authority I have become over the years a figure cloaked in substantial authority. I write screenplays and I write books about writing screenplays. I lecture at universities and colleges all around the world. I consult with governments and with film development corporations. I testify as an expert in legal actions involving screenwriting issues, for example plagiarism and copyright infringement.

Attorneys who retain my services do not appreciate my assertion that even an expert opinion is merely an opinion. Likewise, many among my academic colleagues do not welcome my insistence that even the most highly educated guess is still just that: a guess.

Horsehair, Sheep Gut and Screenwriting

My father, I have said, is a musician who makes his living playing the bass.

But what precisely is a bass player's job?

It entails entrails.

And not just any entrails, but the intestines of sheep, for it is from sheep gut that bass strings are manufactured.

It also involves horsehair.

Horsehair constitutes the bow's filament, the threadlike fiber running its length.

For years I permitted myself the luxury of believing that sheep gut was a figurative term representing something other than what it actually is. Alas, as I inevitably learned, this is not the case. Sheep gut is exactly what it is: the digestive tract of sheep. The coiled, convoluted bowel is removed from its owner and soaked, smoked, oiled, boiled, dried, fried and otherwise curdled and cured.

What the professional bassist does in the narrowest sense, therefore, is to pass his life dragging horsehair across sheep gut.

Day after day, year after year, he saws the tail of a horse up and back across the intestines of a sheep.

By itself, such behavior sounds sufficiently bizarre as to warrant court-ordered psychiatric evaluation. Is it not on its face a ludicrous, indeed perverse, activity for any human being, no less for one calling himself an artist?

If that were the end of it we might on appearance alone consider the offender to be daft. But it's not the end; it's only the beginning.

The player does not merely saw sheep gut with a horsehair blade but, as one might expect, in doing so he produces a sound. Contemplating the circumstances, it would seem a safe bet the sound should be ugly.

But what if the player were to claim that in the hands of a capable practitioner the sound is in fact so beautiful, so mellifluous, so compelling as to cause people to line up four abreast around the block for days on end, tolerating snow, sleet, rain, hail, panhandlers and worse, for the privilege of paying perhaps a hundred dollars in order to pass a couple of hours in a chamber listening to that sound? Would we not be within our rights to consider the claimant clinically deranged?

Yet that's precisely what the talented, disciplined, trained professional bassist does. He scrapes horsehair against sheep gut, causing the latter to vibrate. And in exchange, listeners put money in his pocket and food in his children's mouths.

It's crazy.

So, too, is all creative expression.

Principle 25: Art's not smart. It's deliriously dumb, sweetly stupid, full-tilt schizophrenic. Creativity as a profession is not intelligent and reasonable; it's wacky and eccentric, mad-as-a-hatter, jerky as sin.

Creative expression is not logical, circumspect or responsible; it's illogical, unreasonable, manic and irresponsible, especially as an activity preoccupying grown women and men.

Is screenwriting any different from the other arts?

Yes.

It's crazier.

Recollections of dreams, and dreams themselves, provide interesting parallels to the art of screenwriting. Everyone has related a dream at least once in a lifetime. And everyone has been approached by at least one acquaintance who recounted the details of his own dream.

Surely there is nothing the least bit quirky in that.

Consider, for a moment, a friend who wishes to tell you his dream but, prior to relating it, asserts two conditions. First, he insists that you pay attention not for several seconds or even a handful of minutes, but for two full hours.

Would that not all by itself cause you to wonder about your pal's mental health?

And what if prior to his description of the dream you were required also to remit seven or eight dollars for the privilege of hearing it?

Would you not laugh in his face?

Would you not summon paramedics?

Would you not urgently consider cranking up the lithium in his IV drip?

Yet that is what each and every screenwriter does in each and every screenplay. He orchestrates, choreographs, arranges and rearranges his dreams. And he expects audiences not only to tolerate those dreams but to give them their undivided attention.

And not a little bit of money.

Narrative expression is a bizarre activity and a uniquely human enterprise. As near as we can determine, it is not tigers, not toads, but human beings alone who traffic in professional fantasy. No wonder such a life and such a living are so devoutly to be desired. Is there a greater glory than to spin tales and in the bargain have folks feed your family and pay your rent?

When it works, when it fulfills its purpose, screenwriting is a noble and nourishing and healing endeavor for creator and audience alike. However, it is anything but sensible. In fact, it is richly nonsensical. Perhaps the most destructive mistake any artist can make, therefore, is to plan and calculate rigidly and to exercise reasonable caution, because reason and caution are for airplane pilots and civil engineers, not screenwriters.

Do You Believe in Magic?

Earlier in this chapter I talked a bit about musical instruments. Let us for a moment examine one such instrument, the Stradivarius violin.

Thanks to technological advances in medical imaging, it is now possible to clone a Strad. The wood from which violin bodies are constructed is, after all, organic matter. Using magnetic resonance imaging, plus positron-emission and computer-analyzed tomography, scientists are able to map with perfect precision the inner and outer dimensions of the instrument, a heretofore impossible task. These techniques allow scientists to extrapolate computer models, enabling them to replicate the exact dimensions of the original. Moreover, the wood for the "new" Strads is itself salvaged from cabinetry of the period so that even this element is in every respect identical.

There is only one difference between the true Strad and the clone: the latter has a lousy tone.

What can account for this?

Clearly, what is missing is the magic.

And the most serious mistake any artist can make is to leave out the magic.

Good books on screenwriting, thorough and astute seminars, well-thought-out academic programs are useful. But they are no replacement for plain, old-fashioned magic.

Writers can strategize and computerize, can plan and calculate and intellectualize, but in the end, we need to let go of all that and just stumble around, plod on blindly, bounce and buffet and bump and bumble along.

Because that, too, is crazy art's way.

And if from time to time we cannot find the magic, we need to set all the books and schemes and software aside. And we need to apply our fingers still more diligently to the keys.

And we might just find that, if we persevere, eventually the magic finds us.

The Movie Theater as Church

Why are so many movies so bad?

First of all, as I argue elsewhere, they're not.

Movies are merely as bad—and as good—as any and all other forms of creative expression. If most films lack merit, the same can be said for most paintings, books, sculpture, music, batik, macramé, papier-mâché, bread dough, chopped liver and forms and formats yet to be created.

Even so, the question remains: Why is *any* movie *ever* bad? After all, a screenwriter can read all of the books treating the subject; one can attend a myriad of seminars now offered across the country and around the globe. One can enroll in Master of Fine Arts screenwriting programs.

One can work with an experienced consultant, or two or three, or a veritable squadron of such consultants.

And, notably, one can take all the time one wants. Writers can write and rewrite, and re-rewrite, and re-re-rewrite ad infinitum until the script is robust, ready and right.

Still, the vast majority of movies fail to merit our time, our attention, our consideration, to say nothing of our dollars.

Why?

I don't know.

That is, of course, an answer that is simply not permitted in most disciplines and at most institutions of advanced study. To admit that one does not have The Answer to virtually any question displeases boards of directors of corporations that fund research grants, to say nothing of editorial boards who decide what to publish in scholarly journals. But during all those years on the faculty of a learning institution, I have learned one thing above all others: it is not answers but questions that artists and scholars ultimately seek. And even the most refined questions engender not answers but only further, finer questions.

And it is the particular question posed here—Why are so many movies so bad?—that I find most interesting.

For it is the same question asked not of screenwriting educators but of God.

Why does an all-knowing, all-powerful ruler of the universe create *this* universe, riddled as it is with famine, fire, flood, and frustration in every form? In other words, why does a perfect God create an imperfect universe?

This question is by its nature religious. And why shouldn't it be? Movies are, after all, very much a religious enterprise. They take place in a theater that in many ways resembles a church, a mosque, an ashram, a synagogue. Lots of people sit in ranked pews, chairs or benches. And they observe a smaller number of people philosophizing, pontificating, preaching, performing.

People go to movies for the same reason they attend church. We seek to explore the difficult questions that befuddle our existence. We seek to understand the mysteries and the myths, to solve the puzzles and riddles that surround, astound and confound us.

Movies, therefore, are no mere frill but instead a fundamental component of contemporary human experience.

My late UCLA colleague Dr. Norman Cousins was not the first person to understand that spirit and soul are closely connected to flesh, blood, bone. Given film and television's ability to reach billions of people all around the globe, more hearts are healed by them, and more bodies mended, than by legions of doctors.

Creative expression—art—is something that is uniquely human. Beavers do not engage in it. Neither do termites, plankton or krill.

Only humans.

And humans who fail to engage in creative expression—as creators, as observers—are not a whole lot different from walking, talking, breathing, sweating pieces of flesh.

For they miss the opportunity to fulfill their nature. They deny themselves the chance to interact with the rest of the human family in the grand and glorious spirit of integration and cooperation that lies at the heart of creative expression.

They miss the whole picture.

RECOMMENDED READING

■ ■ ■ ■ ■ ■ ■ ■ ■ ■ ■ ■ ■ ■ ■ ■ ■ ■ ■ ■

If there is anybody out there who is not writing a screenplay, it is probably because he has taken a break to write a book about writing screenplays.

Certainly in recent years the volume of such volumes has sky-rocketed. I am, of course, partly to blame. Not dreadfully long ago I contributed a slim title to the fray and here I am adding yet another.

Somebody stop me before I write again!

At the conclusion of my earlier effort I recommended a list of books, and I stand behind every one of them. Rather than repeat their titles here, I'll refer readers first of all to that book. It's a tactful way of recommending my own book—*Screenwriting: The Art, Craft and Business of Film and Television Writing*—without appearing to wallow in self-aggrandizement.

The authors of screenwriting books do not really compete with one another. People do not purchase either my book or somebody else's, but instead buy several. Screenwriting titles compare in that way to cookbooks. People collect them. Perhaps authors of these screenwriting books are to no small extent actually contributing to writer's block: screenwriters read our books instead of writing their scripts.

The same can be said for the flurry of screenwriting seminars and workshops. Instead of attending to their screenplays, writers attend these events. It is so much easier to spend a weekend sitting in a chamber with a group of folks listening to a skillful speaker—or even a lousy one—than to sit alone in a room, hour after hour, endeavoring to fill blank pages or glowing phosphor with dramatic material meriting the time and attention and consideration of an audience.

Recently I met a writer who had attended one such popular seminar. I asked him his opinion of the event and he said he had found it to be worthy in the extreme. "I took over a hundred and fifty pages of notes," he told me proudly.

"And how's your script coming along?" I asked him.

He hesitated, and then admitted that he was still collating those notes.

Having said that, let me quickly assert my belief that there is no such thing as too much education. The more books and screenplays you read, the more courses you take, the more seminars and workshops you participate in, the more you expand your opportunities for commercial and critical success in screenwriting.

Even bad books—like bad movies—can contain good lessons. Sometimes confronting an alien approach helps a writer form his own aesthetic, develop his own style, find his own voice. To discover the disagreeable is in a certain sense just one more way to find accord.

In my view, the best among the more recent contributions to screenwriting literature is clearly *Lew Hunter's Screenwriting 434* (New York: Putnam, 1994). Professor Hunter is my partner in crime in Westwood. If my own first book compacts and compresses the basic principles extolled in our two-year Master of Fine Arts screenwriting program into a manageable volume one can hold in one's hand, Lew's book leads readers week by week through his own version of our bread-and-butter course, UCLA's Advanced Screenwriting Workshop.

Enrollment in Hunter's feature-writing workshop is among the luckiest experiences a writer could have. But alas, it is an opportunity available to only a handful of individuals each year, all of them fully matriculated UCLA graduate students. For writers unable to enroll in the class—that is to say, the vast majority—the next best thing is to read Hunter's book.

A book that does not directly concern screenwriting but that nevertheless addresses questions screenwriters are well advised to consider is Dr. Roderic Gorney's *The Human Agenda* (New York: Simon & Schuster, 1972). Here is a book that is long overdue for a new printing. Dr. Gorney takes history back only as far as the Big Bang and forward merely to the future. And most appropriately so. Among his many other titles of distinction, he served as director of the Program in Psychosocial Adaptation and the Future at UCLA's Neuropsychiatric Institute.

Professor Gorney has much to say regarding the relation of choice to the human condition. As screenplays—like all creative expression—represent first of all a catalogue of choices, not only screenwriters but all artists can benefit in bounteous and surprising ways by reading Rod Gorney's provocative, informative tome.

Writer, actor, producer and director Garry Marshall (contributing in one or another or several of these capacities to such TV shows and feature films as *Happy Days*, *Mork & Mindy*, *Laverne & Shirley*, *Pretty Woman*, *Flamingo Kid* and many more) has written a book that constitutes an unlikely but welcome contribution to the field: *Wake Me When It's Funny* (Holbrook, Massachusetts: Adams Publishing, 1996).

Marshall has sage advice for both writers and writing educators. Besides providing insightful commentary regarding navigation of the ever-treacherous show business waters, he elucidates the importance of upbeat and affirmative attitudes for writers and writing instructors alike. Here is an enormously enjoyable book that sheds light upon some of the central concerns writers have confronted, from *Agamemnon* through *Joanie Loves Chachi*.

Jurgen Wolff and Kerry Cox are two formidable writers for

film and television who have also written books treating the art and craft of screenwriting. I recommend any book by either or both of them. Perhaps best known is their *Successful Scriptwriting* (Cincinnati: Writer's Digest Books, 1988). Another volume to consider is their recent collection of interviews with writers, *Top Secrets: Screenwriting* (Los Angeles: Lone Eagle Press, 1993).

Kerry and his wife, Leah, herself a tireless warrior for screenwriting education, publish *Hollywood Scriptwriter* (1626 N. Wilcox, Suite 385, Hollywood, CA 90028), an upbeat and savvy screenwriting newsletter I read regularly and recommend highly.

Various screenwriting books treat, among other subjects, professional script format. Few, however, focus exclusively upon that item. And none among them is clearer or more useful than Rick Reichman's *Formatting Your Screenplay* (Lexington, Kentucky: Booksmiths, 1994). It is an oversized trade paperback and able, therefore, to present the various forms and formats full-scale.

I admit I'm fairly weary of the overkill that has characterized the promotion of Joseph Campbell's various mythology books. While they are certainly worthy, I think that screenwriters would benefit more by reading Christopher Vogler's *The Writer's Journey: Mythic Structure for Storytellers and Screenwriters* (Studio City, California: Michael Wiese Productions, 1992). Vogler is a wonderful scribe whose prose is clear as light; he articulates Campbell's lessons and principles in a screenwriter-friendly manner.

There is a perky, provocative book that is also occasionally flat-out hilarious. Even if that's all there were to it I would commend it most vigorously. But beyond that it is also an insightful guide into the nature of writing. Its peculiar title is *Honk if You're a Writer* (New York: Simon & Schuster, 1992), and I believe Arthur Plotnik's book should be returned to print. It does not concern screenwriting alone but more broadly confronts the questions of writers' attitude. Here is a book I keep handy so that I can thumb through it whenever I want or need to, which is frequently.

Good news for writers: there is a new volume from Plotnik that is every bit as useful as *Honk. The Elements of Expression* (New York: Henry Holt and Company, 1996) is written in the writer's unique voice, which blends throwback rap-your-knuckles-with-a-ruler schoolmarm discipline with laugh-out-loud humor that never fails to shine new, fresh light on any number of screenwriting issues.

Professor Paul Lucey, who for ten years taught screenwriting at USC, has written *Story Sense—Writing Story and Script for Feature Films and Television* (New York: McGraw-Hill, 1996). Paul is a generous, effective educator, and there is no substitute for sitting in his classes and listening to his lectures, but the best stuff is contained right here in this wonderful no-nonsense, totally accessible book.

Kenneth Atchity, a writer and literary scholar with solid academic credentials, and also a successful writers' manager, has contributed *A Writer's Time* (New York: W. W. Norton, 2nd edition, 1995). It describes practical methods that can enable writers to overcome the daily distractions confronting them. It demonstrates techniques for apportioning one's hours and energy so as to address most effectively the daunting challenge of getting words onto the page.

The modern godfather among screenwriting book authors has to be Syd Field. His first book, *Screenplay* (New York: Dell, 1979), is criticized occasionally for being too rigidly formulaic with regard to story structure. Frankly, these criticisms smack of jealousy among competitors, as Syd has sold hundreds of thousands of copies of this one book alone. Surely at the time it was written the suggestion that there is an underlying structure beneath every well-crafted film was sorely needed. Over the years Syd has softened his views, as is evidenced in his later works.

I recommend all of them. Syd's tender and generous soul shines brightly in each volume.

An underappreciated, too-long-out-of-print book is Stephen Geller's *Screenwriting* (New York: Bantam, 1985). Professor Geller has taught screenwriting for some years at Boston University, among other institutions. In addition, he is an accomplished screenwriter, and his hands-on experience informs the book. Examples of dramatic works he cites for illustration range from *Macbeth* to Mel Brooks's *The Producers*, which ought all by itself provide a clue to the freewheeling, expansive, funny and affectionate lilt that is available to readers on every page.

Michael Hauge conducts screenwriting seminars all around the world. He is an accessible educator whose book, *Writing Screenplays That Sell* (New York: McGraw-Hill, 1988), contains abundant useful information. My pal and colleague, UCLA Professor Lew Hunter asserts that Michael's chapter dealing with agents is the best of its kind in all of screenwriting literature, and I concur.

Another volume that deals with agents is written not for screenwriters but for authors of books. Nevertheless, *Literary Agents* (Cincinnati: Writer's Digest Books, 1986) by Michael Larsen is one of the brightest works treating the subject. The advice is worthwhile for consideration by writers seeking representation in any medium.

Among the freshest and best-grounded general books treating written expression is Thomas S. Kane's *Oxford Guide to Writing* (New York: Oxford University Press, 1980). Because writers in film depend, first of all, on language to express whatever characters, stories, scenes, themes and situations they have in mind, they would be well advised to study the basics of English in the approachable, available voice that is Kane's. Instead of a dull-as-dust list of rules, Kane celebrates expression as an affirmation of the human spirit.

Professor Richard A. Blum, who teaches in the University of Central Florida's Motion Picture Division, has revised, retitled and expanded his television writing book. *Television and Screen Writing: From Concept to Contract* (Boston: Focal Press, 1995) is everything the title implies, a feast of information from the petty to the profound. Have you ever considered writing sketch material, as an example, for comedians or talk shows? Among many other offerings, Dr. Blum provides an actual sample of such fare from David Letterman's show.

I asserted earlier that I would not repeat references from my own first screenwriting book. Nevertheless, one of screenwriting education's most generous servants, Dr. Linda Seger, has contributed yet a new edition of her now-standard rewriting text, *Making a Good Script Great*, plus two completely new books. One treats adaptation. The other, *Creating Unforgettable Characters* (New York: Henry Holt and Company, 1990), is an indispensable resource for writers of any and all dramatic narratives.

There is a new edition of Alan A. Armer's *Writing the Screenplay* (Belmont, California: Wadsworth, 1993) available now. It is worth any screenwriter's attention—a beginner as well as one who is experienced. Professor Armer has been a central figure in developing film education at a truly excellent institution, California State University's Northridge campus. Much of the expertise he has garnered both as a writer and an instructor is available now to writers everywhere who read his book.

Three rich volumes crammed with useful information are *The Screenwriter's Bible* (Silman-James Press, 1995) by David Trottier; Chistopher Keane's *The New Screenwriter's Workshop* (The Maine Photographic Workshop, 1995); and *Opening the Doors to Hollywood* (Custos Morum Publishers, 1995) by Carlos De Abreu and Howard J. Smith. All of these books are useful references brimming with tips touching on every aspect of screenwriting art and business. Each can be read from cover to cover or seductively browsed in an order created by every individual reader.

Professor Andrew Horton of Loyola University's exceptionally fine film school makes a significant contribution with his *Writing the Character-Centered Screenplay* (University of California Press, 1994). Some will argue that all good screenplays are "character-centered," but what is particularly notable in Horton's book is the manner in which he relates character to tale and demonstrates the way each relates to the other. He offers a remarkably clarifying look at an especially difficult—and important—aspect of screen art and craft.

Two dense but nonetheless enlightening philosophical examinations of story theory are Richard Michaels's *Structures of Fantasy* (Washington: MES Press, 1992) and Archibald Coolidge, Jr.'s *A Theory of Story* (Iowa City: The Maecenas Press, 1989). Here are a couple of truly weighty, scholarly treatises that are not exactly a breeze to read but that contain rare and thoughtful insights into the nature of dramatic narrative.

Sol Saks is a television writer with credits in some of the medium's classic comedy series over many years. His *Funny Business: The Craft of Comedy Writing* (Cincinnati: Writer's Digest Books, 1985) is fresh and funny and contains, as one might well expect, wonderful advice for writers of comedy. Saks's advice, however, is in my view useful for writers in any film or television genre. For writers, there is no challenge greater than comedy, and to polish up one's comedic skills generally expands a writer's strength across the board. Sol Saks reminds us that there are really only two kinds of screenplays: good ones and the other kind.

Another book that might prove invaluable for writers of comedy is *The Comic Toolbox* (Los Angeles: Silman-James Press, 1994) by John Vorhaus. Its straightforward approach employs various workbook exercises that cannot help but engage any writer. Vorhaus informs the book with his substantial experience creating television comedy over an impressive career. It is impossible even to glance at *The Comic Toolbox* without getting caught up in its great wit and abundant insight into the nature of drama.

Writers of short films are well advised to read any or, preferably, all of the above-referenced books. The major difference between a long film and a short film, after all, is that a long film is long and a short film is short. Both have beginnings, middles and ends, and they confront the same challenges: character, tale, dialogue and everything else.

Having said that, however, permit me to assert that a uniquely approachable book designed especially for writers of short films is *Writing Short Scripts* (Syracuse: Syracuse University Press, 1990) by William H. Phillips, a professor at California State University's campus at Stanislaus. Phillips addresses in particular student films, but also commercial, industrial, corporate, instructional and educational movies. This market, it will surprise many writers to know, is actually far larger than the combined Hollywood film and television arenas. It is a world that writers ignore at their own peril.

Writers hoping to enter the mainstream commercial film and television world can learn a lot from Jason Squire's *The Movie Business Book* (New York: Simon & Schuster, 1983). Available now in an updated, revised edition and containing interviews with major movie business figures, it provides useful information not only to screenwriters but to all other folks interested in film.

There is a new edition of Linda Buzzell's *How to Make It in Hollywood* (New York: HarperCollins, 1996). The title makes the book seem, in my opinion, less substantial and substantive than it actually is. Frankly, it contains some of the smartest advice I've ever heard proffered to writers. It's not only about the art and craft of writing, it's about the meaning of the writing life. My favorite section explains why a writer's day job is not his enemy but his very best friend, not merely because it keeps him solvent, but because it keeps him sane.

Robert McKee's Story Structure (New York: HarperCollins, 1996) has been threatened for many years. It was announced for publication at another time—years ago—by another publisher. Perhaps McKee feared that a book containing the information in his seminar would render attendance at that event unnecessary and might cut, therefore, into his gate. Does the appearance of the book signal the end of his seminars? It's anybody's guess.

McKee is an authentic phenomenon in the screenwriting education dodge. He lectures across the globe to thousands of producers, actors, story editors and even writers. Extraordinarily intelligent professionals whom I respect most highly testify that his three-day seminar is worthwhile in every way. But even his staunchest, most adoring groupies whisper that sitting still hour after hour—it is said that he does not permit people to go to the bathroom—day after day is an experience that has been characterized as "butt-numbing."

McKee, according to many of his own fans, gargles razor blades every morning. He can be enormously disrespectful to his colleagues in the trade. He has never (yet) directly attacked me, but in public tantrums and tirades he slams, among others, our compatriots. He says he regrets that Syd Field, for example, published *Screenplay*, a book McKee considers to be "dangerous." Apparently, even glancing at Syd's book invites the risk of eyeball cancer.

He even slams Dr. Linda Seger, an extraordinarily gifted and respected teacher and sought-after consultant, who also happens to be among the gentlest, truest people to ever walk God's earth. Blasting Linda is like mugging Mother Teresa.

McKee protests too much.

I say to him, Lighten up, Bob! Some suggest God placed him here on earth so that there could be someone beside whom I, myself, could stand and appear by comparison to be modest and self-effacing.

Robert McKee is an uncommonly erudite, literate figure with tons of information for scholars and writers. But according to some, the downside to the McKee experience is that it provides producers and story executives with "intelligent" and "informed" reasons to reject screenplays.

If a story editor tells a writer he's rejecting his script because "the climax comes before the crisis and it expresses the root idea intellectually but not emotionally," likely that executive has sat through McKee's long-weekend extravaganza, or at least had it covered. Frankly, I'd prefer that a producer simply tell me "I just don't like this script" rather than launch into some educated, intellectual, convoluted authorization for his opinion.

Additionally, it needs to be noted that even if writers can

wrest a wealth of information from McKee, the way he teaches is not the way writers write. His daylong, frame-by-frame analysis of *Casablanca*, for example, is masterful to be sure, but it is not the way the Epstein brothers and Howard Koch actually wrote the movie. They wrote it, of course, without Bob's help.

Having said that, I'll go on record as proclaiming that no screenwriter's library is complete without Bob's long-awaited volume.

I don't doubt that by the time this book reaches readers' hands, a dozen more screenwriting titles will be available. Read all of them. But leave yourself time also to write your screenplay. After all, if you fail to do that, you'll have missed the whole picture.

For information regarding screenwriting programs, seminars and workshops, write:

Professor Richard Walter
Department of Film and Television
UCLA
Box 951622
Los Angeles, CA 90095-1622

Or call 1-800-755-2785

DUTTON **PLUME**

THAT'S SHOW BUSINESS

☐ **REBEL WITHOUT A CREW** *Or How a 23-Year-Old Filmmaker with $7,000 Became a Hollywood Player* **by Robert Rodriguez.** The author discloses all the unique strategies and innovative techniques he used to make *El Mariachi* on the cheap—including filming before noon so he wouldn't have to buy the actors lunch. You'll see firsthand his whirlwind, "Mariachi-style" film-making, where creativity—not money—is used to solve problems. Culminating in his "Ten-Minute Film School," this book may render conventional film-school programs obsolete. (271878—$11.95)

☐ **LIVING IN OBLIVION by Tom DiCillo.** This book includes the original screen-play of *Living in Oblivion,* a movie about the making of a movie, in this case a very low-budget film being shot on a shoestring on the seedy side of Manhattan. Included as a bonus second feature is *Eating Crow: Notes from a Filmmaker's Diary,* in which the author offers a very uncensored story of rais-ing cash and assembling the people to shoot the film and reveals what really goes on and goes down at the Sundance Film Festival. (275997—$12.95)

☐ **MAKING PRISCILLA The Hilarious Story Behind** *The Adventures of Priscilla, Queen of the Desert* **by Al Clark.** The author and director Stephan Elliott survived various natural disasters and acts of God, such as floods, earth-quakes, bushfires, bomb threats, film festivals, confused critics, the outré L.A. bar scene, and power lunches, lurching from crisis to crisis to make the most hysterical film of the year. (274842—$12.95)

Prices slightly higher in Canada.

Visa and Mastercard holders can order Plume, Meridian, and Dutton books by calling
1-800-253-6476.
They are also available at your local bookstore. Allow 4-6 weeks for delivery.
This offer is subject to change without notice.

PLF239

DUTTON **PLUME**

LIGHTS, CAMERA, ACTION!

☐ **WHAT I REALLY WANT TO DO IS DIRECT** *Seven Film School Graduates Go to Hollywood* **by Billy Frolick.** This unique book follows seven talented and ambitious would-be moviemakers through three years of struggle, misadventure, and triumph in the film business. Added to the first-person narratives are original, insightful commentaries from notable Hollywood directors, writers, and agents. Frank, funny, and entertaining—it serves as both a road map and a cautionary tale for anyone either curious about the industry or considering a filmmaking career. (937706—$24.95)

☐ **FOR KEEPS** *30 Years at the Movies* **by Pauline Kael.** Kael's breadth of knowledge of film history and technique, her insight into the arts of acting and directing, and her unfailing wit and candor are alive in this volume of more than 275 reviews. A boon to serious moviegoers and an indispensable companion in the age of the VCR! "Movie analysis with a serrated edge. . . . Intellectual improvisation that soars."—*Time* (273080—$19.95)

☐ **LEONARD MALTIN'S MOVIE & VIDEO GUIDE 1997** *Annual #1 Bestseller.* This edition is packed with the films that you don't want to miss and those you *will*—from box-office smashes to cult classics to forgettable bombs—all listed alphabetically with a concise summary and capsule review of each film. (276810—$19.95)

Prices slightly higher in Canada.

Visa and Mastercard holders can order Plume, Meridian, and Dutton books by calling
1-800-253-6476.
They are also available at your local bookstore. Allow 4-6 weeks for delivery.
This offer is subject to change without notice.

PL259